UNIVERSITY OF WISCONSIN STUDIES
IN LANGUAGE AND LITERATURE
NUMBER 17

WILLIAM WORDSWORTH
HIS DOCTRINE AND ART IN THEIR HISTORICAL
RELATIONS

BY

ARTHUR BEATTY
ASSISTANT PROFESSOR OF ENGLISH

"—The Mind of Man—
My haunt, and the main region of my song."

MADISON
1922

PREFACE

This study deals mainly with the mature theories and poetry of Wordsworth: that is, with the period beginning with the year 1798, and extending to the end of his active career. However, since I regard Wordsworth's doctrines and art as a developing unity and explain that unity by making as clear as possible how the later forms develop out of the earlier, sufficient attention has been paid to the earlier period of his career to make this development intelligible. The carrying out of this design has led to a somewhat detailed study of some of his long poems which have suffered comparative neglect on the part of critics, such as *The Excursion, The River Duddon,* and *The White Doe of Rylstone,* with a closer examination than has hitherto been attempted of the relationship of his mature theories to his actual poetical performance. This attempt to unify and harmonize two aspects of Wordsworth which are frequently regarded as hostile may fairly be put forward as a claim by this volume to a distinct place in Wordsworth criticism.

A second mark of individuality which is the outcome of the attempt to view all the poet's writings in their relationships the one to the other, proceeds from the deliberate and somewhat detailed study of Wordsworth's prose. It is hoped that the study of the prose will present important results; but regardless of the value of our examination of the *Preface* of 1800 and its enlarged form of 1802, it remains true that never before have some of the central passages of this *Preface* been even commented upon. The same rather surprising thing is true of the *Letter* to "Mathetes"; and, also of the *Preface* of 1815, especially in its original unabbreviated form. Furthermore, the prose writings have never been seriously studied as an integral part of the poet's expression supplementary to the poetry and essential in any evaluation of his work as a writer. This serious defect in Wordsworth criticism it is the aim of this book to correct.

It is to be hoped that the connection of Wordsworth with the English philosophers may throw new light on his poetic intentions and methods and may aid in the solution of the very puzzling aesthetic problems presented to the critic by many of the longer and shorter poems. By connecting Wordsworth with English philosophy we may the more clearly see why he approached his theories by way of associationism, and discussed them in such terms as nature, emotion, imagination, fancy, activity, power, reason, and so on. If the study of Wordsworth in his connections with the philosophers will give aid in the solution of these difficult critical problems and in the elucidation of difficult passages, it will be its own abundant justification, and will suggest a new way of studying the relationship between Wordsworth and his contemporary poets; for he who touches Wordsworth touches an age, and the explanation of Wordsworth involves the explanation of all his contemporaries. This more distinctly literary relationship has merely been glanced at in the present book, fuller consideration of this subject being deferred to another time. Furthermore, the fortunes of Wordsworth's doctrine may be seen in a new aspect, when we view him in connection with the philosophic and scientific thought of a later day, as we see him reflected in the criticism and poetry of Matthew Arnold and in the aesthetic theories of John Ruskin. Into these fascinating fields I have not entered on this occasion, but have left them for future ventures.

I have been as little controversial as possible, and on almost every page I have repressed the desire to turn aside from my main argument to answer an opposing view or interpretation. This procedure has been adopted because I have expended my energies in making the poet speak for himself; and because in his presence I have not wished to indulge in brawls of the market-place. This attitude of pacifism does not argue a lack of conviction on my part; quite the contrary; but I am persuaded that my attack on those who regard Wordsworth as an advocate of vague emotion and flabby, sentimental expansiveness will be more effective if it is made in the poet's own words and in accord with his own dispassionate method. To their assertions I have opposed the calm and deliberate statements of Wordsworth, and have allowed the reader to weigh the evidence. I trust that it will be clear that I am in no sense the defender of Wordsworth's poetry and thought. Into a discussion regarding the ultimate value of his art and thought I have not entered, because they need no defense if they are understood. I have consistently taken the attitude that an earnest attempt to understand is to be regarded as the best and only defense of this great poet. In every case where I have acted as the interpreter of the poet's thought and art, I have done my best to follow "in the footing of his feet," and to couch my explanation in his language, in the hope that Dante's prayer might be answered in this, my journey through the dark passages of our poet's thought:

"Vagliami 'l lungo studio, e 'l grande amore."

In my quotations from the poems I have made use of the earliest text of the *Lyrical Ballads* of 1798 and of 1800, and of the *Poems* of 1807, because it is contemporary with important statements of his doctrine, and so is a more perfect reflection of his mind at the time of publication than that which came from later consideration and self-criticism. I use the final text of the other poems, except in certain specified cases, either because the changes in the later text are not significant, or, as in the case of *The Prelude,* because the original text which is contemporary with the writing of the poem is not available, the poem having been published from a late revision of the earlier manuscript. My quotations from these poems are based on the admirable Oxford edition, edited by Thomas Hutchinson.

August 23, 1922.

CONTENTS

PART I

WORDSWORTH'S DOCTRINE—EARLIER FORMS

"Poetry, and not only poetry, but every other channel of emotional expression and aesthetic culture, confessedly moves with the general march of the human mind, and art is only the transformation into ideal and imaginative shapes of a predominant system and philosophy of life."

John Morley, 1877.

CHAPTER I

THE APPROACH TO WORDSWORTH

What Mr. Wordsworth *will* produce, it is not for me to prophecy: but I could pronounce with the liveliest conviction what he is capable of producing. It is the FIRST GENUINE PHILOSOPHIC POEM.

Samuel Taylor Coleridge, 1817.

In a recent book[1] Salvador de Madariaga presents the attitude of Matthew Arnold towards Wordsworth in a very striking manner. Opposite Arnold's prophecy that Wordsworth will have his due in Europe, and will be recognized as holding a place "after Shakespeare, Molière, Milton, Goethe, indeed, but before all the rest,"[2] he places the rather obvious fact that this prophecy has not yet been fulfilled even after the lapse of some forty years, with the probability that it never can be.[3] Señor Madariaga then proceeds to show that Arnold, in common with English critics in general, stressed the unimportant thing in Wordsworth; and endeavors to demonstrate in a series of chapters that Wordsworth has a strong intellectual and utilitarian bent, which accounts at once for his comparative popularity in England and his utter lack of vogue on the continent. I shall follow Señor Madariaga's arguments no further, and endorse them only in so far as they express a much-needed method of approach to Wordsworth, in that they stress the intellectual side of Wordsworth as of great importance to our understanding of his poetry. There is a curious contradiction in Arnold's judgment of Wordsworth. He classes him with the very greatest poets—Shakespeare, Molière, Milton, Goethe—and yet refuses to grant any value to his philosophy or system of thought, which the poet himself fully expressed in *The Prelude* and *The Excursion*. It is very difficult to say

---

[1] Salvador de Madariaga, *Shelley and Calderon and Other Essays on English and Spanish Poetry*, 1920. "The Case of Wordsworth" is discussed on pages 125-190.

[2] Preface to Arnold's *Poems of Wordsworth*, 1879; reprinted in *Essays in Criticism*, Second Series, 1888.

[3] *Op. cit.*, 127.

what influence Arnold's essay may or may not have had on
foreign appreciation of the poet whom it appraised; but it is
not at all improbable that the prospective foreign reader would
be but slightly attracted toward a poet whose philosophy was
held up to ridicule as "illusion," and hateful to "every disinterested lover of poetry." Whatever may be said of foreign
opinion of Wordsworth and the influence of Arnold on it,
there can be no doubt that he has been enormously influential
on English and American critical opinion; and it is owing to
his example that many critics have denied to Wordsworth any
critical or reasoning power, with the consequent deliberate
neglect of all the poet's attempts to explain himself in essay
and letter. This attitude of Arnold's has been of great importance in determining the sort of Wordsworth criticism
that is representative of a large class of critics, and I characterize it as the first false approach to the study of his work.
As a result of this attitude to the poet it has come about
that only in 1907[4] was there anything like a tolerably full collection of his letters, and that there are not as yet in existence
any adequately annotated editions of his prose writings in
whole or in part. Thus we have the rather startling situation
of having no fully edited edition of the *Prefaces* of 1800
and 1802, despite the fact that they are foundation documents
in the discussion of Wordsworth's much used terms. Fancy
and Imagination, and in the whole question of the relationships
between language and poetry as they were carefully thought
out by the poet in explanation of his method in the art of
poetry. These early *Prefaces* are, indeed, almost unknown
documents. The *Preface* of 1800 was not generally accessible
until 1903,[5] as it does not appear in the *Prose Works,* edited by
Grosart and by Knight.[6] That it is hardly known yet is
shown by the fact that within recent years two eminent scholars
have quoted a famous passage, as from the *Preface* of 1800,
which does not occur until 1802. The original form of the

---

[4] William Knight, *Letters of the Wordsworth Family,* 3 vols. 1907.

[5] George Sampson, *Lyrical Ballads, 1800-1805,* 1903, Methuen, London. The
Preface has since been reprinted, with the 1802 revision carefully collated,
in Harold Littledale, *Lyrical Ballads, 1798,* 1911, Frowde, Oxford.

[6] *Prose Works of William Wordsworth,* edited by the Rev. Alexander B.
Grosart, 3 vols, 1876; *Prose Works of William Wordsworth,* edited by
William Knight, 2 vols. 1896.

Preface of 1815 is almost equally unknown. It has been reprinted apart from the poetical works only once, unless we accept the notes of the latest editor as a part of the text.[7] Moreover, in no form has the *Preface* been given any serious study which would connect it with his poetic activity; and the same is even more true of his other prose writings, such as the longer and more formal letters and the *Letter* to "Mathetes." The only exceptions to this are the elegant editions of the *Guide to the Lakes* and the *Tract on the Convention of Cintra,* with Mr. A. V. Dicey's study of the statesmanship of Wordsworth.[8]

This neglect of the prose explanations of his life and art extended in almost equal measure to his explanatory poem *The Prelude* until Professor Emile Legouis published his elaborate study of the poem.[9] Since the study of Legouis the poem has been treated with respect; but little has been done to carry forward our understanding of the poet, and the view that Wordsworth had any development is so little held that he is persistently studied as a static poet, and is judged in his entirety by the *Preface* of 1815: that is, he is treated as a poet who had no history until he arrived at the age of forty-five. Prose explanations and *The Prelude* and *The Excursion* alike are avoided, because the notion of Wordsworth is that these are mere indiscretions and must be sedulously avoided, lest our pure enjoyment of the poetry may be diverted, or destroyed by the "system of thought," or the "philosophy."[10]

---

[7] First reprinted in *Prose Works of William Wordsworth,* edited by William Knight, 2 vols. 1896. Vol. II, 199-221. Coleridge, *Biographia Literaria,* Chs. I-IV, XIV-XXII, and *Wordsworth's Prefaces and Essays on Poetry, 1800-1815, With Notes,* edited by George Sampson, Cambridge University Press, 1920. The first collected edition of Wordsworth's Prose Works was made by Alexander B. Grosart, in three volumes, 1876. Grosart does not print the 1815 version of the *Preface* to the *Collected Poems,* but a later one.

[8] Wordsworth's *Guide to the Lakes* (Fifth Edition, 1835), Reprinted with Introduction, Appendices, and Notes, by Ernest de Selincourt, Oxford, 1906. Wordsworth's *Tract on the Convention of Cintra,* Reprinted with an Introduction by A. V. Dicey, Oxford, 1915; A. V. Dicey, *The Statesmanship of Wordsworth, An Essay,* Oxford, 1917.

[9] *The Early Life of William Wordsworth, 1770-1798,* 1897, Translated by J. W. Matthews; from *La jeunesse de William Wordsworth, 1770-1798,* published in 1896. New Edition, 1921, with Appendix dealing with facts that have come to light in the interval between 1896 and 1921.

[10] Arnold's essay has had tremendous influence in academic circles. It seems to have thrown discredit on Leslie Stephen's essay on *Wordsworth's*

This ignoring of chronology is a second form of approach to Wordsworth, and is a dogma with Professor Herford, who in his excellent study of the age of Wordsworth says that the chronological method profits little in a study of this poet.[11] This principle does not do any great harm in Professor Herford's case; but it is mischievous in forcing alien meanings upon the poet, varying with the special period in the history of the poet which it may please the critic to choose as his standpoint, or the particular aspect of the poet's work which he may be pleased to select. It will be an important part of our study to emphasize the importance of chronology as a guide to the clear understanding of Wordsworth.

A third wrong method of approach is that of explaining Wordsworth by his supposed relationship with foreign thought. Professor Bradley plainly enunciates as a principle what Pater apparently takes for granted, that Wordsworth's poetry must be interpreted in the light of German, rather than English philosophy.[12]

"The English philosophy of the time," he explicitly says, "seems to me to have much less community than the German with our poetry." He further says, "The matter, the ideas of the English philosophers, Locke, Berkeley, and Hume, do not present matter, ideas, which correspond with those pictures of the world that are painted by our most imaginative poets," and he declares plainly, "We find ourselves in the presence, not merely of an inferior degree of genius, but of a view of the world incongruous with the substance of the poetry."[13]

This position is open to two serious objections. In the first place, it denies the validity of the "plain historic method" in

---

Ethics, against which it was in part aimed, to the great detriment of our understanding of Wordsworth. Stephen's essay is reprinted in *Hours In a Library,* II, 250-284.

[11] C. H. Herford, *The Age of Wordsworth,* 1897, Eighth Edition, 1911, p. 155.

[12] A. C. Bradley, *English Poetry and German Philosophy in the Age of Wordsworth,* Manchester, 1909; Walter Pater, "Essay on Wordsworth," in *Appreciations.*

[13] *Op. cit.,* p. 10. Against this indictment of the value of English philosophy may be set the opinion of L. A. Selby-Bigge in his Introduction to *British Moralists, Being Selections from Writers Principally of the Eighteenth Century,* 2 vols., Oxford, 1897. Mark Pattison in "Tendencies of Religious Thought in England," 1688-1750, also gives a quite different impression; *Essays,* 2 vols., Oxford, 1889. Pattison's essay originally appeared in the famous *Essays and Reviews,* 1860.

criticism by which we explain the development of genius from influences of various sorts to which it is exposed in the formative years; and in the present case it would lead us to believe that a philosophy, of which Wordsworth almost certainly knew very little and of which he was entirely ignorant in his earlier years, had a determining influence on his poetry. In the second place, this opinion is open to the serious objection of denying that the German philosophy can have developed from Locke and Hume, if it is held that Wordsworth's poetry cannot have so developed. But the fact is that the German philosophy did so develop. I hope to show that Professor Bradley has failed to note the similarities and the spiritual kinship between Wordsworth and his English predecessors, and that he has failed to perceive that the poet is in the direct line of succession to the inheritance of their thought—an heir who found his ancestral city one of brick and left it marble.

A fourth method of approach to Wordsworth, not distantly related to that which is illustrated by Professor Herford, is that which deals with him as one of the many "sons of Rousseau." This attitude is well illustrated by Professor Emile Legouis and Professor Babbitt.[14] While both these critics may be spoken of at once by virtue of this fundamental assumption on the part of both, they are utterly distinct and even largely contradictory in their individual development of their theme. I shall say nothing of Professor Babbitt's position in this chapter,[15] but shall examine that of Legouis. First we shall see exactly what he says regarding Wordsworth's alleged connection with Rousseau. The following passage gives it very clearly:

In Wordsworth, we find Rousseau's well-known fundamental tenets: he has the same semi-mystical faith in the goodness of nature as well as in the excellence of the Child; his ideas on education are almost identical; there are apparent a similar diffidence in respect of the merely intellectual processes of the mind, and an equal trust in the good that may accrue to man from the cultivation of his senses and feelings. The differences between the two, mainly occasional and of a political nature, seem secondary by the side

---

[14] Emile Legouis, "William Wordsworth," in *The Cambridge History of English Literature,* XI (1914) 103-128; Irving Babbitt, *Rousseau and Romanticism,* 1919, pp. 83, 145, 285, etc.

[15] For discussion of Babbitt's views, consult pages 120-124.

of these profound analogies. For this reason, Wordsworth must be placed by the general historian among the numerous "sons of Rousseau," who form the main battalion of romanticism; though, if we merely regard the ideas he expressed and propagated, his personality may, thereby, lose some of its originality and distinctness.[16]

The first remark that one must make on this judgment is that it is, for the most part, profoundly and manifestly true. One must agree with all the analogies which are drawn by Professor Legouis between these two authors, with the exception of that of faith in the excellence of the child. But, while this is true, it is equally certain that it is but one side of the case. The world into which Wordsworth was born was one deeply influenced by Rousseau; and that the young poet should have been influenced deeply by Rousseauistic influences was absolutely inevitable. The ways of thinking, of individual attitude towards the world of the senses and emotions, were determined in a measure for Wordsworth by virtue of his environment, with consequent opinions and actions on his part which we may admire or condemn. But there is another aspect of Wordsworth which is not Rousseauistic, and it is that part of him which gives him "originality and distinctness." For Wordsworth has his own originality and distinctness, not in the simple and naive absorption of influences which permeated him from his surroundings, but in his reasoned reaction against the surrounding ideas and influences which earlier in his career determined his thinking and action. Professor Legouis, like most of the critics who are mentioned in this chapter, assumes that Wordsworth is a naive and simple soul, weakly buffeted about by the storms of life, driven into error, and fearfully shrinking into solitude there to pass his remaining days. But this is far from being the truth. Wordsworth in his reasoned expression, does not acquiesce, but revolts. He revolts against Rousseauism; but at the same time he is in a world so thoroughly brought to the ways of Rousseau that in a large measure even the very terms which he is forced to use to combat Rousseau have a coloring which was imparted to them by the system of thought which he opposes. But he speaks a language other than that of Rousseau, and in a large part of his poetry

---

[16] *Op. cit.*, 103.

he attempts to define society, nature, emotion, experience, and life as a whole, in terms which bear the very opposite of the meanings which Rousseau attached to them. Wordsworth was a reactionary in the fullest sense of the term, both in art and in his general theory of morals and conduct, and his reaction was toward those earlier authors and philosophers whose teachings and practice had been distorted by later practitioners. This is a clue to much of Wordsworth; and must be grasped by anyone who would see his theory and art in their true proportions and relationships. In the sphere of art he revolts against poetic diction and harks back to Milton and Shakespeare and Chaucer; in doctrine he revolts against Rousseau[17] and Godwin, and appeals to Hartley, Locke, and the general tradition of English philosophy. This is Wordsworth's true originality; and it is also the source of his complexity and difficulty. It is also the source of the confusion which is so easy to find in his thought; for he was a genuine pioneer, only gradually clearing his notions on fundamental questions of art and life, and only gradually working toward as clear a conception of both as he was ever to attain. But whatever the obscurities and contradictions of Wordsworth's doctrine may be, it is fundamentally opposed to that of Rousseau in the ultimate implication of both. If Wordsworth began as a "son of Rousseau" he spent his best and most productive years in denying his father.

With this complexity in Wordsworth goes a very large technical vocabulary involving an exact use of terms which are largely philosophical, such as could have been mastered only by a rather intimate knowledge of the philosophies of the seventeenth and eighteenth centuries. Not only in vocabulary but also in substance the poetry and prose of Wordsworth is philosophic, in that it is an analysis of the human mind and an examination into the validity of the knowledge on which men act and form moral and social judgments and institutions. He himself regarded this work as important because he treated of the "intellectual instincts, affections, and passions of man-

---

[17] That he contradicted Rousseau openly and in a reasoned manner is shown in the *Tract on the Convention of Cintra*, in which he speaks of "the paradoxical reveries of Rousseau."

kind,"[18] and his endeavor was constantly to find out the truth
concerning them in their manifestations in real life among real
men and women.   Hence we find that he studied life not only
directly, but also its reflection in books that dealt with realities,
such as books of travel; in philosophers, in scientists; and in
the whole body of English poetry, especially his favorite poets,
Spenser, Shakespeare, and Milton.

This we conceive to be the true approach to Wordsworth.
He is a poet of reaction; but a poet whose reaction is not merely negative.   He lived through one period of the Revolution
and was a part of it, and he revolted against the attitude of life
which it approved as well as against the disillusion and loss of
hope which revolutionary thought and action brought upon the
world.   It is at this point that the mature work of Wordsworth
begins.   His work in *The Prelude* is at once a repudiation of
the Revolution and a record of personal readjustment in accordance with another code of ethics; and *The Excursion* is a
poem of reconstruction of the moral life of the world on the
ruins of the Revolution.   But in neither of these poems does
Wordsworth merely revolt, or merely sink back into the old,
but looks forward into the future, using the means which the
present supplies.   He thus envisages a new world of thought
and feeling; and a new poetic practice.   But, as in the world
of doctrine he does not merely revolt, so in the world of poetic
theory he attempts a new synthesis.   By the authority of
Shakespeare and Milton he judges the riot of external sensuous imagery in which the theorists and practitioners of "poetic
diction" indulged, and sets out to classify the ideas of the time
on poetic theory by calling attention to the great tradition of
the English language and by pointing out that any permanent
and "philosophic" language must be based, not on the mere
authority of self-constituted critics, but on the real experiences
of real people.   The whole endeavor of Wordsworth may thus
be briefly expressed as, first, an attempt to obtain a true view
of life as a whole; and, secondly, to give a theory of poetry
which is in harmony with his view of life.   This order of the
two problems in the mind of the poet must be observed.   Life
first, poetry afterwards, was always his attitude: the perplex-

[18] *Letters of the Wordsworth Family,* I, 58.

ity of most of the critics discussed in this chapter comes from forgetting this elemental fact. How Wordsworth connected and reconciled his world and his art will be discussed in the following chapters.

CHAPTER II

EARLY THEORY OF LIFE AND POLITICS—RELATION TO GODWIN

"Throw aside your books of Chemistry," said Wordsworth to a young man, a student in the Temple, "and read Godwin on Necessity."

William Hazlitt, The Spirit of the Age, 1825.

We shall deal mainly with the mature Wordsworth; but as a preliminary to a study of his mature doctrine it is essential to understand the subjects which held his interest before the composition of the *Lyrical Ballads* of 1798 and the inception of his prose explanations in the same year. To do this we must study his earlier connections with theorists on action and thought, and with theorists on art and poetry. This will involve a study of Wordsworth's connection with William Godwin and with the School of Taste. His connection with both of these is of prime importance in understanding the intellectual habits of Wordsworth, for they had great educative force upon him, not because they furnished him with ultimate judgments or final methods, but because they imparted to him the love of generalization and the habit of theorizing. Godwin taught him to generalize about politics, society, ethics, and matters of conduct; the various authors of the school of taste taught him to generalize about art. The influence of these teachers came early in his career, at a period which antedates both his mature poetry and his mature criticism; but so powerfully was he affected by them that their influence remains with him throughout his career, in term, in phrase, and even in an occasional argument, projecting like the bed rock through the later geological deposits.

The obscure period of Wordsworth's life is the term from 1793 to 1797. We have almost no written record of this period, as Wordsworth himself wrote few letters, and only a few from the whole Wordsworth family and group survive. His sister Dorothy's *Journals* do not begin until 1798, and the poet himself is very reticent in his account of these years in *The Prelude*. No very great amount of information has been gathered even by those who have given particular attention to these years, especially to the poet's early love affair in France.[1] When he was recalled from France at the end of 1792, he came fresh from the Rousseauistic and revolutionary teaching of General Michel Beaupuy, with whom he had formed a close friendship at Blois and who had first awakened his slumbering humanitarian sentiments. He was at once plunged into the turmoil and contradictions of English sentiment regarding the revolution; was soon thrown into anger by the declaration of war against the new republic of France, "when with open war Britain opposed the liberties of France";[2] and in his resentment against his country he went so far as to hope for her defeat. But his anger against his country was quickly changed into despair, for very soon "Frenchmen had changed a war of self-defense for one of conquest,"[3] and the war was directed against England and her allies. Then it was that the young poet turned from man as he is to man as he ought to be, and laid his hope upon "evidence safer, of universal application," which he sought elsewhere than among men.[4] In other words, he turned to theory and to books. We know that he associated with companions of a distinctly revolutionary turn of mind, like the preacher Joseph Fawcett, who was later to sink to the role of misanthropic Solitary in *The Excursion:* and it was the most natural thing in the world that a young intellectual being such as he was and keeping the company he did, should turn for comfort to the *Political Justice* of William Godwin.

This book, published in February, 1793, was an event of the first importance to many of the young intellectuals of the day, and Wordsworth has clearly indicated to us the debt which he owed to it—

> yet I feel
> (Sustained by worthier as by wiser thoughts)
> The aspiration, nor shall ever cease
> To feel it;[5]

---

[1] G. McLean Harper, *Wordsworth's French Daughter,* 1921; Emile Legouis. *The Early Life of William Wordsworth,* Revised Edition, 1921. (Appendix).

[2] *The Prelude,* XI, 175.

[3] *Op. cit.,* XI, 207-208.

[4] *Op. cit.,* XI, 203-205.

[5] *Op. cit.,* XI, 255-257. These lines were written towards the end of 1804.

and Hazlitt reports that Wordsworth said to a young man, a student in the Temple, "Throw aside your books of Chemistry, and read Godwin on Necessity"—a piece of advice unconsciously followed by Shelley almost a score of years later, with portentous results. The book advocates the ascendency of Justice and Reason, and is animated by a glow of universal beneficence. The effect on Crabb Robinson is thus recorded by the diarist:

> I read a book which gave a turn to my mind and in effect directed the whole course of my life. . . . It made me feel more *generously*. I had never before, nor, I am afraid, have I ever since felt so strongly the duty of not living to one's self, but of having for one's sole object the good of the community.[6]

This is parallel to the testimony of Wordsworth; and the later characterization by Hazlitt adds strong confirmation as to its significance for the time:

> Five and twenty years ago he (Godwin) was in the very zenith of a sultry and unwholesome popularity; he blazed as a sun in the firmament of reputation; no one was more talked of, more looked up to, more sought after, and wherever liberty, truth, justice was the theme, his name was not far off. . . . No work in our time gave such a blow to the philosophical mind of the country as the celebrated *Enquiry Concerning Political Justice*. Tom Paine was considered for the time as a Tom Fool to him, Paley an old woman, Edmund Burke a flashy sophist. Truth, moral truth, it was supposed, had here taken up its abode; and these were the oracles of thought.[7]

Surely such glowing tributes to Godwin's work by contemporaries should put us on our guard against some modern critics who attempt to minimize the importance of the book by strictures on the book itself and the character of the author.[8] At a day so late as this one can frankly acknowledge the importance of the book in the history of the time without running the risk of being a Godwinian, or even of implying that the book is a great intellectual performance. *Political Justice* is not the only second-rate book that has made a stir in the world

---

[6] Crabb Robinson, *Diary, Reminiscences, and Correspondence,* edited by Thomas Sadler, 2 vols. 1872, I, 18.

[7] *The Spirit of the Age,* 1825, Essay on William Godwin.

[8] For instance, Edward Dowden, *The French Revolution and English Literature,* 1897, II.

of contemporary thought; its special claim to distinction is that it is, perhaps, one of the few second-rate books which have had the good fortune to touch the finest spirits of their time to somewhat surprising issues.

An outstanding feature of the book, and one which must have commended it to the perplexed Wordsworth, is its extreme simplicity. All this complex world of thought is reduced to a sole principle, namely reason. All the modern systems of thought are laid under contribution and the parts of each which suit the purposes of the system are chosen. Locke's rejection of innate principles is approved, the attack on vested rights by the revolutionary theorists, such as Helvétius and d'Holbach,[9] is adopted as Godwin's own; and Rousseau and Hartley[10] are frankly adopted in due course, with full acknowledgment to Swift and the Latin historians.[11] But this borrowing does not lend to the book the complexity which we might expect: on the contrary, all the borrowings are subordinated to the illustration of the leading ideas of Godwin's thoughts—the primary importance of reason. Before this principle all traditional knowledge and practice, all accepted ethics and privileges and instincts, together with the institutions which are based on these, sink into insignificance. Truth and truth alone is supreme, and all else is secondary. As Godwin proceeds with his demonstration, and as churches, kingdoms, property, princes, and potentates disappear from the earth, before his inflexible logic, small wonder that so many readers succumbed and believed.

A second reason why Wordsworth adopted Godwin as his guide is the revolutionary humanitarianism which pervades his writings. Godwin is a "leveller," not because he feels hatred towards those who enjoy special privileges, but because the very heart of his theory is the principle that all are equal, and equality must be carried out for the benefit not only of the oppressed but of the oppressor. In the book is a vision of an emancipated humanity which will allow the natural goodness of man to assert itself and so to bring that natural justice to all which is delayed only through the perversity of institutions

[9] Preface viii.
[10] I, 18.
[11] Preface, viii.

and customs that are the result of prejudice and ignorance and not of reason. Godwin does not present this emancipation in an abstract form only, but also in his novel *Caleb Williams,* published in 1794, where a philanthropic outlaw is represented as being the leader of a band of brigands, a character prophetic of the time when justice shall be attained for all in the reign of reason. This philanthropic brigand reappears as the Marmaduke of Wordsworth's *Borderers,* written in the years 1795-1796, the philosophic philanthropist who leads the band of border outlaws, who, like his forerunner in *Caleb Williams,* is betrayed by a mad, irrational world. That Marmaduke represents Wordsworth's real ideas is shown in his correspondence, in which he expresses in Godwinian terms his belief that every enlightened friend of mankind "should let slip no opportunity of explaining and enforcing those general principles of social order, which are applicable to all times and places," and that "he should diffuse by every method a knowledge of those rules of political justice, from which the further any government deviates the more effectually must it defeat the object for which government was ordained."[12] *The Borderers* and the passage just quoted confirm the statement of the *Memoirs* regarding Wordsworth's opinions in these years:

He expresses a deep feeling of sorrow and commiseration for the wrongs suffered by human nature under existing governments; and, having fixed his mind on these melancholy results, and brooding upon them, he identified monarchy with its abuses, and looked for a correction of them all to the unexplored Utopia of democracy.[13]

Wordsworth's belief in the "Utopia of democracy" as presented by Godwin and his followers was the more ardent, in that it was based on the belief in the original goodness and the ultimate perfectibility of man, and justified the most absolute optimism. For the great consummation to which all tends is nothing less than a perfected race, all base appetites crushed under man's feet, old age averted, and the immortality of a perfect body attained on earth, under the law of perfect reason, when man would remain

---

[12] *Letters of the Wordsworth Family,* I, 69-70. The date is 1794.
[13] Christopher Wordsworth, D.D., Canon of Westminster, *Memoirs of William Wordsworth,* 2 vols., London, 1851.

> Sceptreless, free, uncircumscribed, but man
> Equal, unclassed, tribeless, and nationless,
> Exempt from awe, worship, degree, the king
> Over himself; just, gentle, wise.[14]

To a war-weary world the anti-military doctrines of Godwin were most welcome; and that Wordsworth accepted them we have abundant evidence. The connection between autocracy and war made the cure for war very simple: banish kings, and war will disappear. It is very easy to show that Godwin does not hesitate to connect autocracy with war, in the relation of cause and effect.[15] War arises from autocracy, that product of unreason and imposture; for an offensive war is contrary to the very nature of democracy.

It is perhaps impossible to show that a single war ever did or could have taken place in the history of mankind, that did not in some way originate with those two great political monopolies, monarchy and aristocracy.[16]

What could be the source of misunderstanding between states, where no man or body of men found encouragement to the accumulation of privileges to himself at the expense of the rest? A people among whom equality reigned, would possess everything they wanted, where they possessed the means of subsistence. Why should they pursue additional wealth or territory? These would lose their value the moment they became the property of all. No man can cultivate more than a certain portion of land. Money is representative, and not real wealth. If every man in society possessed a double portion of money, bread and every other commodity would sell at double their present price, and the relative situation of each individual would be just what it had been before. War and conquest cannot be beneficial to the community. Their tendency is to elevate a few at the expense of the rest, and consequently they will never be undertaken, but where the many are the instruments of the few. But this cannot happen in a democracy, till the democracy shall become such only in name. If expedients can be devised for maintaining this species of government in its purity, or if there be anything in the nature of wisdom and intellectual improvement which has a tendency daily to make truth prevail more over falsehood, the principle of offensive war will be extirpated. But this principle enters into the very essence of monarchy and aristocracy.[17]

---

[14] Shelley's *Prometheus Unbound*, IV, 194-197.
[15] *Political Justice*, Book V, Chs. XVI-XX, Vol. II, 511-549.
[16] *Op. cit.*, II, 511-512.
[17] *Op. cit.*, II, 512.

He then warns his readers against certain of those who glorify patriotism; and insists that love of country is excellent and valuable only when it is directed by Reason:[18]

A wise man will not fail to be the votary of liberty and equality. He will be ready to exert himself in their defense wherever they exist. It cannot be a matter of indifference to him, when his own liberty and that of other men with whose excellence and capabilities he has the best opportunity of being acquainted, are involved in the event of the struggle to be made. But his attachment will be to the cause, and not to the country. Wherever there are men who understand the value of political justice and are prepared to assert it, that is his country. Wherever he can most contribute to the diffusion of these principles and the real happiness of mankind, that is his country. Nor does he desire for any country any other benefit than justice.[19]

On the basis of this principle of reason, Godwin judges and condemns war; and notes the unreason which induces men deliberately to seek each other's lives. This unreason might be explained so long as men are blinded by the extremity of exasperation and rage; but civilized man has converted war into a trade. "One part of the nation pays another part to murder and be murdered in their stead; and the most trivial causes, a supposed insult or a sally of youthful ambition, have sufficed to deluge provinces with blood."[20]

Men deal in war largely because they fail to realize its horrors:

We can have no adequate idea of this evil, unless we visit, at least in imagination, a field of battle. Here men deliberately destroy each other by thousands without any resentment against, or even knowledge of, each other. The plain is strewed with death in all its various forms. Anguish and wounds display the diversified modes in which they can torment the human frame. Towns are burned, ships are blown up in the air while the mangled limbs descend on every side, the fields are laid desolate, the wives of the inhabitants exposed to brutal insult, and their children driven forth to hunger and nakedness. It would be despicable to mention, along with these scenes of horror, and the total subversion of all ideas of moral justice they must occasion in the auditors and spectators, the immense treasures which are wrung in the form of

---

[18] *Political Justice*, II, 513-515.
[19] *Op. cit.*, II, 515. Wordsworth's letter to Matthews, *Letters of the Wordsworth Family*, I, 68-76, is an echo of this passage.
[20] *Political Justice*, II, 516.

taxes from those inhabitants whose residence is at a distance from the scene.[21]

Such a terrible monster is not to be lightly invoked, even in the most righteous cause. There are only two justifiable causes of war; "these are the defense of our own liberty and of the liberty of others."[22] The last principle will not justify invasion of another's territory, "to force a nation to be free."[23] "But, when the people themselves desire it, it is virtue and duty to assist them in the acquisition."[24] But, even though this is true, war is such an evil instrument, so evil in its nature, "that it ought never to be selected as a means of promoting our best purposes, in any case in which selection can be practiced."[25]

Finally, the foster mother of Anarchy is despotism. Destroy despotism, and you destroy war and anarchy together. This is the final word of Reason on this theme:

It is to despotism that anarchy is indebted for its sting. If despotism were not ever watchful for its prey, and mercilessly prepared to take advantage of the errors of mankind, this ferment, like so many others, being to itself, would subside into an even, clear, and delightful calm. Reason is at all times progressive. Nothing can give permanence to error, that does not convert it into an establishment, and arm it with powers to resist an invasion.[26]

He identifies war and murder in more than one passage, especially in the second edition, developing a hint in the first edition:

It would be unjust to dismiss the consideration of this most dreadful, yet in the present state of things sometimes unavoidable, calamity . . . of war, without again reminding the reader of its true character. It is that state of things where a man stands prepared to deal slaughter and death to his fellow man. Let us imagine to ourselves a human being remaining alone in the midst of the carnage he has made, surrounded with the dying and the dead, his arms bathed to the very elbow in their blood. What manner of creature shall we esteem him to be? What had these men done to him? Alas! he knew them not; they had never of-

[21] *Op. cit.*, II, 516-517.
[22] *Op. cit.*, II, 520.
[23] *Op. cit.*, II, 520.
[24] *Op. cit.*, II, 520.
[25] *Op. cit.*, II, 525.
[26] *Op. cit.*, II, 549.

fended; he smote them to the death, unprovoked by momentary anger, coldly deliberating on faults of which they were guiltless, and executing plans of wilful and meditated destruction. Is not this man a murderer? Yet such is the man who goes to battle, whatever be the cause that induces him. Who that reflects on these things, does not feel himself prompted to say, "Let who will engage in the business of war; never will I, on any pretense whatever, lift up a sword against my brother."[27]

These passages from Godwin express Wordsworth's attitude to war in his own early poems. It is made use of by the powers of the aristocracy and monarchs as an instrument against the helpless masses, and then against the young democracy. It is to be condemned because it is an enemy of the social order, because it grinds down the poor, on whom democracy depends and who are least fitted to bear the calamities and burdens which war lays upon mankind. Hence, when we find poems against war, wholly or in part, such as *The Evening Walk,* 1787-1793; *Margaret,* 1793-1797; *The Female Vagrant* (later called *Guilt and Sorrow*), 1793-1798; and *The Old Man Travelling, Animal Tranquillity and Decay,* 1798, we meet with the condemnation of war not on purely sentimental, humane, or vaguely "Romantic" grounds, but on the reasoned basis of revolutionary philosophic doctrine. That hatred of war the poet continued to hold until the wars of the Revolution changed from the struggle for freedom to conquest of free peoples. Then he advocated war as the only instrument against a tyrant Napoleon who fought against liberty itself in his conquest of Switzerland, Venice, and Spain, and his attempted invasion of England.[28] This justification of war by the mature Wordsworth is no real change either of Godwin's attitude or of his own early years. Neither Godwin nor Wordsworth was a pacifist or conscientious objector, as some critics of Wordsworth seem to suppose. Godwin expressly says that wars of self-defense are always justifiable; and in this Wordsworth certainly agreed with him. In Wordsworth's later years the pattern of a tyrant who waged war against democracy and liberty was Napoleon: hence his implacable hatred of Bona-

---

27 *Political Justice,* 167 (Second Edition, 1796).
28 His attitude toward war is fully explained in the little read *Tract on the Convention of Cintra.*

parte and the nobly patriotic sonnets dedicated to national independence and liberty.

Finally, an aspect of Godwin's doctrine, which the author of *Political Justice* held in common with many revolutionary theorists, is his necessitarianism. The doctrine of necessity makes the progress of the race an inevitable one, taking place by reason of the nature of things and independent of the whim of individuals. That this belief in necessity was taken up by Wordsworth and made his own appears not only in *The Borderers* and poems like *Guilt and Sorrow,* but also in a poem as late as 1798, in a famous passage in *Tintern Abbey:*

> A motion and a spirit, that impels
> All thinking things, all objects of all thought,
> And rolls through all things,[29]

on which Hazlitt remarks: "Perhaps the doctrine of what has been called philosophical necessity was never more finely expressed than in these lines."[30] The notion of necessity also appears in a passage now forming a part of the fourth book of *The Excursion,* but written about 1796:

> So build we up the Being that we are;
> Thus deeply drinking-in the soul of things,
> We shall be wise perforce.[31]

Both these passages belong to the days of his belief in necessity: but it is significant that he never changed those passages in the many revisions of his poems.

Fired by the spirit of Godwin and by the kindred spirits of Paine, Priestley, Fawcett,[32] Horne Tooke, and Thelwall, in the year 1793, after he had published his two poems *An Evening Walk* and *Descriptive Sketches,* Wordsworth came to the defense of the French Revolution and democracy against the attacks of Bishop Watson, in a pamphlet which was never published, *Letter to the Bishop of Llandaff, by a Republican.*[33]

---

[29] *The Excursion,* IV, 101-103.

[30] *Philosophical Necessity,* Works, XI, 277-278.

[31] *The Excursion,* IV, 1264-1266.

[32] Wordsworth's relationship to Fawcett is indicated in my paper *Joseph Fawcett; The Art of War,* University of Wisconsin Studies in Language and Literature, No. 2, 1918, 225-270.

[33] *Prose Works of William Wordsworth,* edited by William Knight, 2 vols. 1896. I. 1-27.

In this pamphlet he uses the arguments which his mentors employed against monarchy, the aristocracy, the clergy, and special privileges, and in favor of democracy and parliamentary reform, and in an order which very strongly suggests the order in Godwin's book. The same zeal and beliefs mark him during the following year, when he still neglected the "paths of preferment and the law as too narrow, tortuous, and unseemly to bear the pure and broad light of reason," as Hazlitt says, and was attempting to found a review, *The Philanthropist,*[34] in order to give him an opportunity "of explaining and enforcing those general principles of the social order, which are applicable to all times and to all places." As he tells his friend Matthews, he disapproves of "monarchical and aristocratical governments, however modified. Hereditary distinctions, and privileged orders of every species, I think must necessarily counteract the progress of human improvement: hence it follows that I am not amongst the admirers of the British Constitution."[35] Furthermore, he was not an admirer of the government of the day, and with his friend Wrangham proposed and partly executed a translation of Juvenal, which should lash the follies of society and government. This was the poet's attitude in 1795; and, judging by the fragments which we have, the projected satire on existing institutions and their governors was to have been bitter enough. But he had already in 1794 found a subject more to his taste. This was the resumption of a poem begun in 1791 and dealing with the sorrows of the poor, *Guilt and Sorrow,* developed in a characteristically Godwinian direction and exposing "the vices of the penal law, and the calamities of war as they affect individuals."[36] In 1794 was also begun his tragedy *The Borderers,* which was finished in the following year, and shows at once his application of Godwinian principles as a rule of life and his recoil from the consequences involved in them, by his development of the character of Oswald the philosophical murderer. Here he arrives at what he conceives to be the dangers of

[34] *Letters of the Wordsworth Family,* I, 68-76; Letter of Wordsworth to William Matthews, Oct. 1, 1794.

[35] *Letters of the Wordsworth Family, loc. cit.*

[36] Letter of Wordsworth to Francis Wrangham, Nov. 20, 1795. *Op. cit.,* p. 90.

Godwinianism: "What delight!" he ironically exclaims in the eleventh book of *The Prelude*,

> How glorious! in self-knowledge and self-rule,
> To look through all the frailties of the world,
> And, with a resolute mastery shaking off
> Infirmities of nature, time, and place,
> Build social upon personal Liberty,
> Which, to the blind restraints of general laws
> Superior, magisterially adopts
> One guide, the light of circumstances, flashed
> Upon an independent intellect.[37]

This passage is paraphrased from *Political Justice,* and part of it is taken over from *The Borderers*. It expresses the deliberate opinion of Wordsworth that such hopes, abstracting "the hopes of man out of his feelings," must fail miserably and lead all like himself to "yield up moral questions in despair."[38]

> This was the crisis of the strong disease,
> This the soul's last and lowest ebb,[39]

the poet tells us in the eleventh book of *The Prelude*. This was the time when despair came to him; for, as he says, he was attempting to solve the riddle of existence without taking into account the most important thing of all—choice and hope and fear. He was making the fatal mistake of attempting

> to abstract the hopes of Man
> Out of his feelings.[40]

Just how he recovered from this moral crisis we do not know from the poet himself; for Wordsworth's usual reticence in *The Prelude* here becomes almost absolute silence. He says, however, that it was his sister Dorothy who maintained for him a saving intercourse with his true self, and in the midst of all preserved him still a Poet. While this testimony has great value, it is weak in that it in no way explains how it was that by 1798 Wordsworth was in possession of a theory and method in poetry with which he was utterly unacquainted in 1795. Whatever the influence of Dorothy may have been, it cannot

---

[37] *The Prelude*, XI, 236-244. The lines which this passage echoes are found in *The Borderers*, 1484-1496.
[38] *The Prelude*, XI, 305.
[39] *Op. cit.*, XI, 306-307.
[40] *Op. cit.*, XI, 225-226.

have been in the direction of furnishing the poet with a philosophy and an aesthetic. And yet he was furnished with both
during this crucial period of his life; so the problem of the
critic is to cast about for the source whence Wordsworth derived his inspiration and knowledge. It cannot be said that to
give in general the right answer to this problem is a difficult
thing to do; for obviously a most important source is the general stock of English thought, especially the stock of English
philosophic thought, as expressed in the system of David Hartley. But the influence of Godwin remained, especially of the
more reasonable and less extreme Godwin. Wordsworth perceived in Hartley a deeper philosophy of life, and he deserted
the less profound philosopher for one who was more adequate
to his mental needs. And yet he never deserted the thought of
Godwin at its best, and the spirit of Godwin at his best remained with him. And justly so, for where else could Wordsworth find a truer counsellor as to the aims and limits of the
enquiry in which he was engaged?

> It is the madness of philosophy only, that would undertake to
> account for everything, and to trace out the process by which every
> event in the world is generated. But let us beware of falling into
> the opposite extreme. It will often happen that events, which at
> first sight appear least to associate with that regularity and that
> precise system to which we are accustomed, will be found upon a
> minuter and more patient inspection really to belong to it. It is
> the madness of philosophy to circumscribe the universe within the
> bounds of our narrow system; it is the madness of ignorance to
> suppose that everything is new, and of a species totally dissimilar
> from what we have already observed.[41]

In this spirit, under the guidance of Hartley he proceeded
to enquire into the origin and nature of the art which he practiced, arriving at a theory which transcended not only Godwin
and his school but also Hartley and his system of associationism as well.

---

[41] *The Enquirer*, 1797, p. 24.

CHAPTER III

EARLY THEORY OF ART—RELATION TO THE SCHOOL OF TASTE

He who thinks nature, in the narrow sense of the word, is alone to be followed, will produce but a scanty entertainment for the imagination; everything is to be done with which it is natural for the mind to be pleased, whether it proceeds from simplicity or variety, uniformity or irregularity; whether the scenes are familiar or exotic; rude and wild, or enriched and cultivated; for it is natural for the mind to be pleased with all these in their turn. In short, whatever pleases has in it what is analogous to the mind, and is, therefore, in the highest and best sense of the word, natural. . . .

We may therefore conclude that the real substance, as it may be called, of what goes under the name of taste, is fixed and established in the nature of things; that there are certain and regular causes by which the imagination and passions of men are affected; and that the knowledge of these causes is acquired by a laborious and diligent investigation of nature, and by the same slow process as wisdom or knowledge of every kind, however instantaneous it may appear when thus acquired.

Sir Joshua Reynolds, *Seventh Discourse*, Dec. 19, 1776.

In the poetry and prose of Wordsworth, especially in the poems and prefaces which antedate the publication of the *Preface* of 1815, there occur terms and arguments, some of which form no part of his later doctrine of the Imagination as expounded in *The Preface* of 1815; while others are so re-stated in that preface and in *The Excursion* that they have a quite altered significance, though, as we shall see, they do not drop out of sight altogether. These terms and arguments, in the particular significance attached to them by Wordsworth and in the relationships assigned to them, indicate very cleary that he began his literary criticism as an adherent of the school of taste as it is represented by such writers as David Hartley, Lord Kames, Sir Joshua Reynolds, Hugh Blair, Archibald Alison, and Eras-

3

mus Darwin.[1] In these writers and in Wordsworth there are certain principles fundamental to their exposition of poetry and art, chief among which are the three following: (1) A very important principle, amply recognized by Wordsworth, is the dictum that taste is acquired by the study of the masters of art. This is the main guide to correctness of taste and the sole means by which we can study nature. This is, of course, a fundamental rule in the classic school of criticism, from which the school of taste borrowed it, and nowhere more succinctly summed up than in Pope's *Essay on Criticism*. Instances of the use of this principle by the writers listed above and by others of minor importance are so numerous that too much space would be consumed if all were recorded. A few cases may be cited, however, so as to present the standpoint of the school.

Blair deals with this matter in his second lecture. He recognizes the many fluctuations in taste from age to age; but insists that the standard is uniform in "men who are placed in such situations as are favorable to the proper exertions of taste." Even among nations of high civilization, accidental causes "may warp the proper operations of taste; sometimes the taste of religion, sometimes the form of government, may for a while pervert; a licentious court may introduce a taste for false ornaments, and dissolute writings. The usage of one admired genius may procure approbation for his faults, and even render them fashionable." But in the course of time "the genuine taste of human nature" will assert itself and triumph, because it is "founded on sound reason, and the native feelings of men." His conclusion is that "taste is far from being an arbitrary principle, which is subject to the fancy of every individual, and which admits of no criterion for determining whether it be false or true." On the contrary, it is universal, being founded on nature and reason:

---

[1] David Hartley, *Observations on Man*, 2 vols. 1749; Henry Home, Lord Kames, *Elements of Criticism*, 1762; Hugh Blair, *Lectures on Rhetoric and Belles Lettres*, 1783; Sir Joshua Reynolds, *Discourses*, 1769-1790; First Seven Discourses published in one volume, 1778; first published complete (fifteen discourses), 1790; Archibald Alison, *Essays on The Nature and Principles of Taste*, 1790; Erasmus Darwin, *Zoönomia; or, the Laws of Organic Life*, 3 vols. 1794-1796.

Its foundation is the same in all human minds. It is built upon sentiments and perceptions which belong to our nature, and which, in general, operate with the same uniformity as over other intellectual principles. When these sentiments are perverted by ignorance and prejudice, they are capable of being rectified by reason. Their sound and natural state is ultimately determined by comparing them with the general taste of mankind. Let men declaim as much as they please concerning the caprice and the uncertainty of taste, it is found, by experience, that there are beauties, which, if they be displayed in a proper light, have power to command lasting and general admiration. In every composition, what interests the imagination, and touches the heart, pleases all ages and nations. There is a certain string to which, when properly struck, the human heart is so made as to answer.

Hence the universal testimony which the most improved nations of the earth have conspired, throughout a long tract of ages, to give to some few works of genius; such as the Iliad of Homer, and the Æneid of Virgil. Hence the authority which such works have acquired, as standards in some degrees of poetical composition; since from them we are enabled to collect what the sense of mankind is concerning those beauties which give them the highest pleasure, and which therefore poetry ought to exhibit. Authority or prejudice may, in one age or country, give a temporary reputation to an indifferent poet or a bad artist; but when foreigners, or when posterity examine his works, his faults are discerned, and the genuine taste of human nature appears. "Opinionum commenta delet dies; naturæ judicia confirmat." "Time overthrows the illusions of opinion, but establishes the decisions of nature."[2]

Almost identical views are expressed by Hartley,[3] by Alison,[4] and by Sir Joshua Reynolds. As Reynolds discusses the matter from the artist's point of view and presents parallels to Wordsworth, we shall present the outline of his statement. The sixth discourse on the general subject of imitation has much to say on the value of study of great artists to anyone who would form a correct taste.[5]

Invention is one of the great marks of genius; but if we consult experience, we shall find, that it is by being conversant with the inventions of others, that we learn to invent; as by reading the thoughts of others we learn to think.

Whoever has so far formed his taste, as to be able to relish and feel the beauties of the great masters, has gone a great way in his

---

[2] Blair, *op. cit.*, Lecture I.
[3] *Op. cit.*, I, 418-442.
[4] *Op. cit.*, Essay I.
[5] Delivered December 10, 1774.

study; for, merely from a consciousness of this relish of the right the mind swells with an inward pride, and is almost as powerfully affected, as if it had itself produced what it admired. Our hearts, frequently warmed in this manner by the contact of those whom we wish to resemble, will undoubtedly catch something of their way of thinking; and we shall receive in our own bosoms some radiation at least of their fire and splendor. That disposition, which is so strong in children, still continues with us, catching involuntarily the general air and manner of those with whom we are most conversant; with this difference only, that a young mind is naturally pliable and imitative; but in a more advanced state it grows rigid, and must be warmed and softened before it will receive a deep impression.[6]

From these considerations, which a little of your own reflection will carry a great way further, it appears, of what great consequence it is, that our minds should be habituated to the contemplation of excellence; and that, far from being contented to make such habits the discipline of our youth only, we should, to the last moment of our lives, continue a settled intercourse with all the true examples of grandeur. Their inventions are not only the food of our infancy, but the substance which supplies the fullest maturity of our vigour.

The mind is a barren soil; a soil which is soon exhausted and will produce no crop, or only one, unless it be continually fertilized and enriched with foreign matter.

The conclusion of the sixth discourse is:

Study, therefore, the great works of the great masters, forever. Study, as nearly as you can, in the order, in the manner, and on the principles, on which they studied. Study nature attentively, but always with those masters in your company; consider them as models, which you are to imitate, and at the same time as rivals with whom you are to contend.[7]

The seventh discourse has as its subject the reality of a standard of taste, dealing with the relationship between nature and taste with all the vigor and freshness with which he deals with the relationship between imitation and genius in the preceding one. The term Taste is defined as that act of the mind by which we like or dislike, whatever be the subject. This principle by which we judge has its unalterable and fixed foundations in nature, and can, therefore, be equally investigated by reason and known by study:

---

[6] Compare Darwin, *op. cit.*, Section xxii, 3, on Imitation.

[7] Delivered December 10, 1776. This is also the subject of much of the twelfth *Discourse*, delivered December 10, 1784.

The first idea that occurs in the consideration of what is fixed in art, or in taste, is that presiding principle of which I have so frequently spoken in former discourses,—the general idea of nature. The beginning, the middle, and the end of everything that is valuable in taste, is comprised in the knowledge of what is truly nature; for whatever notions are not conformable to those of nature, or universal opinion, must be considered as more or less capricious.

My notion of nature comprehends not only the forms which nature produces, but also the nature and internal fabric and organization, as I may call it, of the human mind and imagination. The terms beauty, or nature, which are general ideas, are but different modes of expressing the same thing, whether we apply these terms to statues, poetry, or pictures.

This nature must therefore be studied; and as the minds of men are uniform the one with the other, the resulting judgments will be uniform, and hence the Taste of men formed on these judgments will be uniform. Thus we learn to know "what are the general feelings and passions of mankind," and so we acquire a true idea of what imagination and art are. The man of taste is a man of judgment, disciplined, and trained in the methods of reason.

A man of real taste is always a man of judgment in other respects; and those inventions which either disdain or shrink from reason, are generally, I fear, more like the dreams of a distempered brain, than the exalted enthusiasm of a sound and true genius. In the midst of the highest flight of fancy or imagination, reason ought to preside from first to last, though I admit her more powerful operation is upon reflection.

I illustrate this principle of imitation and respect for authority, not to prove the well-known fact that it forms an important part of the theory of the school of taste and of the classic school of criticism: I do so to make clear that when Wordsworth defended his "experiments" in a new kind of poetry in the *Lyrical Ballads* of 1798, he did not use the arguments in favor of "genius," but those of imitation. That he had the argument of the school of taste in mind is not a mere inference: he himself quotes Sir Joshua Reynolds, and gives a brief summary of the great painter's position.[8] He first appeals to nature, and claims that these "attempts" must not be judged

---

[8] *Advertisement* to the *Lyrical Ballads*, 1798. Repeated in the *Preface* of 1800 and 1802.

by a narrow definition of poetry but by truth to nature. I quote the entire passage:

> Readers accustomed to the gaudiness and inane phraseology of many modern writers, if they persist in reading this book to its conclusion, will perhaps frequently have to struggle with feelings of strangeness and awkwardness: they will look round for poetry, and will be induced to enquire by what species of courtesy these attempts can be permitted to assume that title. It is desirable that such readers, for their own sakes, should not suffer the solitary word Poetry, a word of very disputed meaning, to stand in the way of their gratification; but that, while they are perusing this book, they should ask themselves if it contains a natural delineation of human passions, human characters, and human incidents; and if the answer be favorable to the author's wishes, that they should consent to be pleased in spite of that most dreadful enemy to our pleasures, our own pre-established codes of decision.

This is said in the very spirit of Sir Joshua Reynolds, who thus defines his main purpose in addressing the pupils of the Royal Academy:[9]

> The tendency of this Discourse, with the instances which have been given, is not so much to place the artist above rules, as to teach him their reason; to prevent him from entertaining a narrow confined conception of art; to clear his mind from a perplexed variety of rules and their exceptions, by directing his attention to an intimate acquaintance with the passions and affections of the mind, from which all rules arise, and to which they are all referable.

But Wordsworth well knew that most of his readers did not have any such view of art; and he now proceeds to answer those readers whose taste may be offended because the subjects of the poems may seem too "low." He challenges the soundness of the taste of such, and retorts that the more conversant the reader is "with our elder writers," and "with those in modern times who have been the most successful in painting manners and passions, the fewer complaints of this kind will he have to make." This defense of the "low" in poetry may be reminiscent of Reynolds' similar defense of the "low" in painting in his discussion of the "Grand style" in his third discourse;[10] which, in turn, was not improbably inspired by the lively controversy on this aspect of literature by the presenta-

---

[9] The eighth *Discourse,* delivered December 10, 1778.
[10] Delivered December 14, 1778.

tion of his friend Goldsmith's *The Good-Natured Man* and *She Stoops to Conquer,* with the resulting condemnation of both plays by Horace Walpole and other critics, on the ground of their low characters and low humor. No doubt not only Reynolds, but Wordsworth also, remembered well Goldsmith's own retort to this criticism in his famous, "Damn anything that's low!"[11]

This supposed condemnation of his poetry by his supposed critics, Wordsworth next proceeds to meet by giving the grounds on which good taste is founded; and here he quotes Sir Joshua Reynolds by name:

An accurate taste in poetry, and in all the other arts, Sir Joshua Reynolds has observed, is an acquired talent, which can only be produced by severe thought and a long-continued intercourse with the best models of composition. This is mentioned not with so ridiculous a purpose as to prevent the most inexperienced reader from judging for himself; but merely to temper the rashness of decision, and to suggest that if poetry be a subject on which much time has not been bestowed, the judgment may be erroneous, and that in many cases it necessarily will be so.[12]

Thus it is by no "romantic" argument, but by the most "classical," that Wordsworth defends these "experiments" in the volume of 1798. He claims that he is in the great English tradition of "the best models of composition"—Chaucer, Spenser, Shakespeare, Milton,—and he appeals to the educated taste of his readers for proper appreciation of the seriousness of his endeavors.

(2) A second principle of the school of taste is the presence in every poem, or painting, or piece of sculpture, of unity or uniformity, and its contradictory quality, variety; of similitude or resemblance, and dissimilitude. Hartley declares that the only things that can be set up as "natural criterions" of "artificial beauty," are "uniformity with variety, usefulness in general, and the particular subserviency of this or that artificial beauty to improve the mind, so as to make it suit best with our present circumstances and future expectations."[13] Lord

---

[11] *She Stoops to Conquer,* I, ii.

[12] This is repeated in the *Preface* of 1800.

[13] *Op. Cit.,* I, 442, a passage summarizing his position. The principle is also discussed on page 419, 422, and 428.

Kames devotes two chapters to the discussion of Resemblance and Dissimilitude, and Uniformity and Variety.[14] Reynolds makes simplicity and variety, uniformity and irregularity essentials in any art which is to satisfy the imagination of the natural man;[15] and Alison develops at great length the thesis that uniformity and variety are the essential qualities of art. He summarizes his position in the following words:

Nothing is more delightful, than in any subject where we at first perceived only confusion, to find regularity gradually emerging, and to discover, amid the apparent chaos, some uniform principle which reconciles the whole to reduce a number of apparently dissimilar particulars, under one general law of resemblance, as it is one of the strongest evidences of the exertion of wisdom and design, so it is also productive of one of the strongest emotions of beauty, which design can excite.[16]

Hartley's exposition of the principle is the same as Alison's in its general outline; but he gives a special coloring to it, so that it is rather clear that Wordsworth probably had it in mind when explaining the principle of his own poetry. Hartley first lays down the general principle and its importance in art:

Uniformity and variety in conjunction are also principal sources of the pleasures of beauty, being made so partly by their association with the beauties of nature; partly by that with the works of art, and with the many conveniences which we receive from the uniformity and variety of the works of nature and art. They must therefore transfer part of the lustre borrowed from the works of art, and from the head of convenience, upon the works of nature.[17]

He proceeds to use this principle in explanation of figures of speech as one of the chief sources of beauty in poetry:

Now figurative words seem to strike and please us chiefly from that impropriety which appears at first sight, upon their application to the things denoted by them, and from the consequent heightening of the propriety as soon as it is duly perceived. For when figurative words have recurred so often as to excite the secondary idea instantaneously, and without any previous harshness to the imagination, they lose their peculiar beauty and force; and in order to recover this, and make ourselves sensible of it, we are obliged to re-

---

[14] *Observations on Man,* Chs. VIII and IX.
[15] The seventh *Discourse.*
[16] *Op. cit.,* Essay II, *Of the Sublimity and Beauty of the Material World,* Ch. IV, Sect. II, Part I. Sect. I especially develops the principle.
[17] *Observations on Man,* I, 419, Proposition XCIV.

call the literal sense, and to place the literal and figurative senses close together, so that we may first be sensible of the inconsistency, and then be more affected with the union and coalescence.[18]

Again, he deals with the reason for metrical language in poetry, offering an explanation which is based on the principle of uniformity and variety, just as Wordsworth does in dealing with this question, as we shall presently observe:

The beauties and excellencies of good poetry are deducible from three sources. First, the harmony, regularity, and variety of the numbers or metre, and of the rhyme. . . . That the versification has of itself a considerable influence may be seen by putting good poetical passages into the order of prose. And it may be accounted for from what has been already observed of uniformity and variety; from the smoothness and facility with which verses run over the tongue, from the frequent coincidence of the end of the sentence, and that of the verse, at the same time that this rule is violated at proper intervals in all varieties, lest the ear should be tired with too much sameness, from the assistance which versification affords to the memory, from some faint resemblance which it bears to music, and its frequent association with it, etc.[19]

The words of Alison and Hartley are reiterated by several authors who are the avowed followers of Hartley, such as Darwin[20] and Priestley.[21]

As has already been said, Wordsworth appeals to uniformity

---

[18] *Op. cit.,* I, 429, Proposition XCIV.

[19] *Op. cit.,* I, 428-429, Proposition XCIV.

[20] *Op. cit.,* Section XXII, 2 ; *Loves of the Plants,* Interlude III.

[21] Joseph Priestley, *Lectures on Oratory and Criticism,* 1777. Lecture XVII, volume XXIII of Rutt's edition. Priestley acknowledges his indebtedness to Hartley as openly as Godwin. For instance, in the preface to his *Examination of Dr. Reid, Dr. Beattie, and Dr. Oswald,* 1774, he says: "Those who are not fond of much close thinking, which is necessarily the case with the generality of readers, and some writers will not thank me for endeavoring to introduce into more public notice such a theory of the human mind as that of Dr. Hartley. His is not a book that a man can read over in a few evenings, so as to be ready to give a satisfactory account of it to any of his friends who may happen to ask him what there is in it, and expect an answer in a few sentences. In fact, it contains a new and most extensive *science,* and requires a vast fund of preparatory knowledge to enter upon the study of it with any prospect of success.

"But in return, I will promise any person who shall apply to this work, with proper furniture, that the study of it will abundantly reward his labour. It will be like entering upon *a new world,* afford inexhaustible matter for curious and useful speculation, and be of unspeakable advantage in almost every pursuit, and even in things to which it seems, at first sight, to bear no sort of relation. For my own part, I can almost say that I think myself more indebted to this one treatise, than to all the books I

and variety of an explanation of the function of metrical language in poetry. The parallelism between his statement and that of Hartley is very apparent:

If I had undertaken a systematic defense of the theory upon which these poems were written, it would have been my duty to develope the various causes upon which the pleasure received from metrical language depends. Among the chief of these causes is to be reckoned a principle which must be well known to those who have made any of the Arts the object of accurate reflection; I mean the pleasure which the mind derives from the perception of similitude in dissimilitude. This principle is the great spring of the activity of our minds and their chief feeder. From this principle the direction of the sexual appetite, and all the passions connected with it, take their origin. It is the life of our ordinary conversation; and upon the accuracy with which similitude in dissimilitude, and dissimilitude in similitude, are perceivable, depend our taste and our moral feelings.[22]

Wordsworth did not write the "systematic defense" of the theory which he held in 1800, and so we do not see the principles of uniformity and variety displayed at length. For, when he again appears in print as an apologist for poetry, this principle had lost its major importance for him. It occupies a rather minor place in the *Preface* of 1815; and does not appear at all in *The Prelude,* or in *The Excursion.* That he held it as rather important as late as 1802, however, and even

ever read beside, the Scriptures excepted." This is only one of many such eulogies by Priestley. He intended to convert Benjamin Franklin to Christianity by prescribing Hartley—a scheme which was interfered with by the Revolutionary War. *Life and Correspondence of Joseph Priestley,* edited by J. T. Rutt, I, 212.

[22] *Preface to Lyrical Ballads,* 1800. In the 1802 *Preface* Wordsworth states that by metre "a dissimilitude will be produced altogether sufficient for the gratification of a rational mind." In the 1815 *Preface* he makes a fundamental use of the principle to explain the *creative* activity of the imagination. See p. 164. It is thus clear that he never repudiated it.

Coleridge, too, clung to it late. In *Table Talk,* December 27, 1831, he speaks of multitude in unity; and in *Anima Poetae,* edited by E. H. Coleridge, 1895, he is quoted as follows: "Now poetry produces two kinds of pleasure, one for each of the two master-movements or impulses of man—the gratification of the love of variety, and the gratification of the love of uniformity." In *Essays on the Principles of Genial Criticism,* 1814, he regards "Multëity in Unity" as The Beautiful: "The sense of beauty subsists in simultaneous intuitive of the relation of parts, each to each and of all to a whole." The principle is a vital Platonic one. *Phaedrus,* 261-262; *Philebus,* 15. Leigh Hunt, *Imagination and Fancy,* 1844, states that poetry modulates its language "on the principle of variety in uniformity." Ruskin, *Modern Painters,* Vol. II, 1846, Part III. Sect. 1, Ch. IV, "Of Unity," deals with unity and variety, deriving variety out of the necessity of unity.

as late as 1815, is abundantly clear; and a recognition of this fact helps us to explain the meaning of more than one passage which would otherwise be dark.

(3) A third doctrine which is intimately associated with most of the members of the school of taste is that of the association of ideas, or associationism. Appearing as a purely psychological concept in Hobbes[23] and Locke,[24] it was taken up by Alison[25] and applied to the field of aesthetics, and by Akenside,[26] who made it the subject of poetry. For our purpose it is important to note that the principle was developed by Hartley, with implications which are peculiar to him; and by Wordsworth with a consideration of the more intimate relationship which it bears to poetry, as the philosopher is interpreted by the poet. As we shall devote a separate chapter[27] to the important relations between Wordsworth and Hartley, we shall say nothing concerning them here.

The principle of associationism is directed against the notion that there are innate ideas, or powers, such as the moral sense, beauty, sublimity, and so on, and in defense of the theory that all these powers, or ideas, are not simple and original, but are very complex and built up out of the simpler elements of the mind, all coming ultimately from experience. This is what makes the theory the opposite of such theories as that of Shaftesbury, and it is important to note that Wordsworth's philosophical connections were with the associationist school and not with the intuitionist, if we are to understand the real bearing of his theories of poetry and of life, especially as developed in his "great philosophic poem," *The Prelude* and *The Excursion.*[28]

Alison applied this doctrine to aesthetics, claiming that the feelings, or emotions, of beauty and sublimity are not simple and innate, but complex, and the result of experience:

The pleasure, therefore, which accompanies the emotion of taste may be considered not as simple, but as a complex pleasure; and

---

[23] *Leviathan,* Ch. II; published 1651.
[24] *Essay Concerning Human Understanding,* Fourth Edition, Book II, Ch. 33.
[25] *Op. cit.,* Essay II, *Of the Sublimity and Beauty of the Material World.*
[26] *Pleasures of the Imagination.* Book III, 278-514. Published 1744.
[27] Chapter VI.
[28] See Chapters XI-XII.

as arising not from any separate and peculiar sense, but from the union of the pleasure of simple emotion, with that which is annexed, by the constitution of the human mind, to the exercise of Imagination.[29]

Qualities of matter are incapable of producing emotion, or the exercise of any affection, yet it is obvious that they may produce this effect, from their association with other qualities; and as being either the signs or expressions of such qualities as are fitted by the constitution of our nature to produce emotion.

Thus, in the human body, particular forms or colours are the signs of particular passions or affections. In works of art, particular forms are the signs of dexterity, of taste, of convenience, of utility. In the works of nature, particular sounds and colours, etc., are the signs of peace, or danger, or plenty, or desolation, etc. In such cases, the constant connection we discern between the sign and the thing signified, between the material quality and the quality productive of emotion, renders at last the one expressive to us of the other, and very often disposes us to attribute to the sign, that effect which is produced only by the quality signified.[30]

Alison proceeds to illustrate this principle in the world of sound, of sight, of forms, of motion, and of the human countenance and form, always insisting on the principle that when the association is dissolved the emotion ceases; and arriving at the conclusion that the beauty and sublimity which are felt in the appearances of matter are to be ascribed to their expression of mind; or to their being the signs of those qualities of mind which are fitted, by the constitution of our nature, to affect us with pleasing or interesting emotion.[31] This is to say that our aesthetic emotions depend on our ideas of things through association, and so are modified and directed by our ideas in an aesthetic product, the ideas in such cases being "ideas of emotion."[32]

That Wordsworth expressed this very principle has not been recognized; but it is nevertheless true that such an opinion is to be found plainly stated in an important passage in his *Preface* to the *Lyrical Ballads* of 1800. In explaining his purpose in composing his poems he uses the following associationistic language:

---

[29] *Essays on the Nature and Principles of Taste*, Essay I, Conclusion, iii.
[30] *Op. cit.*, Essay II, Ch. I.
[31] *Op. cit.*, Essays II, Ch. VI, vi.
[32] *Op. cit.*, Essay I, *Conclusion*.

For all good poetry is the spontaneous overflow of powerful feelings; but though this be true, Poems to which any value can be attached, were never produced on any variety of subjects but by a man who being possessed of more than usual organic sensibility had also thought long and deeply. For our continued influxes of feeling are modified and directed by our thoughts, which are indeed the representatives of all our past feelings.

Hence, since the feelings result from the thought, the reader will be conducted by the feelings which are excited to the thoughts of the poet who recorded the emotions which arose out of the thoughts, "if he be in a healthful state of association." This is true of all poetry; but, says Wordsworth, it will be specially true of his poems, as his purpose will be found principally to be "to illustrate the manner in which our feelings and ideas are associated in a state of excitement."

This statement is clearly couched in the language of associationism, and the same is true of another portion of the same *Preface* of 1800. In speaking of defects that may be found in his poems, he states that he is aware of the possibility that his associations "must have been particular instead of general." This reads like a direct reference to Alison's discussion of this same aspect of associationism.[33] Of these three principles of the school of taste, the last is by far the most important in considering the mature Wordsworth. The doctrine of taste and imitation plays no part in his theory after 1798, except in the general form of the commonly accepted notion that all good authors follow a tradition; the doctrine of uniformity and variety was allowed to drop into comparative obscurity soon after 1800; but the doctrine of association became an essential part of his most mature doctrine. After 1800 the doctrine becomes more profound, as he studies Hartley with fuller understanding, and as interpreted in the light of Locke and other English philosophers, with the result that in the great essays and poems from the publication of the *Poems* of 1807 onward he becomes absorbed in the discussion of deeper problems of life and art from the Hartleian point of view. In the light of Hartley's interpretation of the doctrine of the association of ideas he furnishes a new and original theory of Nature, of Fancy, and of

[33] *Op. cit.*, Essay II, Ch. I; Ch. VI, vi.

Imagination, and becomes at once the interpreter and poet of associationism. To this period of maturity we now turn, considering first the theory of Poetic Diction, a matter which occupied his early years of criticism and practice, but which also remained with him as worthy of consideration in the earlier portion of his period of maturity.

PART II

WORDSWORTH'S DOCTRINE—MATURE FORMS

"Last, and pre-eminently, I challenge for this poet the gift of IMAGINATION in the highest and strictest sense of the word."

Samuel Taylor Coleridge, 1817.

CHAPTER IV

POETIC DICTION

If there be, what I believe there is, in every nation, a stile which never becomes obsolete, a certain mode of phraseology so consonant and congenial to the analogy and principles of its respective language, as to remain settled and unaltered; this stile is probably to be sought in the common intercourse of life, among those who speak only to be understood, without ambition of elegance. The polite are always catching modish innovations, and the learned depart from established forms of speech, in hope of finding or making better; those who wish for distinction forsake the vulgar, when the vulgar is right; but there is a conversation above grossness and below refinement, where propriety resides. . . .

Samuel Johnson, *Preface to Shakespeare*, 1765.

Accordingly such a language arising out of repeated experience and regular feelings is a more permanent and a far more philosophical language than that which is frequently substituted for it by Poets, who think that they are conferring honour upon themselves and their art in proportion as they separate themselves from the sympathies of men, and indulge in arbitrary and capricious habits of expression in order to furnish food for fickle tastes and fickle appetites of their own creation.

William Wordsworth, *Preface* of 1800.

While it is true that not so much needs to be said on the language of poetry as on the subject matter of poetry, Wordsworth's special point of view must be put forward in a manner that will make clear his general purpose and intention, in order to guard against the misunderstandings to which the poet has been subjected, partly because of his own meagre statement of his case.

In the beginning it should be said that the language of poetry is not a major question with him, as we can see in all his discussions of the questions of poetry; for everywhere it is made clear that the important question is the matter rather than the manner of the art. In the *Advertisement* of 1798, and in the *Preface* of 1800-1805, it is distinctly secondary to the content of poetry, and in his remarks concerning the language of

4

poetry he refers rather to those poems which he calls "Lyrical ballads," as distinguished from the "other poems" spoken of on the title-page of all editions of the *Lyrical Ballads.* Such a poem as *Tintern Abbey* can hardly be in his mind when he speaks of this subject in the *Advertisement* of 1798, and all through this statement of his principles he defends the ballads rather than the "other poems." In regard to his statement of 1798 we must also remark that when speaking of the language of *The Ancient Mariner,* he plainly says, "The language adopted in it has been equally intelligible for these last three centuries." That this general ideal was present in the mind of both the authors appears from Hazlitt's account of his visit to them in the summer of 1798:

> He (Coleridge) said the *Lyrical Ballads* were an experiment about to be tried by him and Wordsworth, to see how far the public taste would endure poetry written in a more natural and simple style than had hitherto been attempted; totally discarding the artifices of poetical diction, and making use only of such words as had probably been common in the ordinary language since the days of Henry II.[1]

Coleridge's statement is that in Samuel Daniel there are to be found "many and exquisite specimens of that style which, as the *neutral ground* of prose and verse, is common to both."[2] It seems clear that when Wordsworth spoke of "the real language of men," he was thinking of the language which is permanent and basic in English, the "neutral style" which is neither new nor old, nor the result of artifice.

With this ideal he contrasted the practices of his contemporaries, and what did he find? In place of truth to life, he found "frantic novels, sickly and stupid German Tragedies, and deluges of idle and extravagant stories in verse." Corresponding to these departures from truth in substance was the departure from reality in style which is known as "poetic diction," and against this he carried on a campaign by theory and practice.

In this campaign he had in mind a central idea which is present in "poetic diction," that of personification; and on that he

---

[1] *My First Acquaintance with Poets.* Surely this is a slip for "Henry VII."

[2] *Biographia Literaria,* Ch. XVIII.

made particular war. The particular variety of "poetic diction" which Wordsworth attacked is nevertheless a perfectly natural product of the philosophy of the age, which comes down through a continuous English tradition. Samuel Johnson explains that we had not a "poetical diction" in the time of Dryden, "no system of words at once refined from the grossness of domestic use, and free from the harshness of terms appropriated to particular arts. . . . Those happy combinations of words which distinguish poetry from prose had been rarely attempted; we had few elegances or flowers of speech."[3] Gray had likewise stated that "the language of the age is never the language of poetry";[4] and Goldsmith warmly championed this same idea.[5] In this tradition Addison stands as a most important figure, for it is he who does much to give the theory of poetical diction the particular and special form which it had assumed by Wordsworth's time. He does this by connecting his theory of the Imagination with Locke's distinction between primary and secondary qualities in objects. This distinction is fully accepted by Addison in his influential papers on the "Pleasures of the Imagination," in the *Spectator,* as we see from his explicit statement, June 24th, 1712, No. 413:

I have here supposed that my Reader is acquainted with that great Modern Discovery, which is at present universally acknowledged by all the enquirers into Natural Philosophy; namely, that Light and Colours, as apprehended by the Imagination are only Ideas in the Mind, and not Qualities that have any Existence in Matter. As this is a Truth that has been proved incontestably by many Modern Philosophers, and is indeed one of the finest Speculations in that Science, if the *English* Reader would see the Notion explained at large, he may find it in the Eighth Chapter of the Second Book of Mr. Locke's Essay on Human Understanding.

This statement of Addison is of very great importance, for it shows very clearly that the theory *Ut pictura poesis* had a distinctive English and native tradition founded anew on English philosophy and quite distinct from the general Renaissance literary tradition which had its origin in the Horatian precept. This is to say that through Addison's influence this

---

[3] *Life of Cowley; Life of Dryden.*
[4] *Letter to Richard West,* April 4, 1742.
[5] *Life of Thomas Parnell.*

theory took on a quite specific form, with the result that through Akenside, the expounder of Addison,[6] Beattie,[7] Erasmus Darwin,[8] Alison,[9] and Priestley,[10] and the whole school of taste,[11] the general problem came to Wordsworth in a form which is quite different from that in which it presented itself to Gray, Johnson, and Goldsmith.   This specific form of "poetic diction" takes its origin in accordance with Addison's

---

[6] Mark Akenside, *Pleasures of the Imagination, The Design,* First Edition, 1744.

[7] James Beattie, *An Essay on Poetry and Music,* 1779.   Part II, *Of the Language of Poetry,* Section II, *Natural Language is improved in poetry by the use of poetical words.*   This section gives an account of seven ways in which this improvement is accomplished.   Despite the fact that Beattie recognizes a "poetic diction," he has many similarities to Wordsworth.   For instance, he deprecates the idea that poetical words are all of poetry: "Many passages there are of exquisite poetry, wherein not a single phrase occurs that might not be used in prose," page 230.   Like Wordsworth, too, he looks back to Shakespeare.   In the Section III, *Natural Language is improved in poetry, by means of Tropes and Figures,* he quotes a passage from *Othello,* IV, iii:

> "My mother had a maid call'd Barbara;
> She was in love, and he she loved proved mad,
> And did forsake her. She had a song of willow;
> An old thing it was," etc;

and in a footnote he comments:
"This charming passage, translated into the *finical style,* which, whatever be the subject or speaker, must always be descriptive, enigmatical, and full of figures, would perhaps run thus:

> Even now, sad memory to my thought recalls
> The nymph Dione, who with pious care,
> My much-loved mother, in my vernal years,
> Attended; blooming was the maiden's form,
> And on her brow Discretion sat, and on
> Her rosy cheeks a thousand Graces played.
> O! luckless was the day, when Cupid's dart,
> Shot from a swain's alluring eye,
> First thrill'd with pleasing pangs her throbbing breast!
>
>   . . . . From morn to dewy eve,
> From Eve till rosy-finger'd Morn appear'd,
> In a sad song, a song of ancient days,
> Warbling her wild woe to the pitying winds,
> She sat; the weeping willow was her theme,
> And well the theme accorded with her woe," etc.

He then adds: "I hope my young readers are all wiser; but I believe there was a time, when I should have been tempted to prefer this flashy tinsel to Shakespeare's fine gold."

[8] *Loves of the Plants,* Interludes, 1791.

[9] Archibald Alison, *Essays on Taste,* 1790.

[10] Joseph Priestley, *Lectures in Theory of Language and Universal Grammar,* 1762; *Lectures on Poetry and Criticism,* 1777.   In Vol. XXIII of *Complete Works,* edited by J. T. Rutt; (25 Vols.) 1817-1832.

[11] Francis Jeffrey, "On Beauty," first contributed to the *Encyclopedia Britannica,* 1816, shows that the school of taste retained its vitality well into the nineteenth century.

statement, and largely through his influence. He has been called "the discoverer of the Imagination,"[12] was enormously influential, and was the first to note that Locke's philosophy led to the belief that the human mind by Imagination could supply qualities to objects which do not inhere in these objects; that is, that the imagination operates in an independent way with regard to the "secondary qualities," as contrasted with the "primary qualities" of things. These "secondary qualities" are colors, sounds, light, and smells; and as these exist in the mind, and are creations of the mind, they are capable of being transferred from one sense to another without loss, and frequently with great gain. As it was a settled principle that vision is the most dominant of all our senses, and as both Locke and Berkeley gave great importance to this sense, this transference of ideas from sense to sense took the form of the translation from all the other senses to sight.

This is clearly shown in Erasmus Darwin's theory of poetry. His *Loves of the Plants,* published in the year 1789, "with Philosophical Notes," was composed to illustrate the process of converting the system of botany into poetry by the process of personification in terms of vision. In the *Interludes* to this poem, the second part of *The Botanic Garden,* which were added to the second edition of 1791, he gives very clear expression to the theory. The *Interludes* are cast into the form of conversation which is carried on between a *Bookseller* and a *Poet*:

Bookseller: Your verses, Mr. Botanist, consist of pure description. I hope there is sense in the notes.

Poet: I am only a flower painter, or occasionally attempt a landscape; and leave the human figure with the subjects of history to abler artists.

Bookseller: It is well to know what subjects are within the limits of your pencil; many have failed of success from the want of this self-knowledge. But pray tell me, what is the essential difference between Poetry and Prose? Is it solely the melody or measure of the language?

Poet: I think not solely, for some prose has its melody, and even measure. And good verses, well spoken in a language unknown to the hearer are not so easily to be distinguished from good prose.

---

[12] W. B. Worsfold, *The Principles of Literary Criticism*, Ch. V. entitled "Addison's treatment of the Imagination as a separate faculty of the mind introduces a new principle into Criticism."

Bookseller: Is it the sublimity, beauty, or novelty of the senti-ments?

Poet: Not so, for sublime sentiments are often better expressed in prose. Thus when Warwick, in one of the plays of Shakespeare, is left wounded on the field after the loss of the battle, and his friend says to him, "Oh, could you but fly!" what can be more sub-lime than his answer, "Why then, I would not fly." No measure of verse, I imagine, could add dignity to this sentiment. And it will be easy to select examples of the beautiful or new from prose writ-ers, which, I suppose, no measure of verse could improve.

Bookseller: In what then consists the essential difference be-tween Poetry and Prose?

Poet: Next to the measure of the language, the principal distinc-tion appears to me to consist in this: that Poetry admits of but few words expressive of very abstracted ideas, whereas Prose abounds with them. And as our ideas derived from visible objects are more distinct than those derived from the objects of our other senses, the words expressive of these ideas belonging to vision make up the principal part of poetic language. That is, the Poet writes prin-cipally to the eye, the Prose-writer uses more abstracted terms. Mr. Pope has written a bad verse in the Windsor Forest:

"And Kennet swift for silver Eels renown'd."

The word renown'd does not present the idea of a visible object to the mind, and is thence prosaic. But change this line thus.

"And Kennet swift, where silver Graylings play,"

and it becomes poetry, because the scenery is then brought before the eye.

Bookseller: This may be done in prose.

Poet: And when it is done in a single word, it animates the prose; so it is more agreeable to read in Mr. Gibbon's History, "Germany was at this time *over-shadowed* with extensive forests;" than "Germany was at this time *Full* of extensive forests." But where this mode of expression occurs too frequently, the prose ap-proaches to poetry, and in graver works, where we expect to be in-structed rather than amused, it becomes tedious and impertinent. Some parts of Mr. Burke's eloquent orations become intricate and enervated by superfluity of poetic ornament, which quality of orna-ment would have been agreeable in a poem where much ornament is expected.

Bookseller: Is, then, the office of Poetry only to amuse?

Poet: The Muses are young Ladies; we expect to see them dressed, though not like some modern beauties, with so much gauze and feather that "the Lady herself is the least part of her." There are, however didactic pieces of poetry which are much admired, as the *Georgics* of Virgil, Mason's *English Garden*, Hayley's *Epistles*. Nevertheless Science is best delivered in Prose, as its mode of rea-soning is from stricter analogies than metaphors or similies.

Bookseller: Do not Personifications and Allegories distinguish Poetry?

Poet: These are other arts of bringing objects before the eye, or of expressing sentiments in the language of vision, and are indeed better suited to the pen than the pencil.

Bookseller: That is strange when you have just said they are used to bring their objects before the eye.

Poet: In poetry the personification or allegoric figure is generally indistinct, and therefore does not strike us so forcibly as to make us attend to its improbability, but in painting the figures being all much more distinct, their improbability becomes apparent, and seizes our attention to it. Thus the person of Concealment is very indistinct, and therefore does not compel us to attend to its improbability in the following beautiful lines of Shakespeare:

> "She never told her love;
> But let Concealment, like a worm i' th' bud,
> Feed on her damask cheek."

But in these lines below the person of Reason obtrudes itself into our company, and becomes disagreeable by its distinctness, and consequent improbability:

> "To Reason I flew and intreated her aid,
> Who paused on my case, and each circumstance weigh'd;
> Then gravely reply'd in return to my prayer,
> That Hebe was fairest of all that were fair.
> That's the truth, replied I, I've no need to be taught.
> I came to you, Reason, to find out a fault.
> If that's all, says Reason, return as you came.
> To find fault with Hebe would forfeit my name."[13]

The importance which Darwin attaches to Personification is shown by a portion of his concluding remarks:

And in one respect, I believe, the English language serves the purpose of poetry better than the ancient ones; I mean in the greater ease of producing personifications, for as our nouns have in general no genders affixed to them in prose-compositions, and in the habits of conversation, they become easily personified only by the addition of a masculine or feminine pronoun, as,

> "Pale Melancholy sits, and round *her* throws
> A death-like silence, and a dread repose."
>
> Pope's *Abelard.*

And, secondly, as most of our nouns have the article *a* or *the* prefixed to them in prose-writing and in conversation, they become personified even by the omission of these articles, as in the bold figure of Shipwreck in Miss Seward's *Elegy on Captain Cook:*

---

[13] Interlude, I.

"But round the steep rocks and dangerous strand
   Rolls the white surf, and SHIPWRECK guards the land."[14]

Against this whole theory Wordsworth rebels, as it negatives his fundamental conception of poetry. For poetry is
real, dealing with human passions, human characters, and human incidents that are real and natural, and as a necessary
consequence it follows that the language that expresses these
things must be handmaid to the thought. And so poetry must
be expressed in language that is real,—"the real language of
men."

And what is this real language? In answering this, as we
have seen, Wordsworth had recourse to no absolute or abstract test. He believed that "poetic diction" is a perversion of
the real language of poetry, and he harked back to the Eliza-
bethans, especially to Samuel Daniel, and to a long line of
poets and prose writers from Chaucer down to Collins.[15] He
believed that a reform had been begun in Percy's *Reliques of
Ancient English Poetry,* 1765, in which he thought the real
speech of the people was used. Hence came his enthusiasm
for that work and his imitations of it. If we grant that his
zeal in this direction led him to infelicities of expression and
to over-statement of theory, we must keep in mind that it resulted for the greater part in solid achievement. The infelicities of *Goody Blake and Harry Gill,* or the *Idiot Boy* are a
very little thing when balanced against *We are Seven, Anecdote For Fathers, Lines Written in Early Spring, The Mad
Mother, Expostulation and Reply,* and *The Tables Turned.*
Any influence which encouraged, even in small part, these last
two poems must have been founded on something which is in

---

[14] *The Loves of the Plants,* Interlude III. This theory is referred to and
endorsed in the *Zoönomia,* published 1794-1796, Part I, Section XXII, ii.
The theory of ideas on which the whole system of Darwin's poetic diction
is founded is given in *Zoönomia,* Part I, Section XV, under the heading
Classes of Ideas. There is found the familiar classification of ideas into
1st, Ideas of Sensation, and 2nd, Ideas of Perception. The whole system
of Darwin is Hartleian, but Darwin goes beyond Hartley in holding that
characteristics acquired through education can be transmitted to posterity.
Nowadays Darwin is best known through the parody in the *Anti-Jacobin,*
1797, entitled *The Loves of the Triangles;* but we shall the more clearly
realize Wordsworth's independence of judgment if we recollect that Horace
Walpole was pleased with Darwin's verse, and that to Cowper his verses
were "strong, learned, and sweet," and his whole poem marked him as
"Sweet harmonist of Flora's court."

[15] *Essay Supplementary to the Preface,* 1815.

close relationship with the genius of the English language at its simple best.

The quarrel over the theory of language has been a bitter one, and Wordsworth's enemies have had an easy victory because they have not paid due attention to what he has said. His main statement is that low and rustic life was generally chosen, in the "experiments" which appeared in the volumes of 1798 and 1800-1805,

because in that situation the essential passions of the heart find a better soil in which they can attain their maturity; are less under restraint, and speak a plainer and more emphatic language; because in that situation our elementary feelings exist in a state of greater simplicity and consequently may be more accurately contemplated and more forcibly communicated; because the manners of rural life germinate from those elementary feelings; and from the necessary character of rural occupations are more easily comprehended; and are more durable; and lastly, because in that situation the passions of men are incorporated with the beautiful and permanent forms of nature. The language, too, of these men is adopted (purified indeed from what appear to be its real defects, from all lasting and rational causes of dislike or disgust) because such men hourly communicate with the best objects from which the best part of language is originally derived; and because, from their rank in society and the sameness and narrow circle of their intercourse, being less under the action of social vanity, they convey their feelings and notions in simple and unelaborated expressions. Accordingly, such a language arising out of repeated experience and regular feelings is a more permanent and a far more philosophical language than that which is frequently substituted for it by Poets, who think that they are conferring honour upon themselves and their art in proportion as they separate themselves from the sympathies of men, and indulge in arbitrary and capricious habits of expression in order to furnish food for fickle tastes and fickle appetites of their own creation.

Now, if this passage is read carefully and in this connection, it is clear that what Wordsworth has in mind is "poetic diction" and nothing more. Thus, it is very unfair to argue that he is here setting himself and peasant speech up against Shakespeare and other English authors, for his footnote to this very passage which we have quoted, reads: "It is worth while here to observe that the affecting parts of Chaucer are almost always expressed in language pure and universally intelligible even to this day." Clearly, what he is doing is not

opposing "the real language of men" to that of Shakespeare
and Milton, but identifying these and opposing them to the
perversions of language which had been brought about by
"poetic diction." Against these perversions Wordsworth directs his arguments, which are based on the belief that "the
real language of men" is the language of real men who speak
it in its most unperverted, idiomatic form; and he cites, as
striking illustrations of this "real language," the language of
the lower and middle classes and the great English poets. This
is the "philosophical language" of which he speaks in the passage quoted, because it is based on real experience and knowledge and is not the product of the "false, secondary power, by
which we multiply distinctions" and build up a vocabulary
which does not arise out of actual contact with reality. This
is the "permanent" language; for both in the case of the unsophisticated person and in the case of the poet, it arises out of
"repeated experience and regular feelings," and is shared alike
by both classes.

In the same line of reasoning, there is "no essential difference between the language of prose and metrical composition."
Here again, the real language of men and the language of
Shakespeare, Milton, and Chaucer have the quality of reality,
permanence, philosophical character, or as we should say, propriety and idiomatic quality, as contrasted with "poetic diction." This is the "philosophic language" so much sought
after by many writers in the eighteenth century, a quest which
made research into the nature of language an integral part of
philosophic systems and gave to the study of grammar all the
aspects of a philosophic search for the first principles of
mind. Hence we find Locke and Berkeley dealing with the
abuses which language is forced to undergo, and hence is
traced the origin of the philosophico-grammatical treatises of
Hermes, and *The Diversions of Purley.*[16] The general endeavor of all these writers was to establish a grand common

---

[16] It seems clear that Wordsworth was acquainted with Locke's treatment of Language in the *Essay on the Human Understanding,* Book III,
and he can hardly have been ignorant of Berkeley's *Principles of Human
Knowledge.* J. Harris, *Hermes,* 1751, a philosophical treatise on Grammar,
not improbably encouraged him in his idea of the "permanent language,"
Book III, p. 345. Horne Tooke's *Diversions of Purley,* 1736-1798, was
famous.

language which should be the medium for the clear and effective transference of thoughts from mind to mind; and an obvious conclusion to be drawn from this was that poetry, if it is to be such a medium, must not differ from prose in *essentials*. It was equally inevitable that in supporting this position, Wordsworth should have appealed to the common man and to the poets and prose writers who are the glory of English literature. This is precisely what Wordsworth did, and opposed them to the language of those who employed "poetic diction" and proclaimed that it was all of poetry.

With regard to the further development of poetic language and its use in certain poetic situations, it may be said that Coleridge has very correctly pointed out the weaknesses of Wordsworth's reasoning on the aesthetic side of poetry. But it may also be remarked that Coleridge is singularly disregardful of Wordsworth's point of view and obvious meaning. In those famous chapters of *Biographia Literaria*,[17] in which he criticizes Wordsworth's theories of poetry, he pays no attention to the related subjects of Imagination as Wordsworth conceives it, nor does he refer to Wordsworth's explanation of the effect of metre by the principle of similitude in dissimilitude. By this method of procedure he drives the argument into fields not contemplated by Wordsworth and so gains an easy victory. It is a pity that he did not carry his arguments along the same line as that of Wordsworth, for if he had done so we should have had a discussion, from Coleridge's side, of the relationships that exist between imaginative activity and verse,—a subject which he does not even touch on, and one which Wordsworth merely sketches out in his *Preface*. If Coleridge had taken up the principle of similitude in dissimilitude, by means of which Wordsworth justifies metre, we might have had a discussion of associationism, and of the importance which was attached to the principle of uniformity and variety, and possibly of other fundamentals of the school of taste.

However, Coleridge did not proceed in this manner, nor did Wordsworth develop his argument much beyond a mere outline of what he probably would have said if he had been writing "a systematic defence" of the theory upon which the poems

---

[17] Ch. XIV-XX.

in the *Lyrical Ballads* were written. We are thus deprived of
a most interesting chapter in literary criticism by both author
and critic which would have given greater significance both to
the *Preface* to the *Lyrical Ballads* and to these critical chapters of *Biographia Literaria*.

In behalf of Wordsworth, however, it must be said that in
the *Appendix* of 1815 to the *Preface* to the *Lyrical Ballads* he
returned to the subject of poetic diction, and clearly indicated
that his objections to this species of poetic language were based
on the grounds of reality and truth:

> The earliest poets of all nations generally wrote from passion ex-
> cited by real events; they wrote naturally, and as men: feeling pow-
> erfully as they did, their language was daring and figurative. In
> succeeding times, Poets, and Men ambitious of the fame of Poets,
> perceiving the influence of such language, and desirous of produc-
> ing the same effect without being animated by the same passion, set
> themselves to a mechanical adoption of these figures of speech, and
> made use of them, sometimes with propriety, but much more fre-
> quently applied them to feelings and thoughts with which they had
> no natural connection whatsoever. A language was thus insensibly
> produced, differing materially from the real language of men in *any
> situation*. The Reader or Hearer of this distorted language found
> himself in a perturbed and unusual state of mind: when affected by
> the genuine language of passion he had been in a perturbed and
> unusual state of mind also: in both cases he was willing that his
> common judgment and understanding should be laid asleep, and he
> had no instinctive and infallible perception of the true to make him
> reject the false; the one served as a passport for the other. The
> emotion was in both cases delightful, and no wonder if he con-
> founded the one with the other, and believed them both to be pro-
> duced by the same, or similar causes. Besides, the Poet spake to
> him in the character of a man to be looked up to, a man of genius
> and authority. Thus, and from a variety of other causes, this dis-
> torted language was received with admiration; and Poets, it is
> probable, who had before contented themselves for the most part
> with misapplying only expressions which at first had been dictated
> by real passion, carried the abuse still further, and introduced
> phrases composed apparently in the spirit of the original figurative
> language of passion, yet altogether of their own invention, and
> characterized by various degrees of wanton deviation from good
> sense and nature.

Thus it is that language, though differing from the ordinary
language, because it becomes the language of extraordinary

occasions, becomes hardened into an artificial one which is never the real language of men *in any situation;* and thus it is that when tried by his test of reality the principle of poetic diction is found wanting. An artificial, unreal language can never be the medium of the reality of life which is contemplated by the Imagination; only the real language of real men and real poets can express imaginative truth and reality.[18]

[18] For a statement of the case, see William Minto, *Literature of the Georgian Era,* pp. 159-165.

CHAPTER V

THE THREE AGES OF MAN

I can compare human life to a large mansion of many apartments
. . . The first we step into we call the thoughtless Chamber, in
which we remain as long as we do not think. We remain there a
long while . . . but are at length imperceptibly impelled by
the awakening of the thinking principle within us—we . . . get
into the second Chamber, which I shall call the Chamber of Maiden
Thought. . . . Your third Chamber of Life shall be a lucky and
a gentle one—stored with the wine of Love—and the bread of
Friendship.

John Keats to John Hamilton Reynolds, 1818.

The imagination of a boy is healthy, and the imagination of a
man is healthy; but there is a space of life between, in which the
soul is in a ferment, the character undecided, the way of life un-
certain, the ambition thick-sighted.

John Keats, *Preface* to *Endymion*, 1818.

As has already been said, Wordsworth was habitually occupied with philosophical and moral problems, which he discussed fundamentally, and which he chose to furnish the principal subjects of his poems. Chief among these problems is
that of the unity of consciousness in the individual and the
mystery of personal identity, through a long series of years
and the most disparate experiences—a mystery which was
heightened for him by the strange fact that in spite of the sorrows, fears, pains, and agonies experienced in early years, the
life of the adult is one which is guided chiefly by Hope, Love,
and Sympathy. In other words, the poet sought to explain the
strange anomaly that in a world of real pain and sorrow all
that we see may be "full of blessing"; that is, to explain the
life of man and society in terms of optimism. This explanation of the problem is made by Wordsworth in a quite personal
way: namely, by a study of the origins of knowledge and individual consciousness, beginning with childhood through youth
to the mature individual. This method of approach to the
problem of the unity of mind is so fundamental with Words-

worth that it forms the basis of all his other ideas and is the point of approach to all the other main problems of ethics, art, and politics with which he deals in his poetry and prose. It is, therefore, the first problem which we shall study.

Wordsworth deals with this matter in a variety of ways: in autobiography, in lyric, in ode, and in prose and poetic philosophical analysis, during the years of his greatest poetic activity, from 1798 to 1820. These years represent the actual period of time in which definite expression is given to his problem, but on his own evidence we can say that this particular way of explaining his world of man and experience was in his mind before 1798,[1] and so we can be certain that his theory was formed rather definitely before the composition of any poem of his which he wished to be regarded as the product of his matured powers. Because of these facts we can proffer as certain the statement that Wordsworth's poetry is at bottom an explanation of theories which antedate the impulse, or the power to give them expression.

It is probable that the transition from theory to poetic expression began before 1798 and began to take vague form as the poem which he calls *The Recluse; or Views of Nature, Man, and Society,* which he probably began about 1797, and which had attained considerable length by March 6, 1798.[2] Judging by the title and by his own statement that he strove to convey in the poem most of the knowledge of which he was possessed, it seems probable that it is the earliest attempt to give expression to his solution of these problems of man, nature, and society which he had already been deeply pondering. What these thirteen hundred lines were we cannot certainly

---

[1] Letter to James Tobin, March 6, 1798, *Letters of the Wordsworth Family,* I, 115; Letter to James Losh, March 11, 1798, *op. cit.,* III, 358.

[2] Letter to James Tobin, March 6, 1798. This statement should supersede or supplement the commonly quoted one in the letter to James Losh, March 11, 1798. In the letter to Tobin, Wordsworth states that he has completed 1300 lines, and in the letter to Losh he mentions 706 lines. I cannot explain the discrepancy; there may be none, as it is entirely possible that the two statements refer to different sets of verses. In any case we credit Wordsworth with at least 1300 lines of his philosophical poem on March 11, 1798. That the plan of the philosophical poem antedates 1798 by some years is shown by a passage in a letter to Sir George Beaumont, December 24, 1804, in which he speaks of the poem as "the chief object upon which my thoughts have been fixed these many years." *Letters of the Wordsworth Family,* I, 173.

say, except that part of them constituted the story of Margaret, now included in *The Excursion,* and that another part, philosophical in nature, is included in another part of the same poem;[3] but it is clear that we have in the lines referred to, the earliest sketch of the "great philosophical poem," thus early conceived, but never carried to completion, even in an unusually long life, the only completed parts being *The Prelude, The Excursion,* and one book of *The Recluse.* In the year 1798 the poem was to suffer an interruption for a full year, on account of a new poetic project, the *Lyrical Ballads,* which appeared anonymously early in September, 1798. In this volume we find the poet committed to his theory of the mind once and for all, in a number of poems; and in the most famous and the most characteristically "Wordsworthian" of them all, his discussion is quite fully developed. This poem bears the long and accurately descriptive title of *Lines Written a Few Miles above Tintern Abbey, on Revisiting the Banks of the Wye during a Tour, July 13, 1798,* and is obviously not one of the "ballads" which are referred to in the *Advertisement* to the volume, the language and substance of which are defended against the taste of those who might find these "experiments" strange. Both the authors of the volume must have known that this poem has nothing "low" or "too familiar" or "not of sufficient dignity"[4] in its language; and it is clear that it belongs to those "few other poems" mentioned in the title page. It has about it nothing either of the ballad or the lyric, being written in blank verse, and in language and spirit akin to the "great philosophical poem" which was then under way and only temporarily interrupted.

In this poem his discussion takes the form of psychological autobiography, and is therefore the forerunner of *The Prelude,* of which it may be called a preliminary outline, or short summary. As the title indicates, it was composed on the thirteenth day of July, 1798; and the occasion was a visit by Wordsworth and his sister Dorothy to the farm of John Thelwall, a revolutionist and poet, who had retired to Lys Wen, an "obscure and

---

[3] *Margaret* is in Book I; the philosophical passage is found in Book IV, 1207-1274.

[4] *Advertisement* to *Lyrical Ballads.*

solitary" spot in Brecknockshire, in Wales, in order to escape from the dangers and turmoil of London and politics, and to bring up his family in peaceful agricultural pursuits. As Wordsworth marked the peaceful landscape and the "pastoral farms" of the beautiful Wye valley, he was reminded of his former visits to these same scenes in earlier years, especially of his visit of 1793, when he was yet but a youth who knew life but little or not at all.

> Five years have passed, five summers, with the length
> Of five long winters,

the poem begins; and in the interval he has seen and experienced much. He writes as one who has come to man's estate; and as his mind runs back in reminiscence over the intervening five years and beyond to childhood, he remembers what he was then as contrasted with what he is now, and he contemplates the strange ways by which in this "unintelligible world," his mind has become what it is. Then, whether by chance or design, he presents the history of his mind's development as a tripartite thing, as it were; divided into three distinct stages or periods, each marked by its distinct attitude to the universe of man and nature. Writing as he does from the standpoint of the experience which produced the poem, he contrasts his present period with the period of life in which he was five years before,[5] and gives a brief characterization of an earlier age.[6] The first part of the poem furnishes us with an analysis of his present consciousness, together with a theory of the processes by which it was produced,[7] an aspect of the subject which is resumed later.[8] Upon this follows an address to his sister Dorothy, who is in the period of youth, but who will also attain to the culminating age of maturity through the inevitable processes of life and rational living,[9] the whole concluding with the declaration that even though he be much changed in the course of his life, he brings to nature a love which is warmer and holier than the ecstatic devotion of his youth.

He characterizes the three periods in the following way:

[5] Lines 66-103.
[6]   "   74-75.
[7]   "   23-50.
[8]   "   103-112.
[9]   "   112-160.

5

1. Childhood, or Boyhood, has its coarser pleasures (as contrasted with the "purer mind" of maturity)[10] and its "glad animal movements." This is the unreflecting period of life, when there is no conscious reaction to experience and nature.

2. The second period is youth, which is marked by mental as well as bodily activity, by "aching joys" and "dizzy raptures." As contrasted with the stage at which he has arrived, this period is marked by the direct emotional responses to life, like "appetite" to food, by "passion," by "feeling," by "love," without any translation into "thought."[11]

3. The third age is the period of thought, Maturity. In this age the immediate joy in sensation has gone; but as an "abundant recompense" comes the deeper and more profound outlook on life, with "thought," which alone satisfies. And what is the wisdom which this "thought," teaches him? That "man" is the center of the universe, the "mind of man" is the culminating point of the "something" which is "interfused" in the universe "and rolls through all things." To this height he has come; but the true optimism of the poem is that what is true of him may be true of all. The wisdom of maturity allows him to see that all "thinking things, all objects of thought," are "impelled"[12] towards higher things, and, as has been noted, he is certain that his sister Dorothy, whose "wild eyes" remind him of his own "past existence," that is, his period of youth, will also reach the culminating period of maturity, by the inevitable processes of life.

---

[10] Lines 74-75 and 30. It is to be noted that the "purer" in line 30 has no moral significance, but a purely philosophical one: purely mental, as contrasted with the more "animal," physical forms of sensation.

[11] Lines 76-84.

[12] Line 101. Compare the phrases "we shall be *wise perforce*," and "impelled by strict necessity, along the path of order and of good," in *The Excursion*, Book IV, lines 1265, 1269-70. These lines were written in 1797-1798, and so are really contemporaneous with *Tintern Abbey*. Hazlitt, who knew Wordsworth's mind at this date, interprets these phrases as expressive of the doctrine of necessitarianism. Commenting on lines 94-103, he says: "Perhaps the doctrine of what has been called philosophic necessity was never more finely expressed than in these lines." See Chapter VI.

Wordsworth's note on lines 107-108 shows the trend of his thought. He is pleading for the inherent value of the primary sensations—"they half-create," as well as "perceive." In the language of Edward Young, to whom he refers, *Night Thoughts*, VI, 424-425:

"And half create the wondrous world they see.
Our *senses*, as our *reason*, are divine."

Thus Wordsworth clearly announces as the source of his belief in the integrity of mind and as the ground of his hope, a scheme of individual mental development in three stages, or ages, each one of which is linked with the other in a causal connection. This scheme, he says, represents the facts of his own development; it represents the facts of his sister's development, so far as she has come down life's way; and it represents the general laws of growth of every individual mind. In the poet's own words, we may characterize the periods in the following terms: 1. Childhood, or Boyhood, is the age of *sensation;* 2. Youth is the age of *feeling;* and, 3, the period of the After Years, or Maturity, is the age of *thought.* Thus each age has its own integrity and at the same time the earlier is essential to the development of the later. In the light of this philosophy the poet found comfort for the loss of the immediate joy of boyhood and youth; for, in accordance with his theory, it is the general law of life that the vividness of sensation and feeling should die away with the coming of maturity, and it is equally the law of life that thought, intellect, the philosophic mind, which are the compensations of maturity, should be attained only in the last stage of development.[13]

---

[13] Robert Bridges notes three stages of development in *Tintern Abbey,* but does not extend the stages into the other poetry of Wordsworth. "In that poem (*Tintern Abbey*) Wordsworth distinguished three stages of mind following by development one on another: 1st, boyhood—mere animal pleasure; 2nd, simple unreflective ecstasy in Nature; 3rd, reflective pleasure in Nature, i. e. pleasure accompanied by or interwoven with that sense of mystery it is the object of his poem to exhibit." Introduction to *The Poems of John Keats,* 2 vols., 1894.

Professor Oliver Elton, in discussing *The Prelude,* notes that the experiences therein related come to the front "in a traceable order and development." 1. There is a long, unreflective, childish phase, which begins early. 2. At sixteen he is submerged, like a Hindoo, in the feeling of impersonal existence, or Being—not yet thought of as Mind. 3. Then his spirit ceases to be merely passive, but seems itself to contribute to Nature, to be her tyrant; she is rather part of him than he of her; the consciousness of self and the intuition of nature become indistinguishable. 4. Next Wordsworth takes his fellow-men into the circle of his feeling, and he is aware of a new "human-heartedness" in his love of nature, *A Survey of English Literature,* 1780-1830, 2 vols., 1912, II, 58.

"Here (*Tintern Abbey*) he describes the mere animal enjoyment of Nature in boyhood; the later period, when beauty and sublimity, reaching him through the eye and ear, became a passion; later still, the tranquillising, and also the elevating and spiritual influences of Nature; and now, a feeling for Nature, touched and chastened by humanity, and, at the same time, a deeper communion with the spiritual Presence at work both through Nature and in man. We might name these periods that of the blood, that of the senses, that of the imagination, and that of the soul." Edward Dow-

This is Wordsworth's first formulation of his doctrine. It is characterized by brevity; but the evidence that he believed it to be fundamental is best seen in the fact that from the year 1798 on to 1820 in prose and in poetry he developed the theory again and again, basing upon it his most fundamental arguments regarding life and poetry; making it the foundation of his great poems *The Prelude,* and *The Excursion;* and from it deriving his famous distinction between Fancy and Imagination. I give a complete list of all the passages in which the three ages are specifically mentioned, with dates; and consider a few typical ones in some detail and in chronological order.[14]

After the publication of the *Lyrical Ballads,* on his return from Germany in 1799, he was urged by Coleridge to go on with *The Recluse;* but Wordsworth was following the impulse which had been imparted to him by the *Lyrical Ballads* volume, and he continued to write short poems which are intimately connected with the theory of the three ages, but which are not expressive of the whole theory. This lasted until 1800, when the second edition of the *Lyrical Ballads* appeared in two volumes, some of the most characteristic of the poems in this edition being studies of the peculiarities of the various

den, *Poems by William Wordsworth,* 1897, 370-371. Dowden also divides Wordsworth's life into three periods: republicanism, patriotic enthusiasm, and his uncourageous elder years. *Studies in Literature,* 123.

C. E. Spurgeon notes stages in the fourth book of *The Excursion:* "It is interesting that the steps in the ladder of perfection, as described by Wordsworth, are precisely analogous to the threefold path or 'way' of the religious and philosophic mystic, an ethical system or rule of life, of which, very probably, Wordsworth had never heard." *Mysticism in English Literature,* 1913, p. 64.

These are the only instances known to me of deliberate statements concerning periods, or phases, in Wordsworth's development. My agreement or disagreement with all or either will be apparent as my discussion proceeds.

[14] (1). 1798, *Tintern Abbey;* (2). 1800, *The Prelude,* Book I, 581-635; (3). *The Prelude,* Book II, 232-450; (4). 1800, *The Recluse,* 1-70; (5). 1802, Letter to John Wilson, in *Letters of the Wordsworth Family,* III, 435-443, especially 436; (6). 1801-1802, *The Excursion,* Book I, 77-433; (7). 1802, *My Heart Leaps Up;* (8). 1802-1806, *Ode. Intimations of Immortality;* (9). 1804, *The Prelude,* Book VIII, 340-364; (10). 1805, *The Prelude,* Book XII, 121-207; (11). 1808, (November and December), *Convention of Cintra,* edited by A. V. Dicey, 1915, 189-190; (12). May 5, 1809, *Letters of the Wordsworth Family,* III, 472; (13). 1809-1812, *The Excursion,* Book IV, 66-196; (14). 1809-1812, *The Excursion,* Book IX, 29-86; (15). 1809, Letter to "Mathetes," *The Friend,* Nos. 17 and 20; (16). 1815, *Preface* to *Collected Poems of 1815;* (17). 1817, *Ode to Lycoris;* (18). 1818, *Composed on an Evening of Extraordinary Splendour and Beauty;* (19). 1820, *The River Duddon,* Sonnet No. XXVI.

ages, and so continuing the method of a number in the first edition. Hence, we have poems like *There Was a Boy,* a study of the earlier experiences of childhood; *The Two April Mornings,* a contrast between youth and age; and *The Fountain,* a presentation of the inability of youth to understand the mentality of maturity; as well as *Michael, Ruth,* and *The Brothers,* which are studies of the mature mind, illustrative of the "primary laws of our nature," showing the fluxes and refluxes of the mind when agitated by the great and simple affections of our nature,[15] such as maternal, paternal, and brotherly love. Many other psychological topics are discussed in the volumes, with which we shall not deal at the present time.[16]

But with the completion of the new edition of the *Lyrical Ballads* and its prose explanation in the *Preface,* in 1800, Wordsworth was ready to heed his friend Coleridge's request to go on with the great philosophical poem; and it is significant that the first endeavors to proceed with his great poem took on the form of the development of the doctrine of the three ages of man, Moreover, the particular method adopted is that of *Tintern Abbey,*—that of autobiography,—the work done in 1800 being what is now the first two books of *The Prelude.*

The purpose of the poem is clearly expressed by both Coleridge and the author. Writing in the summer of 1799, Coleridge says:

My dear friend, I do entreat you to go on with *The Recluse;* and I wish you would write a poem in blank verse, addressed to those, who, in consequence of the complete failure of the French Revolution, have thrown up all hopes of the amelioration of mankind, and are sinking into an almost epicurean selfishness, disguising the same under the soft titles of domestic attachment and contempt for visionary *philosophes.* It would do great good, and might form a part of *The Recluse,* for in my present mood I am wholly against the publication of any small poems.[17]

In almost the same words the author gives his purpose in writing the poem:

---

[15] *Preface* to *Lyrical Ballads,* Second Edition, 1800.
[16] See some useful material on this point in Emile Legouis, *Early Life of William Wordsworth,* 1897, Book IV, Ch. II, "Wordsworth's Relation to Science."
[17] *Memoirs of Wordsworth,* I, 159.

If in these times of fear,
The melancholy waste of hopes o'erthrown,
If, mid indifference and apathy,
And wicked exultation when good men
On every side fall off, we know not how,
To selfishness, disguised in gentle names
Of peace and quiet and domestic love,
Yet mingled not unwillingly with sneers
On visionary minds; if in this time
Of dereliction and dismay, I yet
Despair not of our nature, but retain
A more than Roman confidence, a faith
That fails not, in all sorrow my support,
The blessing of my life; the gift is yours,
Ye winds and sounding cataracts! 'tis yours,
Ye mountains! thine, O Nature! Thou hast fed
My lofty speculations; and in thee
For this uneasy heart of ours, I find
A never-failing principle of joy
And purest passion.[18]

These first two books of *The Prelude* deal with the first of the three periods; and so we must expect to have his discussions of the three ages subordinated to his reminiscences of childhood and youth; but we can plainly see that the doctrine of the three ages is none the less the foundation on which the interpretation of his childhood experience rests.

Addressing Coleridge, he justifies himself for beginning early in the history of his life, and trusts that he is not misled

By an infirmity of love for days
Disowned by memory;[19]

but believes that by connecting childhood with his manhood he might better understand himself and lead his friend to better knowledge how the author's heart was framed.[20] In the first book, by a series of instances he presents characteristic incidents in his boyhood: bathing, skating, card-playing, trapping, and the placid events of an ordinary childhood. In addition, he gives us examples of experiences of other kinds, fears, and pains, as the incident of the stolen boat,[21] illustrating the strange diversity of experience which makes up the

[18] *The Prelude,* II, 432-451.
[19] *Op. cit.,* I, 614-615.
[20] *Op. cit.,* I, 617-635.
[21] *Op. cit.,* I, 357-400.

boy's life and yet develops into the harmonious calm which is the man's. His enunciation of the principle is of primary importance:

> Dust as we are, the immortal spirit grows
> Like harmony in music; there is a dark
> Inscrutable workmanship that reconciles
> Discordant elements, makes them cling together
> In one society. How strange that all
> The terrors, pains, and early miseries,
> Regrets, vexations, lassitudes interfused
> Within my mind, should e'er have borne a part,
> And that a needful part, in making up
> The calm existence that is mine when I
> Am worthy of myself![22]

Childhood is the time of sensations, when pure experiences are being impressed on the young mind; the time of "vulgar joy," and "giddy bliss." All these are soon forgotten, save that now and then "chance collisions and quaint accidents," the joy, or bliss, or fear, all of which have that "visionary" quality on which he so frequently lays stress, combine with the "collateral" objects with which they are associated, become fixed in the mind and remain there until the occasion arises which calls them forth from their hiding place, glorified and raised into the finer mental forms of youth or manhood. Through them the scenes with which they were first associated, even though they are bright, or beautiful, or majestic, become more habitually dear to the adult and so become fastened to the affections.[23] The whole book is a marvelous picture of the "visionary" quality of commonplace childhood experiences, of the mental activity of the child in its self-concentration, of those "dumb yearnings, hidden appetites" which are characteristic of the child, and which "must have their food."[24] It dwells upon that strange vividness of experience, and gives us detailed pictures of

> Those hallowed and pure motions of the sense,
> Which seem, in their simplicity, to own
> An intellectual charm.[25]

[22] *The Prelude*, I, 340-350.
[23] *Op. cit.*, I, 581-612.
[24] *Op. cit.*, V, 506-507.
[25] *Op. cit.*, I, 551-553.

But in sensation the child rests. Wordsworth does not ideal-
ize this period; he shows that this period of life is vital to the
succeeding periods if they are to come to their own fruition;
for sensation is the prerequisite of all higher mental forms.

The second book of *The Prelude* deals more particularly
with the period of youth,[26] but correlates it with the other
ages. As he explains in Book I, the external world was "collateral,"[27] and "extrinsic" to himself when he was a child, so
in the present book, he speaks of "the winning forms of Nature" as being "collaterally" attached to his experience; he
speaks of the "incidental charms" which first attached his
heart to rural objects; and explains that up to the time of
youth nature was but "secondary."[28] But now that youth had
come, nature was "sought for her own sake."[29] "A plastic
power abode"[30] with him; and under the influence of his active,
plastic mind he read into objects a connection which did not
really exist. Under the influence of his strong feelings his
own enjoyments were transferred "to inorganic nature."[31]
Under the stress of his feelings he "coerced" all things into
activity,[32] and observed affinities between things which were
the pure product of his active mind.[33] The mind of youth is
active with the activity of feeling, as the mind of childhood is
active with the activity of sensation.

The next passage we shall examine is found in the first
book of *The Excursion,* written 1801-1802; and this has a
special interest because it shows that Wordsworth applies the
doctrine of three ages to a mind other than his own. The
Wanderer is introduced as a mature man, and we are given a
hasty sketch of the processes which have made his mind what
it is. In the main, it may be said that the description is
couched in terms which are very much like those of *The
Prelude* and that the general scheme is the same. We find that
the age of boyhood was one of activity of mind which grew

---

[26] *The Prelude,* II, 232-451
[27] *Op. cit.,* II, 50-51.
[28] *Op. cit.,* II, 198-202.
[29] *Op. cit.,* II, 201-203.
[30] *Op. cit.,* II, 362-363.
[31] *Op. cit.,* II, 391-399.
[32] *Op. cit.,* II, 390.
[33] *Op. cit.,* II, 383-384. The whole passage, 352-418.

up in intercourse with books and things, nourished by fear and the milder passions.[34] Then followed youth, in which "the animal being was swallowed up in love, sensation, soul, and form." Youth had not acquired "thought."

> Thought was not; in enjoyment it expired;

but he was acquiring the experiences that produce thought.

> And thus before his eighteenth[35] year was told,
> Accumulated feelings pressed his heart.
> With still increasing weight; he was o'erpowered
> By Nature; by the turbulence subdued,
> Of his own mind; by mystery and hope,
> And the first virgin passion of a soul
> Communing with the glorious universe.
> Full often wished he that the winds might rage
> When they were silent: far more fondly now
> Than in his earlier season[36] did he love
> Tempestuous nights—the conflict and the sounds
> That live in darkness. From his intellect
> And from the stillness of abstracted thought
> He asked repose; and, failing oft to win
> The peace required, he scanned the laws of light
> Amid the roar of torrents, where they send
> From hollow clefts up to the clearer air
> A cloud of mist, that smitten by the sun
> Varies its rainbow hues. But vainly thus,
> And vainly by all other means, he strove
> To mitigate the fever of his heart.[37]

It was vain for him to seek rest in thought and intellect; for in youth they are not developed; in no way could the fever of youth be mitigated, for the fever and unrest are of the very essence of that period of life.

With maturity there came to the Wanderer the wisdom of life; and he was now

> Vigorous in health, of hopeful spirits, undamped
> By worldly-mindedness or anxious care;
> Observant, studious, thoughtful, and refreshed
> By knowledge gathered up from day to day.[38]

[34] *The Excursion*, I. 132-196.

[35] It is to be noted that Wordsworth makes the seventeenth year important in his own case: *The Prelude*, II. 386.

[36] Boyhood, or Childhood and Boyhood. The first period is here divided into two parts.

[37] *The Excursion*, I. 280-300. With this compare the similar descriptions of Wordsworth's own experience, *The Recluse*, 703-720.

[38] *Op. cit.*, I. 392-395.

His development through the three ages is thus summed up by the poet, in terms of childhood, youth, and manhood:

> The Scottish Church, both on himself and those
> With whom from *childhood* he grew up, had held
> The strong hand of her purity; and still
> Had watched him with an unrelenting eye.
> This he remembered in his *riper age*[39]
> With gratitude, and reverential thoughts.
> But by the native vigour of his mind,
> By his habitual wanderings out of doors,
> By loneliness, and goodness, and kind works,
> Whate'er, in docile *childhood* or in *Youth*,
> He had imbibed of fear or darker thought
> Was melted all away; so true was this,
> That sometimes his religion seemed to me
> Self-taught, as of a dreamer in the woods;
> Who to the model of his own pure heart
> Shaped his belief, as grace divine inspired
> And human reason dictated with awe.
> —And surely never did there live on earth
> A *man* of kindlier nature.[40]

We shall take as another example, the *Ode. Intimations of Immortality.* While Wordsworth was laboring at *The Prelude* and its related poems, things were going badly with his friend Coleridge. Coleridge's letters at this period are the saddest possible, and we read in Dorothy's *Journals* how the letters dampened their spirits. Evidently the conversations which the friends held still thickened the gloom; and Wordsworth found a challenge in Coleridge for his doctrine of Hope. For Coleridge, to his own horror, was dying as a poet: that Joy, which he and Wordsworth had proclaimed as the essential principle of the universe, had gone from his own heart; and he was in despair. Under the stress of this appalling experience of Coleridge, Wordsworth meditated on the problem, and on the twenty-sixth day of March, 1802, he composed *The Rainbow*,[41] in which he again asserts his fundamental principle of the inevitable progress of the individual mind, in the famous line, "The child is father of the Man"; and on the

---

[39] Compare "unripe time," referring to Childhood, *The Prelude*, VIII, 342.
[40] *The Excursion*, I, 397-415. I have italicized the words which mark the three ages.
[41] That is, *My Heart Leaps Up*.

same day he wrote part of an ode. This, we know, is the famous *Ode,* to which was given much later the sub-title, *Intimations of Immortality from Recollections of Early Childhood;* but how far he progressed we are not informed. Obviously Coleridge's mind was engaged on the same problems, for on April 21 he visited the Wordsworths and brought with him the saddest of all his poems, *Dejection,* which he had written early in that month and addressed to Wordsworth, "the brother of his soul." In this poem Coleridge speaks of the loss of Joy and the eclipse of his feelings:

> O William! in this wan and heartless mood,
> To other thoughts by yonder throstle woo'd,
> All this long eve, so balmy and serene,
> Have I been gazing on the western sky,
> And its peculiar tint of yellow green:
> And still I gaze—and with how blank an eye!
>
> .   .   .   .   .   .
>
> I see them all so excellently fair,
> I see, not feel, how beautiful they are!

As a result he sees no hope such as Wordsworth sees: Joy, "the spirit and power" of life, has gone; and there is no beyond. For not only is his youthful mirth gone, but also the very essence of his poetic powers:

> But now afflictions bow me down to earth:
> Nor care I that they rob me of my mirth;
>   But oh! each visitation
> Suspends what Nature gave me at my birth,
>   My shaping spirit of Imagination.

This, then, is the state to which Coleridge had been brought by life, and in the face of this testimony Wordsworth resumes the problem in the *Ode.*

He acknowledges all that Coleridge asserts, up to a certain point. He, too, no longer sees the "celestial light" and the visionary "glory" and "freshness" in the sensations of life. He, too, can no longer feel the joy of the child and the lamb: the familiar tree known and loved in youth, and the well-known field so intimately associated with the vivid sensations and feelings of youth, tell him of "something that is gone." And what is it that is gone? Nothing more or less than the "visionary gleam" that rests upon our early sensations. And where is it now? Here the poem of 1802 ends, at the forty-sixth line; and when it was resumed four years later it followed in the general course of the three ages, with an idealization of the period of childhood as "coming from afar," but without any alteration of the arguments for Hope, such as we have seen in the previous instances. This expansion of the age of infancy gives the poem and the argument a false proportion, and really lends to it the aspect of being in reality two poems: stanzas i-iv and ix-xii forming a self-consistent poem founded solely on the three ages, and stanzas v-ix a complete intercalary poem on the glory of the child and his derivation from afar, more idealistic and less optimistic than earlier statements. That the *Ode* is one whole in the mind of the author is shown by the fact that the two parts have stanza ix in common, and especially by the fact that stanzas ix-xii form a conclusion absolutely like that of *Tintern Abbey,* but in more splendid and glorified form. Nevertheless, there is a difference of tone between the two parts, as Swinburne pointed out many years ago, but without making any attempt to arrive at the cause of it.[42]

In the last three stanzas of the *Ode* Wordsworth enters the full flood of his main thought that the love, the intellect, the emotion, of maturity are all of more profound importance than those of either childhood or Youth; and this is a reason for Hope; for these are the Permanent. Delight may depart; but the deeper Joy remains.

> Then sing, ye Birds, sing, sing a joyous song! . . . .
> We *in thought* will join your throng,
>   Ye that pipe and ye that play
>   Ye that through your hearts to-day
>   Feel the gladness of the May!
> What though the radiance that was once so bright
> Be now forever taken from my sight,
> Though nothing can bring back the hour
> Of splendour in the grass, of glory in the flower;
>   We will grieve not, rather find
>   Strength in what remains behind,
>   In the primal sympathy
>   Which having been must ever be,

---

[42] "Miscellanies," in the essay *Wordsworth and Byron,* 1886. First printed in *The Nineteenth Century,* April and May, 1884.

> In the soothing *thoughts* that spring
>   Out of *human suffering*,
> In the faith that looks through death,
> In years that bring the *philosophic* mind.

And so in maturity he can say:

> I love the Brooks which down their channels fret,
> Even more than when I tripp'd lightly as they;
> The innocent brightness of a new-born Day
>   Is lovely yet;
> The clouds that gather round the setting sun
> Do take a sober colouring from an eye
> That hath kept watch o'er man's mortality. . . .
> Thanks to the human heart by which we live,
> Thanks to its tenderness, its joys, and fears,
> To me the meanest flower that blows can give
> Thoughts that do often lie too deep for tears.

This is the loftiest expression of the constant theme of his poetry: the justification of hope and the triumph of life in the coming of maturity, with its accompanying deepening of thought and emotion, and that profounder understanding of Man, the heart of man, and human life. For our present purposes it is important to note that this state is reached by the regular and inevitable progress of each individual soul through the three stages of Boy, Youth, and Man,[43] by the demonstration that "the Child is father of the man."[44]

As this interpretation is not by any means the usual one, I wish to add Wordsworth's own statement regarding the doctrine which is taught in the poem. The sub-title, *Intimations of Immortality from Recollections of Early Childhood,* was added in the edition of 1815, the 1807 form being simply entitled *Ode.* In the Fenwick note he says that the visionary qualities of childhood have often been noted, and have been interpreted as intimations of immortality. He says that he could never admit the notion of death, (like the little girl in *We Are Seven*). A characteristic form of deducing immortality from this "visionary quality" in childhood experience, with its related notion of pre-existence, is found in the Platonic philosophy. Why not make use of this philosophy to express

---

[43] Stanza 5.
[44] *My Heart Leaps Up.*

the vividness of the child's sensations? This he does; but, be it noted, he does not do this to argue for pre-existence. On the contrary, he takes the idea of pre-existence as a vivid way of making the reader realize the vividness and "visionary quality" of the child's life. To give his own words on this point will make it clear that he is engaged in establishing this vividness and "visionary quality" of youth, and not in establishing the doctrine of pre-existence:

To that dream-like vividness and splendour which invest objects of sight in childhood, every one, I believe, if he would look back, could bear testimony, and I need not dwell upon it here: but having in the poem regarded it as presumptive evidence of a prior state of existence, I think it right to protest against a conclusion, which has given pain to some good and pious persons, that I meant to inculcate such a belief. . . . I took hold of the notion of pre-existence as having sufficient foundation in humanity for authorizing me to make for my purpose the best use of it I could as a poet.

This distinction which he makes in the Fenwick note is also made in the poem itself, but not clearly. The "intercalary poem" develops the idea of pre-existence to such a degree that it seems to become the main theme, to the obscuring of the real subject—the "visionary quality" of the experiences of youth, and the nobler and purer Hope which comes to the mature man who sees his life as one whole, and by thought and imagination makes that visionary quality which marks youth his own even in his maturity, thus transmuting it into something higher. The introductory stanzas,—that is, stanzas i-iv, written in 1801-2, four years before the rest of the poem, form, with the conclusion, a perfectly clear expression of the three ages of man. The intercalary stanzas divert the thought of the opening stanzas by the development of a symbol and a theory in such a way and to such an extent that the attention of the reader is turned aside from the leading theme of the visionary quality of youthful sensations and their fading and replacement by the much more valuable thought of maturity, to his consequent confusion and the misinterpretation of the poem as a whole. In stanza ix the main theme appears again, and the poem proceeds to its logical close—a close which results not from the idea of pre-existence, but from the thought that precious as is the vividness of youthful sensations, much

more precious are the thoughts that come to the "philosophic
mind" of maturity.   Such stanzas as ix, x, and xi, so full of
hope and joy, are not the conclusion of that part of the poem
which develops the notion of pre-existence, with its hopeless-
ness, but of the other part, so characteristic of Wordsworth
throughout his whole mature career.

In the eighth book of *The Prelude,* which is devoted to the
problem of the transition from youth to maturity, or, as the
poet concretely expresses it, "Love of Nature leading to Love
of Man," he clearly indicates the progress which he describes
in terms of the three ages.[45]   He is describing his mature
mind in detail, especially the relation of man and nature to
his own consciousness, when he turns aside from his discussion to remind Coleridge that his attitude towards nature and
man is the result of a process.   That process is marked by
three stages: (1) The first was an "unripe time," Childhood,
in which Nature was "secondary" to his own pursuits and
animal activities.   (2) This was followed by a second stage,
when Nature, "prized for her own sake," became his joy,
in which man held a place "subordinate to her."   Man was
but an occasional delight, an accidental grace, *"his hour being
not yet come."*[46]   (3) This was followed by a third period,
in which nature became subordinate to man, "when not less
than two and twenty summers had been told,"[47] as the poet
tells us with surprising definiteness.   Putting this definite date
with the other specific dates furnished us, we learn that childhood lasts from the first consciousness, at about five or six,[48]
to ten,[49] and thus youth extends from ten to twenty-three; at
which point maturity begins.   This book of *The Prelude* is of
especial importance in explaining the growth of Fancy and
Imagination; but the discussion of this will be postponed to a
later chapter.

At the close of the eighth book of *The Prelude* he states
that he has brought his life up to the third age,[50] and that in

---

[45] Especially lines 340-364.
[46] Lines 340-356.
[47] Lines 348-349.
[48] *Ode. Intimations of Immortality,* l. 86.
[49] *The Prelude,* V, 552-553.
[50] Lines 676-686.

the remainder of the poem he will deal at length with the coming and consummation of this culminating period. We shall now consider only books twelve and thirteen, which give in summary form the history of his imagination in the third stage of life.[51] During Childhood and Youth the powers of the mind are held "in absolute dominion" by the senses, especially by "the bodily eye," the most despotic of our senses; and are not equipped with a regulating faculty which

> summons all the senses each
> To counteract the other, and ourselves,
> And makes them all, and the objects with which all
> Are conversant, subservient in their turn
> To the great ends of Liberty and Power.[52]

As yet not endowed with the great regulative principle of the Imagination, the youthful poet's activity of mind was directed to the externals of things, insatiably seeking for delights:

> I roamed from hill to hill, from rock to rock,
> Still craving combinations of new forms,
> New pleasure, wider empire for the sight,
> Proud of her own endowments, and rejoiced
> To lay the inner faculties asleep.[53]

But, with the coming of maturity, Imagination freed him; and he stood in Nature's presence, "a creative soul."[54] He was no longer dominated by Nature, but stood above her, a free being who could recombine her into the free forms of art. This is the time of full maturity and the creative Imagination.

The next formulation of the three ages in point of time is to be found in the *Tract on the Convention of Cintra,* written in November and December, 1808, and published in 1809. Near the conclusion of the book he lays down a principle of life, that of perfection and benevolence, in accord with the Christian exhortation, "Be ye therefore perfect, even as your Father which is in Heaven, is perfect." He promises that on another occasion he will point out the steps by which the

---

[51] *The Prelude,* XII. 121-207.
[52] *Op. cit.,* XII, 135-139.
[53] *Op. cit.,* XII, 143-147.
[54] *Op. cit.,* XII, 206-207.

practice of life may be lifted up to these high precepts,[55] and lays down the plan of his future exposition in the following terms: "I shall have to speak of the child as well as the man; for with the child, or the Youth, may we begin with more hope." Then, designating each of these three ages by the leading feature which characterizes it, he speaks of childhood as *animal,* of youth as *sentient,* and of manhood as *intellectual,* and shows the interrelationship of the three ages as follows:

I shall strive to show that these principles and movements of wisdom—so far from towering above the support of prudence, or rejecting the rules of experience, for the better conduct of those multifarious actions which are alike necessary to the attainment of ends good or bad—do instinctively prompt the sole prudence which cannot fail. The higher mode of being does not exclude, but necessarily includes, the lower; the intellectual does not exclude, but necessarily includes, the sentient; the sentient, the animal. . . .[56]

During the years from 1809 to 1812 Wordsworth wrote the fourth book of *The Excursion,* the book which contains the heart of the whole argument of the poem—how despondency may be corrected. With the main argument of the book we shall not deal at present; but shall note that at the basis of all is the division of human life into the three ages, though but little is made of the first. Speaking through the Wanderer, the poet differentiates Youth and Maturity, as the means by which he is to differentiate truth from error, and to give the grounds of hope.[57] And he followed this procedure; for in this way he displays the mind's integrity. The "fervent raptures" of Youth flee in maturity; but despondency should not result; rather Hope; for Duty exists, and conscience, and reason, and love.[58]

Another important use of the scheme of the three ages belongs to the year 1809. In Number 17 of *The Friend,* December 14, 1809, a letter, signed "Mathetes," appeared, complain-

---

[55] Possibly, in a paper in *The Friend.* This is done in his reply to "Mathetes," which we consider presently.

[56] *Convention of Cintra,* Edited by A. V. Dicey, 1915, pp. 189-190. *Prose Works of William Wordsworth,* edited by William Knight, I, 273-276.

[57] *The Excursion,* IV, 66-196.

[58] *Op. cit.,* IV, 73, 152, 160, 269, 332-350.

ing of the weaknesses of the times, and asking for the guidance of one, namely Wordsworth, fitted to guide Youth. It asks that Wordsworth should exert this influence "in a work, adapted by its mode of publication, to address the feelings of the time, and to bring to its readers repeated admonition and repeated consolation." By this the writer doubtless meant that Wordsworth should contribute a series of papers to *The Friend*. Wordsworth's answer to this appeal by "Mathetes" —which pseudonym is identified as John Wilson and Alexander Blair[59]—is in all probability a definite brief formulation of the discussion of the three ages of man which he promised at the conclusion of his *Tract on the Convention of Cintra*, beginning in the same number of *The Friend* and continued in the twentieth number, Thursday, January 4, 1810, occupying all this number but two pages, and extending altogether to eighteen pages of the original issue. It is thus a document of considerable length; and, in view of the amount of thought which Wordsworth had given to the subject, deserves more careful study than it has received. For our present purpose, however, it will suffice to indicate that the arguments are avowedly based on the doctrine of the three ages of man.

"Mathetes" writes as a Youth, and asks to be delivered from those errors which originate in the false education of the times and in the very nature of Youth, specifically indicating Wordsworth as the desired deliverer.

To this Wordsworth replies[60] that the way to virtue is a path that is winding and various, and must be travelled alone. Thus every youth must be thrown back upon himself, and he must be capable of self-examination. Then, in a very minute and methodical way he characterizes the first age of man—

[59] *Coleridge's Works*, edited by Shedd, II, 358. This is the second letter which Wordsworth addressed to Wilson. In 1802 Wilson wrote to Wordsworth regarding the *Lyrical Ballads*. Wordsworth's reply is highly valuable in furnishing us with source notes on certain poems, a statement of certain of his theories, and of his purpose as a poet. He has the development of mind clearly in view; speaking of "full-grown man," and "childhood" as contrasted. *Letters of the Wordsworth Family*, III, 435-443. It is also printed in *The Prose Works of William Wordsworth*, edited by Grosart, II, 208-214, and by Knight, I, 35-42. Wilson's letter, a long and interesting one, is printed in Mrs. Mary Gordon, *Memoir of Christopher North*, 1863, 26-32. It is dated May 24, 1802.

[60] The *Letter* to "Mathetes" and Wordsworth's reply are both in the Introduction to Section II of *The Friend*.

that of infancy, childhood, and boyhood; and also the second age,—that of Youth, as being developed by nature "through joy and gladness, and as a creatress of the faculties by a process of smoothness and delight." But in the transition to the third age, "when youth is passing into manhood," a new faculty must be called upon, "that works after a different course: that faculty is reason; she gives more spontaneously, but she seeks for more; she works by thought, through feeling; yet in thoughts she begins and ends." Then follows the elaborate example of the expiring candle, to illustrate what has just been said; that is, to show the method of mental development in the earlier stages of life under the sway of direct and immediate experience, and the method of reason, into the period of manhood. Childhood and youth are taught "through the affections," by the sympathies, thus "developing the understanding"; manhood is guided by the "reason," by the "thinking mind."

Thus far there is little that is new in the letter; but he develops the characterization of the ages more fully than elsewhere, in a certain direction. In nearly every place in which the three ages are dealt with, he makes it clear that they are not merely a manner of speaking or a figure of speech, but a genuinely important psychological reality. For instance, when speaking of childhood in the fifth book of *The Prelude* he protests against the adult mind meddling with the child's mind and forcing its alien interpretation on what the child experiences. This he does because of his belief that the child mind is an integral whole which must have its integrity preserved if it is to develop into the higher stage of youth.[61] Similarly, he stoutly maintains the integrity of youth in his autobiography: by the activity of his own mind he had created a world of his own, false perhaps, but nevertheless real for him. Wordsworth constantly keeps in mind that self-activity that is the characteristic of every healthy, normal mind; and this activity is the clue which guides him in the dark places of the mental history of himself and others. Now, the way in which we can measure the activity of a mind is by noting how well

[61] *The Prelude*, V, 293-346.

developed are the characteristics of each age; and this Words
worth proceeds to do.

It is commonly known that he stoutly maintains the independence of the child mind; but we should note that he is
equally a champion of youth. He tells "Mathetes" that the
integrity of youth is a fundamental principle:

To expect from youth these virtues and habits, in that degree of
excellence to which in mature years, they may be carried, would
indeed be preposterous. Yet has youth many helps and aptitudes
for the discharge of these difficult duties, which are withdrawn for
the most part from the more advanced stages of life. For youth
has its own wealth and independence; it is rich in health of body
and animal spirits, in its sensibility to the impressions of the
natural universe, in the conscious growth of knowledge, in lively
sympathy and familiar communion with the generous actions recorded in history, and with the high passions of poetry; and, above
all, youth is rich in the possession of time, and the accompanying
consciousness of freedom and power.

If the youth is weak it is not because he lacks some characteristic of manhood but of youth. If the youth feels weaknesses
"let him first be assured, before he looks about for the means
of attaining the insight, the discriminating powers, and the
confirmed wisdom of manhood, that his soul has more to
demand of the appropriate excellences of youth than youth
has yet supplied to it; that the evil under which he labours is
not a superabundance of the instincts and the animating spirit
of that age, but a falling short, or a failure."

And how, then, is the youth to be corrected who thus falls
short? There are obstacles, Wordsworth says, but the way
is obvious:

He cannot recall past time; he cannot begin his journey afresh;
he cannot untwist the links by which, in no undelightful harmony,
images and sentiments are wedded in his mind. Granted that the
sacred light of childhood is and must be for him no more than a
remembrance. He may, notwithstanding, be remanded to nature,
and with trustworthy hopes, founded less upon his sentient than
upon his intellectual being; to nature, as leading on insensibly to
the society of reason; but to reason and will, as leading back to
the wisdom of nature. A reunion, in this order accomplished, will
bring reformation and timely support; and the two powers of
reason and nature, thus reciprocally teacher and taught, may advance together in a track to which there is no limit.

This is to say, in order to correct the mind which has not been normally developed it must be sent back to the sources of experience in first-hand impressions. It must go through, even at a belated period, the process of forming ideas and judgments: it must become as a child and youth, and again drink from the ancient sources of all real knowledge. It will be seen how this principle is applied in the great fourth book of *The Excursion* not only to the individual but to society as a whole. In other words, the way of health in mind is the way of experience; and this is not because in this way the mind is preserved from error. Quite the contrary: the way of life is full of errors; but if we do not know errors we cannot know truth. This attitude is very clearly seen all through Wordsworth, and explains his strange tolerance of error and his refusal to draw a moral.[62] No English poet so fully enters into the spirit of Milton's saying that "good and evil grow up together in the field of the world almost inseparably"; nor so constantly assumes that "a knowledge and survey of vice" is necessary to human virtue, and the scanning of error to the confirmation of truth. "For, as that man cannot set a right value upon health who has never known sickness, nor feel the blessing of ease who has been through his life a stranger to pain, so there can be no confirmed and passionate love of truth for him who has not experienced the hollowness of error." It is only thus that the man attains to truth.

In conclusion, Wordsworth warns his correspondent against teachers, lest they interfere with the youthful mind and make it merely receptive of judgments ready-made, and passive, instead of active. Of a possible teacher he says in warning:

Grant that in the general tenor of his intercourse with his pupil he is forbearing and circumspect, inasmuch as he is rich in that knowledge (above all necessary for a teacher) which cannot exist without a liveliness of memory, preserving for him an unbroken image of the winding, excursive, and often retrograde course along which his own intellect has passed. Grant that, furnished with these distinct remembrances, he wishes that the mind of his pupil should be free to luxuriate in the enjoyments, loves, and admirations appropriated to its age; that he is not in haste to kill what

---

[62] For instance, in the stories told in *The Excursion*.

he knows will in due time die of itself; or be transmuted, and put on a nobler form and higher faculties otherwise unattainable.

There must be "consistency or harmony of the being within itself," as Wordsworth says, and the only way in which that harmony can be maintained is by a due evaluation of each age of man. Each age is integral to itself and must be held inviolable if it is to perform its part in the development of the mind. Childhood and youth are *sentient;* maturity is *intellectual;* and both combined and blended in due order build up the being that we are in due time. But time must be allowed, and the individual must be subjected to first-hand experience and must build up his own world out of the world which he has made for himself, not out of one which has been supplied to him by an outside power. This is the wisdom of life as the poet imparts it to the youthful "Mathetes."

This doctrine of the three ages, if it is vital to Wordsworth's thinking, might be looked for in *The Excursion;* and it can be readily shown to be there throughout the poem and forming its very foundations. But it is not only assumed: it is specifically formulated at all the critical points. I shall indicate two, the first of which is in the fourth book.[63] In the Wanderer's speech, in which he begins his argument against despondency, he raises the question of what is the Permanent; and, in order to answer this fundamental question, he appeals to the testimony of his own development. He speaks of *infancy,* a "cloud" wrapped round us; of *youth* with its "fervent raptures," and "visionary powers of eye and soul"; and of his present period, from which the raptures are gone, and which is characterized by conscious effort and aspiration, in place of the spontaneousness of youth, by reason and by hope.

The second passage which I shall mention is from the culminating argument of the poem.[64] In the beginning of the ninth, and concluding, book, the Wanderer enlarges the idea of the activity of the mind to a more general notion of the "active principle" which rules the universe. In man this impelling activity has as its end Hope:

[63] *The Excursion,* IV, 79-129.
[64] *Op. cit.,* IX, 20-36.

> The food of hope
> Is meditated action; robbed of this
> Her sole support, she languishes and dies.
> We perish also; for we live by hope
> And by desire; we see by the glad light
> And breathe the sweet air of futurity;
> And so we live, or else we have no life.[65]

Then, indicating the two lads, he says that the *boys,* now taken up with their successful fishing expedition, will find before them a field "freshened with the dew of other expectations." The *Youth,* he adds, obeys a like glad impulse; and the *Man,* " 'mid all his apprehensions, cares, and fears," also pursues Hope.

In the following year, 1815, he printed the *Preface* to the *Collected Poems,* in which there appeared a paragraph concerning some extracts from *An Evening Walk* and *Descriptive Sketches,* which were included among the Juvenile Pieces. The extracts were omitted later, and the paragraph in the *Preface* referring to them was cancelled. As a result it is almost unknown. The substantial part is as follows, and shows clearly that the terms "youth" and "youthful" are used in a precise manner:

These Extracts seem to have a title to be placed here [among the Juvenile Pieces], as they were the productions of youth, and represent implicitly some of the features of a youthful mind, at a time when images of nature supplied to it the place of thought, sentiment, and almost of action; or, as it will be found expressed, of a state of mind when

> "the sounding cataract
> Haunted me like a passion: the tall rock,
> The mountain, and the deep and gloomy wood,
> Their colours and their forms, were then to me
> An appetite: a feeling and a love,
> That had no need of a remoter charm,
> By thought supplied, or any interest
> Unborrowed from the eye."

In order to show that this tripartite scheme of human life was not forgotten in later years, it is sufficient to note that a poem written in 1818, *Composed Upon an Evening of Extraordinary Splendour and Beauty,* reminiscent of *Tintern Abbey*

---

[65] *Op. cit.,* IX, 20-26.

and the great *Ode*, draws the distinctions between his "blissful infancy," and the present time of maturity. Now for a
moment is granted "this glimpse of glory," but it departs: and
it reminds the poet of

> the light
> Full early lost and fruitlessly deplored.

None the less the poet rejoices, for his soul now

> Rejoices in a second birth.

Thus we see that from 1797-8 to 1820 Wordsworth made
habitual use of the doctrine of the three ages of man in dealing with all the important problems of his life and art. We
have specially noted with regard to this doctrine of the three
ages that it is a real doctrine and not a mere external manner
of classifying his experiences, for it is to be marked, (1) that
each of the ages is regarded as being distinct the one from the
other, (a distinction consistently maintained throughout the
whole extent of his best productive period); (2) that the ages
are causally related the one to the other; and (3) that they
represent the manner in which every normal mind develops.

In the remaining chapters we shall show how this doctrine
and method is fundamental in the poet's attitude towards all
the main problems of nature and art, and forms an integral
part of his presentation of each.

We shall first deal with the relationships of this doctrine of
the three ages to earlier and contemporary theories, and shall
thus attempt to indicate the sources of Wordsworth's important ideas and the "seminal principle" of his mind. After this
examination of what we may call the seed, we shall follow its
bourgeoning into the blade and the ripened ear of theory and
mature, accomplished art.

CHAPTER VI

WORDSWORTH, HARTLEY, AND ENGLISH PHILOSOPHY

Take, for instance, in Philosophy, Hartley's book upon Man. How many years did it sleep in almost entire oblivion!

William Wordsworth to Richard Sharp, 1808.

We have noted two important stages in the development of Wordsworth toward an aesthetic and philosophy of life. The first we have designated his earlier period,[1] which we can rather accurately limit between the time of his graduation from Cambridge in January, 1791, through his sojourn in France from November, 1791, to November, 1792, his subsequent residence in London, and his wanderings in England, ending in the year 1795. Intellectually, this period is marked by his frank acceptance of William Godwin, as we have indicated in our second chapter, and by his revolt from him, with consequent yielding up all moral questions in despair. Aesthetically the period is marked by his acceptance of the principles of "poetic diction," and culminates in his repudiation of it in favor of the more philosophic principles of the school of taste.

The second stage, which we denominate the period of maturity, begins with his revolt from both Godwin and "poetic diction" with the consequent moral and aesthetic confusion, about the year 1795, comes to its first characteristic expression in both poetry and prose in the *Lyrical Ballads* of 1798, and develops in various directions through subsequent editions of the *Lyrical Ballads,* the *Poems* of 1807, and *The Excursion* and *The Prelude* with their various prose accompaniments. These developments we shall discuss in the chapters that follow, the present one having especially to do with the transition from the early to the mature period.

---

[1] First adequately presented in Emile Legouis, *The Early Life of William Wordsworth,* 1897. New edition, 1921. Much new material on the personal side of Wordsworth in France has been added by G. M. Harper, *William Wordsworth,* 2 vols., 1916; and *Wordsworth's French Daughter,* 1921.

The stages of his recovery from the moral despair caused by his awakening to the evil results of Godwinianism are not by any means so clear. He himself speaks but briefly of this transition in his development: but there is no doubt that he regards it as most important, as he characterizes the change as the passage from errors—"juvenile errors" is his phrase—to the full light of truth. He tells us that the fundamental mistake in Godwinianism is the attempt

> to abstract the hopes of man
> Out of his feelings;[2]

and he regards his passage from error to truth as safely accomplished when he is at last united to his sister Dorothy, who maintained for him a saving intercourse with his true self, preserved him still a poet, and,

> By all varieties of human love
> Assisted, led me back through opening day,
> To those sweet counsels between head and heart
> Whence grew that genuine knowledge, fraught with peace,
> Which, through the later sinkings of this cause,
> Hath still upheld me, and upholds me now.[3]

This explanation of the manner in which he arrived at the view of life and art as we see it in the *Lyrical Ballads* of 1798 is not fully satisfactory; for, while it may give a complete explanation of the peace which he attained in his personal life, it cannot explain altogether the sources of the "genuine knowledge" and the set of doctrines which he found between 1795 and 1798 and worked into a fairly complete system, which express the essential Wordsworth as we know him, and of which he gives no sign in those early poems which were published in 1793.[4] However great and important the influence of Dorothy was upon him, as we have already noted, it cannot have been in the direction of furnishing the poet with a philosophy and an aesthetic. And yet, during this crucial period of his life, he was furnished with both; so the problem of the critic is to cast about in search of the source whence

---

[2] *The Prelude*, XI, 225-226.
[3] *Op. cit.*, XI, 351-356.
[4] *The Evening Walk*, written 1787-1789; *Descriptive Sketches*, written 1791-1792. The first is thus an undergraduate poem; the second is coincident with his sojourn in France.

Wordsworth drew his inspiration and his knowledge. Just as in the first stage, of which we have spoken, the period from October, 1791, to 1795, the important fact is his devotion to the system of Godwin; so in this second stage is his meeting with Samuel Taylor Coleridge, and the intellectual stimulus which resulted from his intercourse with Coleridge and the Bristol group, which led to a renewed devotion to a line of other English thinkers and philosophers, chiefly David Hartley.

I say a renewed devotion; for no more is meant than that the meeting with Coleridge and his group was a great incentive to Wordsworth to follow his original philosophical bent. As has already been indicated in the second chapter, he had been acquainted with Godwin's *Political Justice* since 1793, the very year in which the book was published; and anyone who was acquainted with Godwin could not fail to have his attention drawn to Hartley, for Godwin avowedly based his work partly on him. For instance, his chapter on "The Moral Characters of Men Originate in their Perceptions," Book I, Chapter II, is "An abstract" of Hartley's argument in those things "which relate to experience"; and his chapter "Of the Mechanism of the Human Mind," Book IV, Chapter VII, is accompanied by the following note:

The above will be found to be a tolerably accurate description of the hypothesis of the celebrated Hartley. It was unnecessary to quote his words, as it would be foreign to the plan of the present work to enter into a refutation of any individual writer. The sagacity of Hartley, in having pointed out the necessary connexion of the phenomena of mind, and shewn the practicability of reducing its different operations to a single principle, cannot be too highly applauded. The reasonings of the present chapter, if true, may be considered as giving further stability to his principal doctrine of freeing it from the scheme of material automatism with which it was unnecessarily clogged.

In this note Godwin has the tone of a discoverer of Hartley; and such, indeed, he was. Probably Wordsworth at first took his Hartley on faith from Godwin; and there can hardly be any doubt that one reason for his revolt from Godwin was the conviction that Godwin's system of philosophy, while claiming to be founded on Locke and Hartley, was really a perversion of these philosophers, attributing sentiments and opinions to them which belonged solely to the other writers whom Godwin claimed as his masters,—Helvétius and Rousseau. When he met Coleridge he met one who had proclaimed, and was still proclaiming, the pure doctrine of the master, which was quite a different thing from the anarchistic abstraction of Godwin's interpretation. Thus his change from a faith in Godwin to a faith in Hartley involved no very radical shifting of interests. Both systems begin with Locke and experience, and so shifting from one to the other involved only a new interpretation of the old facts with a new evolution of man and society in the light of that interpretation.

The first meeting between Wordsworth and Coleridge, momentous not only for themselves but for the future of English poetry, took place in the month of September, 1795. The friendship then begun was continued in the following year, and was succeeded in 1797 and 1798 by the almost daily intimacy which produced the *Lyrical Ballads* of 1798. As Wordsworth has left no substantial record of his thoughts in the fertile years 1795 to 1797, we may turn to the more communicative brother poet, and by reading his thoughts we may learn what Wordsworth himself was absorbing and laying up for future use in poetry and theory. We have abundant evidence that what interested Coleridge most during these years and for some years afterwards, was philosophy, and the individual philosophers who most attracted him were Berkeley and Hartley, with the precedence clearly given to the latter. The evidence on this point is so abundant that only a few references need be given. We have, of course, his own late evidence in the *Biographia Literaria,* and the contemporary evidence confirms this. His friend Cottle tells us that he

generally contrived, either by direct amalgamation, or disgression, to notice, in the warmest encomiastic language, Bishop Berkeley, David Hartley, or Mr. Bowles. . . . He urged the purchase of three works, indispensable to all who wished to excel in sound reasoning, or a correct taste; namely; Simpson's Euclid; Hartley on Man; and Bowles's Poems.[5]

This statement of Cottle's refers to 1795; and in *Religious Musings,* a poem written by Coleridge during the years 1794-

---

[5] Joseph Cottle, *Early Recollections,* London, 1837, 21.

1796, we have the following well-known tribute to Hartley:

> and he of mortal kind
> Wisest, he first who marked the ideal tribes
> Down the fine fibres from the sentient brain
> Roll subtly-surging;

and in a note to a passage on the final transformation of the love of the world and self into the love of God, he begins by saying, "See this *demonstrated* by Hartley, vol. 1, p. 114, and vol. 2, p. 329." The poem as a whole has many Hartleian features, and has several passages which have the appearance of being little more than paraphrases from this "wisest of mortal kind," or are written in the spirit of associationism and Hartleian optimism.[6] As corroborative evidence it will be necessary only to remind the reader that in 1796 Coleridge christened his first-born David Hartley, "after the great master of Christian philosophy." Further evidence of the place held in the mind of Coleridge by the system of Hartley, is furnished by Lamb, in a letter written to Coleridge, February 5, 1797. He suggests some subjects for a long poem, and among others recommends this to his friend:

> Or a Five Days' Dream, which shall illustrate, in sensible imagery, Hartley's five Motives to Conduct:—1. Sensation; 2. Imagination; 3. Ambition; 4. Sympathy; 5. Theopathy;

and proceeds to supply hints for the scenery of each of the five books.

Carlyon,[7] our authority for Coleridge in Germany, details conversations belonging to the spring of 1799 which are thoroughly Hartleian in substance; and Hazlitt's account of his visit to the joint authors of the *Lyrical Ballads* in the very year of the publication of the volume, shows that benevolence and association, two fundamentals in the system of Hartley, were fully accepted by Coleridge. In 1801 and 1803 Coleridge writes to his friends that he has overthrown the association

---

[6] For instance: Lines 28-45, which show the discipline of Fear and the growth of the soul to its identity with God; lines 88-104, an account of the transmutation of the Passions to higher forms; lines 198-259, which depict the "unsensualizing" of the mind through Imagination. Lines 395-401 are avowedly Berkeleian in proclaiming "the final happiness of all men"; but this is also Hartley. I quote the reading of 1796.

[7] Clement Carlyon, M.D., *Early Years and Late Reflections*, 3 vols., 1856, I, 33-34.

theory; but in 1803 we also find him making a proposal to prefix to a new edition of Tucker's *Light of Nature* an essay "containing the whole substance of the first volume of Hartley." De Quincey testifies that by 1807 Coleridge had abandoned Hartley; and this is well within the truth. In connection with his statement concerning Coleridge and his abandonment of Hartley, De Quincey adds his own opinion of the system of associationism, which is a partial explanation of the fascination which it exercised over the minds of so many:

> I must contend that the *Essay on Man, his Frame, his Duty, and his Expectations* stands forward as a specimen almost unique of elaborate theorizing, and a monument of absolute beauty in the impression left of its architectural grace. In this respect it has, to my mind, the spotless beauty and the ideal proportions of some Grecian statue.[8]

William Hazlitt had the great good fortune to visit Wordsworth and Coleridge at Alfoxden in the summer of 1798, when they were actively engaged on the composition of the *Lyrical Ballads,* and he has left us a record of his two weeks' stay in the form of one of the very best accounts of that wonderful season.[9] Among other things, he tells us that he engaged in metaphysical argument, and expressly states that he had already adopted the characteristic opinions of what later became his *Essay on the Principles of Human Action: Being an Argument in favour of the Natural Disinterestedness of the Human Mind. To which are added, Some Remarks on the Systems of Hartley and Helvétius,* published in 1805.[10] The main thesis of this book is in substance one of the cardinal doctrines of Hartley, and the whole argument is impregnated with Hartleian influences, despite the fact that it is developed in conscious contradiction of the Hartleian theory.

In the last place, we have direct evidence that Wordsworth esteemed Hartley very highly. In a letter written to Richard Sharp in 1808, he speaks of Hartley as one among the "men of real power, who go before their age"; and exclaims, ob-

---

[8] Masson's Edition, III, 154.
[9] *My First Acquaintance with Poets.* First published in *Winterslow,* 1839.
[10] This essay is to be found in Waller and Glover's edition of Hazlitt, VII, 383-475.

viously referring to his own rediscovery of Hartley's book upon Man, "How many years did it sleep in almost entire oblivion!"[11]

It is thus clear that Wordsworth was familiar with Hartley, whether he accepted the system itself or not. We shall now examine the internal evidence to show the connections between the poet and the line of philosophic thought represented by Bacon, Locke, Berkeley, and Hume, but especially by David Hartley's *Observations on Man, his Frame, his Duty, and his Expectations,* first published in two volumes in 1749; re-issued in 1791 in three volumes, with notes by Pistorius; and also published in selections in one volume by Joseph Priestley in 1775.[12] It will also be necessary to consider the work of Hartley's most conspicuous disciples, Joseph Priestley and Dr. Erasmus Darwin, both contemporaries of Wordsworth, devoting special attention to Darwin in his *Botanic Garden* and his *Zoönomia.* In our examination of these authors we shall have specially in mind the scheme of the three ages of man and its collateral developments, as a fundamental principle in their systems.

In the *Lyrical Ballads,* first published in 1798, in conjunction with Coleridge, the revolt from Godwin and the comfort in a more satisfying philosophy are both plainly to be seen. At the same time, the volume is a composite affair, for of the twenty poems contributed by Wordsworth there are a goodly number which deal with general humanitarian topics common to Godwin and a large class of his contemporaries. *Lines left on a Seat in a Yew Tree, Lines Written in Early Spring, The Convict,* and *The Thorn,* are examples; and they are closely related to another and more numerous class which have to do with the more specialized topic of the horrors of war. Antimilitary poetry was very common at this time, and in this Wordsworth fell in with a prevailing fashion of his day which was being observed by Southey, Thelwall, Coleridge, Bowles, and others. In *The Female Vagrant,* and *Animal Tranquillity,*

[11] Knight, *Letters of the Wordsworth Family,* I, 379.
[12] My preliminary statement appeared in *The Nation,* July 17, 1913, pp. 51 ff., under the title "Wordsworth and Hartley." Passages of this paper are here reproduced and adapted.

we see this special anti-military application of the general and widespread feeling for the sufferings of the poor.[13]

All these poems would have met with the hearty approval of Godwin, as we have observed in the second chapter; but others are of a different quality. The philosopher of the *Political Justice* hailed justice in the abstract as the greatest virtue of society and decried the more human ones, like pity, the family feelings, filial piety,—the "blessed charities of father, son, and brother"—as mere prejudices, to be suppressed and subjected to the clear light of truth. Property, according to Godwin, is an evil; but we find Wordsworth making a protest against the principle in *The Last of the Flock,* a poem written to show the natural love of man for property, its importance in fostering the domestic affections, and the decline of manhood in extreme poverty. This subject of the domestic affections and their importance for the English peasantry continued to engage the attention of Wordsworth, as we see in *The Brothers* and *Michael,* and as he himself explains in the long letter to Fox in elucidation of both these later poems. Another set of his poems inspired by his revolt against Godwin consists of those which have to do with "the primary laws of our nature," as he himself expresses the matter. To these belong *The Idiot Boy* and *The Mad Mother,* founded on the maternal passion; *Simon Lee,* a vindication of the feelings of benevolence and gratitude; *The Forsaken Indian Woman,* a picture of the soul in the face of death, and its counterpart *We are Seven,* a picture of the child's inability to understand what death is; and finally *Goody Blake and Harry Gill,* an account of a soul under a curse. This subject of the soul under a curse is of course the subject of *The Ancient Mariner,* and of those poems which the authors of the *Lyrical Ballads* were engaged on in 1798 but did not publish as yet, *Christabel, Cain, The Three Graves,* and *Peter Bell,* and the same as that of De Quincey's Kate in *The Spanish Military Nun*—"penitential sorrow" in the Opium-Eater's finely descriptive phrase.

After we have named all the preceding titles in the volume of 1798 we have left names that are far more famous still; and these are the titles of poems which deal with the relations

---

[13] See Chapter II.

of Nature to the development and nurture of the individual soul. Here we first arrive at the really "Wordsworthian" poems in the volume, and here it is that we first come into contact with the sort of poetry that the poet developed into his most characteristic work. The titles of these poems are not so much titles as a roll-call of glory—*Lines Written at a Small Distance (To my Sister), Lines Written in Early Spring,* the pair, *Expostulation and Reply* and *The Tables Turned;* and greatest of all, *Lines Written a few Miles above Tintern Abbey, on Revisiting the Banks of the Wye During a Tour, July 13, 1798.* Here, surely, we are at the heart of Wordsworth.

In these poems there are many expressions concerning the educative powers of Nature, which have given a great deal of trouble to commentators; some have called the doctrine in these poems Pantheism, some Platonism; some, like Lord Morley, have treated these expressions as "playful sallies"; while others have treated them as indiscretions to be hushed up and forgiven. I wish to examine them in the light of the Hartleian philosophy, as the first statement of the newly-found solution of the universe and as the poet's first satisfying aesthetic, which gave theoretical support to his own insistent need of joy and hope, and pleasure. In any case, we cannot ignore the poet's statements concerning Nature, for they are not made casually, but frequently and deliberately, and have the air of being the deliverances of a man who is possessed of a body of doctrine which he is ready to apply to life as a whole.

First, it should be noted that while Wordsworth speaks of immediate joy in the presence of Nature, as in the *Lines Written in Early Spring,* this is not his characteristic attitude. His doctrine of Nature does not dwell on the immediate good which Nature brings; but rather on the "future good for years to come," as in the cryptic lines,

> Some silent laws our hearts may make
> Which they shall long obey,

or, as in the words addressed to Dorothy in *Tintern Abbey,*

> Therefore let the moon
> Shine on thee in thy solitary walk;
> And let the misty mountain winds be free

7

> To blow against thee: and in after years,
> When these wild ecstacies shall be matured
> Into a sober pleasure, when thy mind
> Shall be a mansion for all lovely forms,
> Thy memory be as a dwelling-place
> For all sweet sounds and harmonies.

Her mind, like the poet's own, will be educated by Nature, and will be pleased to recognize in Nature and the language of the sense, the anchor of her purest thoughts, the nurse, the guide and guardian of her heart, and soul of all her moral being. This is the education of Nature, which she effects on all souls subjected to her sway; for, whether we will or not, our human souls are linked to her. In these poems Wordsworth is giving first expression to the thought which he was to work out later in such exquisite form as that of *Three Years She Grew,* and at greater length, in "the great philosophical poem," which shows "how exquisitely the individual Mind to the external World is fitted; and how exquisitely too the external World is fitted to the Mind." This, the avowed subject of *The Prelude,* is the subject of *Tintern Abbey:* it is the history of the development of his own mind under the guidance of Nature, or experience. It is to be noted that we find in *Tintern Abbey* the first clear indication of a characteristically Wordsworthian method of poetic procedure, that is, the method of reminiscence or retrospect, combined, as we have noted in the previous chapter, with the method of the three ages of man. It is thus that he vitalizes the commonplace form of retrospect and reminiscence, interpreting the facts of experience by the association philosophy of David Hartley and of some of his later interpreters. In the light of this philosophy it is not mere fancy but sound philosophy to say that the Child is Father of the Man, and the philosopher does not go beyond the warrant of associationism when he gives thanks for

> Those shadowy recollections,
> Which, be they what they may,
> Are yet the fountain light of all our day,
> Are yet a master light of all our seeing;
> Uphold us, cherish us, and make
> Our noisy years seem moments in the being

Of the eternal Silence: truths that wake
    To perish never;
Which neither listlessness, nor mad endeavour
    Nor Man nor Boy,
Nor all that is at enmity with joy,
Can utterly abolish or destroy!

We shall now examine the problems and topics of this last class of poems in the *Lyrical Ballads* in the light of English philosophy in general and of Hartley's system in particular.

Needless to say, one of the main problems of philosophy is the question of how man attains to conscious knowledge; and a question which is vitally connected with this is the way in which the mind of man is wedded to this goodly universe.[14] This and the related question of the unity of consciousness form the main problem of Wordsworth; and we must note at once that the method by which he explains the union of the mind of man with this goodly universe is essentially in line with the general tradition of English philosophy. There can be no manner of doubt that he approaches the problem of mind from the angle of Locke, basing his whole theory on the assumption that thought originates in experience, and that out of the product of sensation, or experience, ideas and the more complex forms of mentality are developed. This is so obvious from our fifth chapter that we do not need to develop the matter here. It is a mark of that fundamental difference between him and Coleridge that the latter so often suspected; for Wordsworth did "treat man as man—a subject of eye, ear, touch, and taste, in contact with external nature," and contrary to Coleridge's opinion, not "informing the senses from the mind," but "compounding a mind out of the senses."[15]

In this he is at one with the general tradition of English philosophy and that of the Continent from which it is in part derived, and on which it reacted, as embodied in the systems of those men with whom Wordsworth is most in sympathy on this point,—Locke and Hartley. We shall note Hartley in particular, indicating certain pertinent relationships which he holds with other philosophers.

---

[14] *The Recluse*, 805-806.
[15] Coleridge, *Table Talk*, July 21, 1832.

Hartley

The qualities of Hartley's philosophy which attracted Wordsworth were its completeness of method; its simplicity; its common-sense foundation; its reactionary tendency toward old standards which had been forgotten in the times which were "out of joint"; together with a deep spiritual enthusiasm, and the necessitarianism of Godwin and Priestley, and an insistence on sympathy and benevolence that satisfied the poet's newly awakened love for his country and his re-established domestic peace. Thus a rational basis was offered him for all his fondest hopes; and a method was furnished him by which he could satisfactorily account for many facts in his own experience which were inexplicable by the systems of thought to which he had hitherto given his allegiance.

Like all systems of philosophy founded on that of Locke, all innate ideas are banished; and all mental states are derived from sensation. These sensations are the primary, ultimate, and irresolvable facts of our mental life, and are the result of our direct contact with external things: and they, through the power of association, are transformed into the complexes of those forms of mental life which succeed those that partake of the simplicity and directness of sensation. According to Hartley, association is the law of the mind, as gravitation is the law of the physical world. He is the original exponent of the law of association, in which he has been followed by the Utilitarians; and we have abundant evidence that Wordsworth gave this law his full credence.

association

Under the influence of this law of association, then, as Hartley conceives it, the primary sensations are transmuted, by a sort of chemical process, into the "purer" forms of thought: first into ideas of a simple sort, and then into more complex ones. Hartley's own words are as follows:

Sensations are those internal feelings of the mind, which arise from the impressions made by external objects upon the several parts of our bodies.

All of our other internal feelings may be called *ideas*. Some of these appear to spring up in the mind of themselves, some are suggested by words, others arise in other ways. Many writers comprehend *sensations* under *idea;* but I everywhere use these words in the senses here ascribed to them.

The ideas which resemble sensations, are called *ideas of sensation:* all the rest may therefore be called *intellectual ideas.*

It will appear in the course of these observations, that the *ideas of sensation* are the elements of which all the rest are compounded. Hence *ideas of sensation* may be termed *simple, intellectual* ones *complex.*[16]

Thus we have a hierarchy of mental complexes:

(1) Sensations, which arise from impressions from external objects.

(2) Simple ideas of sensation; or "sensible" ideas; that is, ideas surviving sensations after the objects which caused them have been removed. This is the mind's first step in the "purer" forms of thought, but such ideas are closely allied to sensations, and are hardly distinguishable from them. It is to be noted that from them arise all the other ideas—"the elements out of which they are compounded."

(3) Complex ideas; that is, intellectual ideas, compounded from the simpler ideas under the power of association.

But Hartley does not look upon man as a mere machine for registering the impressions of external nature. There is from the very earliest and simplest sensation an activity or motion of the human soul, or spirit, which transmutes these experiences into their appropriate personal values, which are classified under the heads of *pleasure* and *pain:*

The *pleasures* and *pains* are comprehended under the sensations and ideas, as these are explained above. For all our pleasures and pains are internal feelings, and, conversely, all our internal feelings seem to be attended with some degree either of *pleasure* or *pain.* However, I shall, for the most part, give the names of *pleasure* and *pain* only to such degrees as are considerable; referring all low, evanescent ones to the head of *mere sensations* and *ideas.*

The pleasures and pains may be ranged under seven general classs, viz.:

1. Sensation;
2. Imagination;
3. Ambition;
4. Self-interest;
5. Sympathy;
6. Theopathy; and,
7. The moral sense; according as they arise from

---

[16] *Observations on Man,* I, i-ii.

1. The impressions made on the external senses;
2. Natural or artificial beauty or deformity;
3. The opinions of others concerning us;
4. Our possession or want of the means of happiness, and
   security from, or subjection to, the hazards of misery;
5. The pleasures and pains of our fellow-creatures;
6. The affections excited in us by the contemplations of the
   Deity; or,
7. Moral beauty and deformity.[17]

That is, these forms are associated with sensations and ideas; but in a way which is in harmony with the particular mental state. Thus they do not all possess the power of association with all ideas alike. The first four are associated with the simple ideas of sensation and the sensations; and the last three—sympathy, theopathy, and the moral sense,—being the highest in quality, are associated, or ought to be associated, with the higher, more complex, and "purer" intellectual ideas. These three alone are worthy of being made our primary pursuit in life.[18]

Although this is true, the principle of transmutation through association holds true: for

all the intellectual pleasures and pains are deducible ultimately from the sensible ones, if one can show of each intellectual pleasure and pain in particular, that it takes its rise from other pleasures and pains, either sensible or intellectual. For thus none of the intellectual pleasures and pains can be original. But the sensible pleasures and pains are evidently originals. They are therefore the only ones, *i. e.* they are the common sources from whence all the intellectual pleasures and pains are ultimately derived.[19]

Hartley also recognizes in men certain powers or faculties:

The human mind may also be considered as indued with the faculties of *memory, imagination* or *fancy, understanding, affection,* and *will.*[20]

He then proceeds to define each of these faculties; the only definitions which are important for our purposes being those of *understanding* and *affection:*

---

[17] *Observations on Man,* I, ii-iii.
[18] *Op. cit.,* II, 283-346.
[19] *Op. cit.,* I, 416-417.
[20] *Op. cit.,* I, iii.

The *understanding* is that faculty, by which we contemplate mere sensations and ideas, pursue truth, and assent to, or dissent from propositions.

The *affections* have the pleasures and pains for their objects as the *understanding* has the mere sensations and ideas. By the affections we are excited to pursue happiness, and all its means, fly from misery, and all its apparent causes.[21]

A most important aspect of Hartley's treatment of these two faculties of the affections and understanding is their mutual relations. Wordsworth follows Hartley, and this has a profound effect on his theory of the affections and emotions, which in turn has a corresponding effect on his theory of poetry. Hartley plainly makes the affections derivative from ideas; from sensitive, or simple ideas primarily, but connected through association the one with the other by the inevitable transmutation of the lower and simple into the higher and complex. This makes emotion, or feeling, secondary to the intellectual processes. Hartley's statement is as follows:

First, That our passions or affections can be no more than aggregates of simple ideas united by association. For they are excited by objects and by the incidents of life. But these, if we except the impressed sensations, can have no power of affecting us but what they derive from association. . . .

Secondly, Since the passions are states of considerable pleasure or pain, they must be aggregates of the ideas, or traces of the sensible pleasures and pains, which ideas make up by their numbers, and mutual influence upon one another, for the faintness and transitory nature of each singly taken. . . .

Thirdly, As sensation is the common foundation of all these, so each in its turn, when sufficiently generated, contributes to generate and model all the rest.

He then proceeds to show how this is done in accordance with the law of association, by which the lower and simpler coalesces with the next in order to produce a third. Thus, sensation will be transmuted into imagination; sensation and imagination will generate ambition; and so on, until we arrive at the moral sense, the highest and most complex of all mental phenomena. Conversely, imagination will re-model sensation, and so on,

---

[21] *Op. cit.,* I, iii.

till at last, by the numerous reciprocal influences of all these upon each other, the passions arrive at that degree of complexness, which is observed in fact, and which makes them so difficult to be analysed.[22]

Thus passion, or emotion, is secondary to ideas, that is, to intellect: and it is also not primary, but "factitious," that is, generated by association. In this way "particular desires" become "general desires"; and even if it is true that after general desires and endeavors are generated, they give rise to a variety of particular ones, "the original source is in the particular ones, and the general ones new-alter and new-model the particular ones, so much as that there are not many traces and vestiges of their original mechanical nature and proportions remaining."[23]

The secondary and "factitious" nature of emotion is explicitly maintained by Wordsworth in many passages, and is always assumed. In a notable passage of *The Prelude,* he says that he "has been sedulous to trace how Nature by extrinsic (*i. e.* "factitious") passion first peoples the mind with forms sublime or fair"; and goes on to develop this idea. As a child he felt "gleams like the flashings of a shield," and,

> the earth
> And common face of Nature spake to me
> Rememberable things; sometimes, 'tis true,
> By chance collisions and quaint accidents
> (Like those ill-sorted unions), work supposed
> Of evil-minded fairies), yet not vain
> Nor profitless, if haply they impressed
> Collateral objects and appearances,
> Albeit lifeless then, and doomed to sleep
> Until maturer seasons called them forth
> To impregnate and to elevate the mind,
> —And if the vulgar joy by its own weight
> Wearied itself out of the memory,
> The scenes which were a witness of that joy
> Remained in their substantial lineaments
> Depicted on the brain, and to the eye
> Were visible a daily sight; and thus
> By the impressive discipline of fear,

---

[22] *Observations on Man,* I, 368-369.
[23] *Op. cit.,* I, 370-371.

By pleasure and repeated happiness,
So frequently repeated, and by force
Of obscure feelings representative
Of things forgotten, these same scenes so bright,
So beautiful, so majestic in themselves,
Though yet the day was distant, did become
Habitually dear, and all their forms
And changeful colours by invisible links
Were fastened to the affections.[24]

This is pure associationism, both in the doctrine of the extrinsic nature of feeling and in the quite definite naming of the particular passions of *fear* and *pleasure* as the leading forces in this association and transmutation of feeling. Hartley classifies the "general passions of human nature" with all the precision of the mediaeval classification of the "seven deadly sins":

After the actual joy and grief are over, and the object withdrawn, there generally remains a pleasing or displeasing recollection or resentment, which recurs with every recurrency of the idea of the object, or of the associated ones. This recollection keeps up the love or hatred. In like manner the five grateful passions, love, desire, hope, joy, and pleasing recollection, all enhance one another; as do the five ungrateful ones, hatred, aversion, fear, grief, and unpleasing recollection. And the whole ten, then together, comprehend, as appears to me, all the general passions of human nature.[25]

This passage is a clue to Wordsworth's frequent use of *fear, grief,* and *aversion,* as well as *joy,* and *hope,* and *love* as discipline of childhood and youth.

Wordsworth is associationistic in his views as to the nature of the affections, and in his classification of them. Much more fundamentally, he is associationistic in his views as to the relationship between ideas and the affections. As we have noted, Hartley regards the affections as derived from ideas; and Wordsworth follows him in this. In his *Preface* to the second edition of *Lyrical Ballads,* 1800, he gives a famous, and always half-quoted, description of poetry. He claims that his poems are differentiated from those of some of his contemporaries "at least by one mark of difference, that each of them has a worthy *purpose."*

---

[24] *The Prelude,* I, 586-612.
[25] *Observations on Man,* I, 373.

Not that I mean to say, that I always began to write with a distinct purpose formally conceived; but I believe that my habits of meditation have so formed my feelings, as that my descriptions of such objects as strongly excite those feelings, will be found to carry along with them a *purpose*. If in this opinion I am mistaken I can have little right to the name of Poet. For all good poetry is the spontaneous overflow of powerful feelings; *but though this be true*, Poems to which any value can be attached, were never produced on any variety of subjects but by a man who being possessed of more than usual organic sensibility had also thought long and deeply. For our continued influxes of feeling are modified and directed by our thoughts, which are indeed the representatives of all our past feelings; and as by contemplating the relation of these general representatives to each other, we discover what is really important to men, so by the repetition and continuance of this act feelings connected with important subjects will be nourished, till at length, if we be originally possessed of much organic sensibility, such habits of mind will be produced that by obeying blindly and mechanically the impulses of those habits we shall describe objects and utter sentiments of such a nature and such connection with each other, that the understanding of the being to whom we address ourselves, if he be in a healthful state of association, must be in some degree enlightened, his taste exalted, and his affections ameliorated.[26]

That is to say, Poetry proceeds from feelings; but the only feelings which are aesthetic ones are those which have their origin in intellectual ideas: any other emotion, or feeling, is not worthy of poetry. He re-states this later on in the *Preface,* illustrating the principle of the priority of thought over emotion by Dr. Johnson's stanza in parody of the ballad stanza:

> I put my hat upon my head,
> And walk'd into the Strand,
> And there I met another man
> Whose hat was in his hand.

Immediately under this Wordsworth places a stanza from *The Babes in the Wood,* a poem which appears in Percy's *Reliques,* and which Wordsworth admired:

---

[26] *Preface* to *Lyrical Ballads,* 1800. I quote this passage here, despite the fact that a large part of it is quoted in Chapter III to illustrate Wordsworth's associationistic connections. It is a very important statement.

> These pretty Babes with hand in hand
> Went wandering up and down;
> But never more they saw the Man
> Approaching from the Town;

and then he asks why the latter stanza is admitted as admirable and Dr. Johnson's as a fair example of the superlatively contemptible. The answer is, "not because of the metre, not because of the language, but because the *matter* expressed in Dr. Johnson's stanza is contemptible."

The proper method of treating trivial and simple verses to which Dr. Johnson's stanza would be a fair parallelism is not to say this is a bad kind of poetry, but this wants sense; it is neither interesting in itself, nor can *lead* to anything interesting; the images neither originate in that sane state of feeling which arises out of thought, nor can excite thought or feeling in the Reader. This is the only sensible manner of dealing with such verses: why trouble yourself about the species till you have previously decided upon the genus? Why take pains to prove that an Ape is not a Newton when it is self-evident that he is not a man?[27]

This derivative nature of emotion, thus clearly maintained, is carried to important conclusions in his theory of Poetry and Imagination, as we shall see later.[28] Meanwhile, it is very clear that those who represent him as exalting emotion at the expense of intellect, read the poet in a careless manner or in the light of a theory rather than of evidence. To accuse Wordsworth of trusting in mere spontaneity, and thus to deny him ethical imagination, is to ignore this definition of emotion, and to forget many passages which expressly state or imply that intellect is the last and final guide in the difficult way to wisdom.[29] Such is the theme of the *Letter* to "Mathetes"— "Nature has irrevocably decreed . . . that the way to knowledge shall be long, difficult, winding, and oftentimes returning upon itself." This is not a trust in sensation, or in Nature, but in reason and intellect.

----

[27] *Preface* to *Lyrical Ballads*, 1800. This reference to the Ape and Newton is to be found in Pope, *Essay on Man*, II, 34 :
"And shew'd a Newton as we shew an ape."
[28] In Chapters VIII and IX.
[29] As, for instance, Irving Babbitt, *Rousseau and Romanticism*, 1919. Contrast the admirable essay in Leslie Stephen, *Hours in a Library*, II, 250-284, "Wordsworth's Ethics."

Another quality in Hartley's system which probably attracted Wordsworth is the optimism. According to Hartley, evil inevitably disappears and good as inevitably grows until we arrive at happiness in the love of God. While Wordsworth never adopted this view he was very familiar with it during his early acquaintance with Coleridge, who made much of Hartley, as we see by his *Religious Musings,* 1794, and who thus expresses the idea of the disappearance of evil:

> And first by Fear uncharmed the drowséd Soul
> Till of its nobler nature it 'gan feel
> Dim recollections; and thence soared to Hope
> Strong to believe whate'er of mystic good
> The Eternal dooms for His immortal sons.
> From Hope and firmer Faith to perfect Love
> Attracted and absorbed: and centered there
> God only to behold, and know, and feel,
> Till by exclusive consciousness of God
> All self-annihilated it shall make
> God its Identity: God all in all!
> We and our Father one![30]

As we have seen, Coleridge directly connects this passage with Hartley by a footnote, stating that the idea thus poetically expressed has been *demonstrated* by Hartley. He also adds that in the third volume of the edition of 1791, the proposition is likewise proved *and freed from the charge of mysticism.*

Thus by the inevitable processes of life every soul under the guidance of association seeks good and happiness and pleasure, and arrives at Sympathy, the love of God, and the highest reaches of the moral sense. In this way the poet in his individual growth to sympathy with men and to moral sense, as he portrays his own development in *The Prelude,* was but following out the laws of growth as laid down by Hartley; and the ultimate end of his own development and of Hartley's philosophy is ultimate good and optimism.

Ultimate attainment of the good was connected by Hartley with necessitarianism, for this attainment of the good was no secondary thing, but a prime necessity in the very nature of things; a doctrine accepted by Wordsworth in his earlier maturity, however modified it may have been in his later years.

---

[30] *Religious Musings,* 34-45.

Another set of related characteristics in the philosophy of Hartley, which attracted Wordsworth and caused him to adopt them and make them his own, is made up of (1) individualism, (2) utilitarianism, and (3) the principle that pleasure, or happiness, is the ultimate test of philosophy and life alike. The whole of the system of Hartley is strongly individualistic, like that of Locke and all those which begin with sensation as the beginning of knowledge. As we have already noted, the proposition that all the constructions of the mind are compounded out of the simple sensations is a fundamental one in Hartley; and quite consistently with this his ethical principles are based on self-interest, ethical progress being the passing from the "gross self-interest" of sensation, imagination, and ambition to the "refined self-interest" of sympathy, theopathy, and the moral sense. All these are "active powers" of the mind, which have always a reference to the self. Even the three last, the highest that man is capable of, have no meaning or content apart from the experience of the individual, for it is utterly impossible to experience the moral sense unless all the previous pleasures and pains, beginning with those of sensation and ending with theopathy, have been experienced. This is a fundamental assumption of his associationism; for all mental life begins with experience, and the highest forms are only transmutations of the lower. Hence moral judgments must be preceded by all the lower judgments out of which it is transmuted.[31]

This position brings certain logical consequences: first Hartley is in direct opposition to the "moral sense" school of Shaftesbury and Butler, who hold that moral judgments are a direct appeal to an ultimate and simple "moral sense." To Hartley such a "sense" is an absurdity, for the higher forms of our mind are not implanted in us, but are a gradual evolution of the higher out of the lower, as a result of experience on the part of the individual, under the law of association. His own formal statement is as follows:

---

[31] It is only "when the moral sense is advanced to a considerable perfection" that "the pleasures of moral beauty and the pains of moral deformity and unfitness, may be transferred, and made to coalesce almost instantaneously." *Observations on Man*, I, 497.

And thus we may perceive, that all the pleasures and pains of sensation, imagination, ambition, self-interest, sympathy, and theopathy, as far as they are consistent with one another, with the frame of our natures, and with the course of the world, beget in us a moral sense, and lead us to the love and approbation of virtue, and to the fear, hatred, and abhorrence of vice. This moral sense, therefore, carries its own authority with it, inasmuch as it is the sum total of all the rest, and the ultimate result from them; and employs the force and authority of the whole nature of man against any particular part of it, that rebels against the determinations and commands of the conscience or moral judgment. It appears also that the moral sense carries us perpetually to the pure love of God, as our highest and ultimate perfection, our end, centre, and only resting-place, to which we can ever attain.[32]

That Wordsworth adopted the associationism of Hartley and most of its consequences we shall make as clear as we can in succeeding chapters. It is essential at this point to note the fundamental difference between Hartley and Shaftesbury and his school, in view of the fact that the influence of the latter over Wordsworth has been maintained by some recent students of the poet. In order to contrast the two on the point in hand, I shall quote Shaftesbury's own statement:

Sense of Right and Wrong therefore being as natural to us as natural affection itself, and being a first principle in our constitution or make; there is no speculative opinion, persuasion, or belief, which is capable *immediately* or *directly* to exclude or destroy it. That which is of original and pure nature, nothing beside contrary habit or custom (a second nature) is able to displace. And this affection being *an original one* of earliest rise in the soul or affectionate part; nothing beside contrary affection, by frequent check and control, can operate upon it, so as either to diminish it in part, or destroy it in the whole.[33]

This is the exact opposite of the opinion of Hartley: with Shaftesbury the moral sense is "a first principle," "original and pure nature," "an original affection of earliest rise," and so is in no sense derivative from something else; with Hartley it is "the ultimate result" of the individual's completed development, derived from all the other and more simple processes of the mind, and utterly dependent on them. All moral judgments are deduced from association only; and the

[32] *Observations on Man,* I, 497.
[33] *Characteristics,* II, 44. (Edition of 1738.)

reason why we think of them as "original and natural disposi-
tions or instincts" or "axioms and intuitive propositions," is
that these associations have been "formed so early, repeated so
often, rivetted so strong" that they have lost all appearance of
being what they really are—"factitious" and derivative from
earlier and simpler mental processes.

A second consequence of Hartley's associationistic philosophy is that virtue and well-being are in no way dependent on
"public interest," "the good of one's kind," "society," or "the
public," as is held by Shaftesbury.[34] Hartley holds that these
are not original instincts, the ultimate end to which they point
being private happiness.[35]

To be sure, the aim of the individual may be toward public
good, but this can be explained by the law of association, in
accordance with which ends and means are often transposed.
This aspect of Hartley Wordsworth very resolutely adopted,
his whole theory of development and rectification of mind
being strongly individualistic. His mature attitude is essentially expressed by saying that it is not the sentimental
humanitarianism represented by Shaftesbury but the utilitarian
individualism represented by Locke and Hartley. Hence his
insistence on the "grand elementary principle of pleasure" in

---

[34] *Characteristics*, II, 77-78.

[35] In introducing his discussion of The Rule of Life, Hartley lays down as
fundamental the proposition that "God sent us into the world to make ourselves and others happy." The order here given to "ourselves" and "others"
is significant of the whole development of the rule of life. *Observations on
Man*, II, 196-210. Hartley derived the idea of association from the Rev.
Mr. Gay's essay prefixed to Archdeacon Law's translation of Archbishop
King's *Origin of Evil*, 1731. A quotation on the connection of a moral sense,
virtue and happiness will show how closely Hartley followed Gay:

"Our approbation of morality and all affections whatsoever, are resolva-
ble into reason, pointing out private happiness, and are conversant only
about things apprehended to be means tending to this end: and whenever
this end is not perceived, they are to be accounted for from the association
of ideas, and may properly enough be called habits. If this be clearly made
out, the necessity of supposing a moral sense, or public affections, to be
implanted in us (since it arises only from the insufficiency of all other
schemes to account for human actions) will immediately vanish." p. 32.

Gay supposes the love of happiness to be an original and implanted principle in us. Wordsworth had his own definition of this happiness or well-
being:

"He called it joy, meaning thereby not mirth or high spirits, or even
happiness, but a consciousness of entire and therefore well being, when the
emotional and intellectual faculties are in equipoise." E. H. Coleridge, "The
Lake Poets in Somersetshire," in *Transactions of the Royal Society of
Literature*, XX, 105-131.

his theories of poetry in his *Preface* of 1800—a principle which he never retracted.[36]

A third consequence which follows from Hartley's doctrine of association is accepted by Wordsworth, which sharply marks him off from the school of Shaftesbury. This is his theological ethics, common also to Hartley and Locke. Locke was attacked by Shaftesbury for this very quality, on the ground that virtue must be disinterested if it is to be real. Conduct which is inspired by the motive of reward and punishment is not virtue at all, for it is not disinterested. Thus he reasons, we cannot appeal to a God for a standard of goodness, "for how can supreme goodness be intelligible to those who do not know what goodness is?" The conclusion is that virtue, or goodness, is ultimate, and in the nature of things, "not arbitrary or factitious, . . . not constituted from without, or dependent on custom, fancy, or will; not even on the Supreme Will itself, which can no-way govern it; but being *necessarily good,* is governed by it, and ever uniform with it."[37] This gets rid of a Deity in summary fashion—a position which was never held by either Hartley or Wordsworth. Both alike posit a God,—the theological Christian God, in the main—as the standard of faith and virtue.

A fourth consequence of Hartley's associationism in which the poet and Hartley agree is the standard of virtue which is to be set up. Contrary to the sentimental, moral sense school, Hartley says that the rule of life must be based on "the practice and opinions of mankind." This includes the testimony of religion, natural and revealed; for all the expressions of mankind must be studied. All men, since the infancy of the race, have sought happiness, and their methods of obtaining it are rather constant and discoverable: moreover, as opinion is less swayed by passion than practice, where men's practice conflicts with their deliberate opinions, we have the latter as more certain guides on moral questions.[38] That Wordsworth made ex-

---

[36] This principle was enunciated by Coleridge as early as 1796 in the *Preface* to his *Poems:* "The communicativeness of our nature leads us to describe our sorrows; and by a benevolent law of our nature from intellectual activity a pleasure results which is gradually associated and mingles as a corrective with the painful subject of the description."

[37] *Characteristics*, II, 267.

[38] *Observations on Man*, II, 198-199.

actly the same statement in *The Excursion* will be demonstrated in due time.[39]   Again, he and Hartley are distinctly utilitarian and practical as contrasted with Shaftesbury, who places virtue on a much more idealistic and absolute basis, as we have seen.   Contrasted with the school of Shaftesbury, the poet is practicality and realism itself.

I have endeavored to make it clear that Wordsworth accepted Hartley's theory as regards (1) the operation of association, (2) the origin of all knowledge in experience, (3) the secondary and derivative nature of emotion, (4) optimism, (5) necessitarianism, (6) individualism, (7) the nature of virtue, (8) the end of man as happiness, and (9) the three stages by which the mind develops.   While all these nine points are important, the fundamental one for our immediate purposes is the last one.   Wordsworth must have had the greater faith in the importance of the three ages as expounded by Hartley, as the form in which they are presented is only the culmination of a tradition dating from Locke and constantly recurring down to Hartley, so that it had become a fixed method by which to indicate mental development.   A brief examination of Locke, Berkeley, and Hume will make this clear.

Locke rejects all innate ideas and dates all knowledge from sensations, out of which are built up our ideas.   These are of three kinds, rising in a scale of complexity: (1) Simple ideas of sensation; (2) simple ideas of reflection; and (3) complex ideas.[40]   This is nothing else than the three ages of man; and the endeavor of Locke was the endeavor of Wordsworth—to arrive at a notion of real knowledge, which would be found valid when applied to the realities of life.   With Locke, as with Wordsworth, the validity of all knowledge depends on the reality of our sensations: for it is only through the sensations that we can be sure that we touch objective reality. Hence Locke lays great stress on one aspect of our simple ideas: that they *are* simple; that is, not made up of simpler elements; and that we are passive with regard to them, in the

---

[39] See Chapter XII.
[40] John Locke, *Essay on the Human Understanding*, Book II.

sense that "the mind can neither make nor destroy them."[41]
In the same way Wordsworth is constantly insisting on the
necessity of accuracy of sense impressions.   In the *Preface*
of 1815, for instance, he places first among "the powers requisite for the production of poetry," "the ability to observe with
accuracy things as they are in themselves, and with fidelity to
describe them, unmodified by any passion or feeling existing in
the mind of the describer"; and in the *Letter* to "Mathetes" he
speaks of the imagination, "with all its imperfections laid
open," one of which is "not having even attended with care to
the reports of the senses, and therefore grossly deficient in
the rudiments of its own power." . This same insistence is expressed in the necessity of allowing the senses to make their
impression and to pay heed to them as the materials out of
which all real knowledge is made, in a familiar and much-dis-
cussed passage in the first edition of the *Lyrical Ballads,* 1798,
in the companion poems, *Expostulation and Reply,* and *The
Tables Turned.*   The central statements are as follows:

> The eye it cannot chuse but see,
> We cannot bid the ear be still;
> Our bodies feel, where'er they be,
> Against, or with our will.
>
> Nor less I deem that there are powers,
> Which of themselves our minds impress,
> That we can feed this mind of ours
> In a wise passiveness.

Hence the argument proceeds,

> Come forth into the light of things,
> Let Nature be your teacher:

that is, let experience be the source of your knowledge, not
fancy, or the mere secondary understanding,[42] which creates
false knowledge.   Hence, too, the conclusion:

> One impulse from a vernal wood
> May teach you more of man;
> Of moral evil and of good,
> Than all the sages can.

---

[41] Locke, *Essay,* Book II, Ch. II, 2.   See James Gibson, *Locke's Theory
of Knowledge in its Historical Relations,* 1917, Ch. III.   Compare Berkeley,
Principles of Human Knowledge, I, 25.
[42] "That false secondary power."   *The Prelude,* II, 216.

That is, to speak in prose, real knowledge gained from experience is better than all the ready-made knowledge in the world. Surely these lines are no more "mystical," or "playful," or "subjective" than the prose statement of Locke: they are identical in their intention of insisting on real knowledge as opposed to the abstract understanding, on the immediate, simple processes of the mind and imagination, as opposed to the supposedly higher "intuitive," and "transcendental" ones. It is exactly the same as the statement of Locke: "The mind is wholly passive in the reception of all its simple ideas."[43]

In spite of differences with Locke, Berkeley is at one with him as well as with Wordsworth in the notion of the progressive growth of the individual mind by stages from Sense to Reason and Deity, from the "grossly sensible" to the "purely intelligible":

By experiments of sense we become acquainted with the lower faculties of the soul; and from them, whether by a gradual evolution or ascent, we arrive at the highest. Sense supplies images to memory. These become subjects for fancy to work upon. Reason considers and judges of the imaginations. And these acts of reason become new objects to the understanding. In this scale, each lower faculty is a step that leads to one above it. And the uppermost naturally leads to the Deity; which is rather the object of intellectual knowledge than even of the discursive faculty, not to mention the sensitive. There runs a chain throughout the whole system of beings. The meanest things are connected with the highest.[44]

In another passage Berkeley ascribes to the Intellect the sovereign part which is given by Wordsworth:

Sense at first besets and overbears the mind. The sensible appearances are all in all: our reasonings are employed about them: our desires terminate in them: we look no farther for realities or causes; till Intellect begins to dawn, and casts a ray on this shadowy scene. We then perceive the true principle of unity, identity, and existence. Those things that before seemed to constitute the whole of Being, upon taking an intellectual view of things prove to be but fleeting phantoms.[45]

---

[43] *Essay*, Book II, Ch. XII, Sect. 1. Locke holds that passivity implies activity and power, Book II, Ch. XXI, Sect. 2.

[44] Berkley, *Siris*, Sect. 303.

[45] *Op. cit.*, Sect. 294.

This last quotation might have been written as an introductory note to *Tintern Abbey,* or to *Ode. Intimations of Immortality.*

Hume, too, in his search for valid knowledge follows the familiar tripartite division. (1) First are impressions of sensation and reflection; (2) from these come simple ideas, which develop into (3) complex ideas.[46]

Thus we see how commonly the development of the mind was regarded by the English school of philosophers as developing in three stages, and so presented itself ready-made to Wordsworth's hand. Hartley lays down the principle in the following terms:

Some degree of spirituality is the necessary consequence of passing through life. The sensible pleasures and pains must be transferred by association more and more every day, upon things that afford neither sensible pleasure nor sensible pain in themselves, and so beget the intellectual pleasures.[47]

All that the poet had to do was to take the stages as they were given him by his predecessors in philosophic thought and give them an autobiographical, or chronological, interpretation, as (1) Childhood, the age of sensation; (2) Youth, the age of simple ideas; and (2) Maturity, the age of intellectual, complex ideas; and the foundation of his greatest poems and of his most characteristic theories and teaching was complete. How he developed this fundamental theory in its various applications to life and art will be studied in the following chapters.

---

[46] *Treatise of Human Nature,* Book I, Sections i-iii; *Enquiry Concerning Human Understanding,* Section II.
[47] *Observations on Man,* I, 82. (Proposition XIV, Corollary 7.)

CHAPTER VII

WORDSWORTH'S DOCTRINE OF NATURE

Not in a mystical and idle sense,
But in the words of Reason deeply weighed.
William Wordsworth, *The Prelude*, II, 1800.

To nature, as leading on insensibly to the society of reason.
William Wordsworth to "Mathetes," 1809.

Wordsworth's doctrine of Nature is of primary importance for the proper understanding of his poetry and criticism, as it forms an essential part of the whole body of his writings, not only of those poems which avowedly deal with matters of doctrine on man and nature, but also of those which seem on the surface to be the simple outpouring of a naïve and simple mind, and to be wholly innocent of theory. This is to say that his doctrine of Nature permeates not only *The Excursion, The Prelude,* and the prose *Prefaces* and *Essays,* but also *Tintern Abbey, The Cuckoo, Michael, Peele Castle, Resolution and Independence, Lines Written in Early Spring, Expostulation and Reply,* and the *Ode. Intimations of Immortality.* I mention specimens of diverse classes of his work quite purposely; for I wish to make clear that, so far as the doctrine of Nature is concerned, Wordsworth has not put his doctrines into one set of poems and his poetry into another.

But, while it is true that Nature is of great importance in the poetry and prose of Wordsworth and permeates the whole body of his work, it is equally true that his doctrine of Nature is strictly subordinate to another and much more fundamental, comprehensive, and complex one, of which it is a part, and a necessary part; but only a part. In other words, his doctrine of Nature is only one aspect of his doctrine of the development of the individual mind, according to the scheme of the three ages of man. It is difficult to stress this too strongly; for it is only by remembering that in the poet's mind the place which nature holds to man is but a part of the larger problem of the mental development of the individual that we can understand his use of the three ages of man. The poet himself has posed his problem for us in unforgetable language in those lines first made public in the *Preface* to *The Excursion,* which now form the conclusion of *The Recluse,* and which he calls "a kind of *Prospectus"* of the design and scope of the whole "great philosophical poem":

> On Man, on Nature, and on Human Life,
> Musing in solitude, I oft perceive
> Fair trains of imagery before me rise,
> Accompanied by feelings of delight
> Pure, or with no unpleasing sadness mixed;
> And I am conscious of affecting thoughts
> And dear remembrances, whose presence soothes
> Or elevates the Mind, intent to weigh
> The good and evil of our mortal state.
> —To these emotions, whencesoe'er they come,
> Whether from breath of outward circumstance,
> Or from the Soul—an impulse to herself—
> I would give utterance in numerous verse.
> Of Truth, of Grandeur, Beauty, Love, and Hope,
> And melancholy Fear subdued by Faith;
> Of blessèd consolations in distress;
> Of moral strength, and intellectual Power;
> Of joy in widest commonalty spread;
> Of the individual mind that keeps her own
> Inviolate retirement, subject there
> To Conscience only, and the law supreme
> Of that Intelligence which governs all—
> I sing:—"fit audience let me find though few!"
> . . . . Not Chaos, not
> The darkest pit of lowest Erebus,
> Nor aught of blinder vacancy, scooped out
> By help of dreams—can breed such fear and awe
> As fall upon us often when we look
> Into our Minds, into the Mind of Man—
> My haunt, and the main region of my song.
> —Beauty—a living Presence of the earth,
> Surpassing the most fair ideal Forms
> Which craft of delicate Spirits hath composed
> From earth's materials—waits upon my steps;
> Pitches her tent before me as I move,
> An hourly neighbour. Paradise, and groves
> Elysian, Fortunate Fields—like those of old
> Sought in the Atlantic Main—why should they be

A history only of departed things,
Or a mere fiction of what never was?
For the discerning intellect of Man,
When wedded to this goodly universe
In love and holy passion, shall find these
A simple produce of the common day.
—I, long before the blissful hour arrives,
Would chant, in lonely peace, the spousal verse
Of this great consummation:—and, by words
Which speak of nothing more than what we are,
Would I arouse the sensual from their sleep
Of Death, and win the vacant and the vain
To noble raptures; while my voice proclaims
How exquisitely the individual Mind
(And the progressive powers perhaps no less
Of the whole species) to the external World
Is fitted:—and how exquisitely, too—
Theme this but little heard of among men—
The external World is fitted to the Mind;
And the creation (by no lower name
Can it be called) which they with blended might
Accomplish:—this is our high argument.

These lines make it as clear as is possible that Wordsworth's chief interest is in the human mind, the problems of knowledge and consciousness, and the relations between character and conduct, for that is what is meant by the fitting of the individual mind to the World and of the World to the Mind. And this deliberate statement is in entire keeping with his *Preface* to the *Lyrical Ballads* of 1800, in which he states his purpose as follows:

The principal object then which I proposed to myself in these Poems was to make the incidents of common life interesting by tracing in them, truly though not ostentatiously, the primary laws of our nature: chiefly as far as regards the manner in which we associate ideas in a state of excitement. . . . But speaking in less general language, it is to follow the fluxes and refluxes of the mind when agitated by the great and simple affections of our nature. This object I have endeavored in these short essays to attain by various means.

This is to say that Wordsworth is primarily a philosophical poet; and in his own mind this is what he consistently was. He looked upon all his poems collectively as forming one work, as he says in the *Preface* to *The Excursion* and in the *Preface* to the *Collected Poems* of 1815:

My guiding wish was, that the small pieces of which these volumes consist, thus discriminated, might be regarded under a two-fold view; as composing an entire work within themselves, and as adjuncts to the philosophical Poem, "The Recluse." This arrangement has long presented itself habitually to my mind.[1]

That he held the same opinions regarding his poetic method much later in life is seen from a letter written to Crabb Robinson, in 1835. A reviewer in the *Examiner* had stated that Wordsworth was superior in "dealing with nature" as opposed to his "treatment of human life." In reply the poet explicitly says:

In my treatment of the intellectual instincts, affections, and passions of mankind, I am nobly distinguished by having drawn out into notice the points in which they resemble each other, in preference to dwelling (as dramatic authors must do) upon those in which they differ. If my writings are to last, it will, I myself believe, be mainly owing to this characteristic. They will please for the single cause, "That we have all of us one human heart."[2]

That this was the opinion of Coleridge is shown in several passages which are classical; as, for example, the declaration that Wordsworth is capable of producing "the first genuinely philosophic poem,"[3] or the longer statement to the same effect in his letter to Wordsworth regarding *The Excursion:*

In the very pride of confident hope I looked forward to "The Recluse" as the *first* and *only* true philosophical poem in existence. Of course, I expected the colours, music, imaginative life, and passion of *poetry;* but the matter and arrangement of *philosophy.*"[4]

Thus we have an abundance of evidence that in intention the whole body of Wordsworth's poetry, the short poems as well as the long poems, are philosophic in content; and therefore their interest is in the problems of psychology and philosophy. This is to say that the problem of Nature is not approached directly as a distinct and separate question, but always in connection with the problem of the development of the mind. The question of Nature is always a part of the question of the development of the individual mind: and the varying attitudes of

[1] *Preface* to the *Poems of 1815.*
[2] *Letters of the Wordsworth Family,* III, 73-75.
[3] *Biographia Literaria,* Ch. XXII.
[4] *Letters of Samuel Taylor Coleridge,* II, 648, May 30, 1815.

the mind toward Nature, or the more general reactions towards Nature, as the mark of the mind's development. More explicitly, the poet deals with Nature in terms of his own peculiar theory of the development of the mind; that is, in terms of the three ages of man. It is absolutely essential to keep this in mind, and to realize that Wordsworth is dealing with the problem of mental development; for only then can we see that he describes his relationships to Nature at each period of life, and that what he holds true of one period he does not regard as true of the others. This is of particular importance in dealing with the attitude of his mind to Nature during youth. He gives a great deal of space to it, and makes some very striking statements regarding it; and as a result those who have read his statements without sufficient care, or, under the influence of some particular theory, have attributed to the poet final opinions regarding his attitude which he expressly assigns to his youth and which he clearly characterizes as *not* being those of his maturity.[5]

It must further be noted that Wordsworth does not use the term "nature" in a naïve way: but in a highly technical meaning, or series of meanings. He inherited the term from the eighteenth century; and not the term only but the controversy which had raged around it for a century and a half; and hence it was almost inevitable that he should make an important use of it in any discussion of man in his social, ethical, or religious associations, making his choice of the various meanings which best suited his purpose. For the meanings which were given to the term were many; but for our purposes we shall consider only two; which, while they are distinct, merge into each other and into other quite distinct uses.[6] There is the use which may be said to derive from Bacon and Hobbes, continued through Locke and the "sensational school"

---

[5] For example, Irving Babbitt, *Rousseau and Romanticism*, 1919, pp. 145, 171, 272 (a striking case of neglecting to note that the passage—*The Excursion*, I, 200-218—refers to youth), 303. This last case shows the failure of the author to note that the poet is dealing with the mind as a developing entity. The same oversight appears in Sir Walter Raleigh, *Wordsworth*, p. 127. It would be easy to extend this list indefinitely.

[6] On the term see Leslie Stephen, "Cowper and Rousseau," in *Hours in a Library*, Vol. II; P. M. Masson, *La formation religieuse de Rousseau*, 3 vols. 1916, especially I, 259-286, and II, 252-294, and C. B. Tinker, *Nature's Simple Plan*, 1922.

of philosophy, in which nature is held as the source of truth and reason. "Natural law" is a favorite phrase with those who view nature in this way; and reason and nature are one. The only validity which anything can claim is its "naturalness," and its naturalness is its reasonableness. In Bacon this takes the form of seeking to master nature by understanding her; in Hobbes, of the "natural" laws of society and the ordering of a commonwealth in the light of those immutable and eternal principles on which both natural and moral laws alike are based; in Locke, of endeavoring to arrive at the reality of "those parts of knowledge that men are most concerned to be clear in," and to investigate the nature and conditions of knowledge that conforms to external reality. This attitude to "nature" sternly subjects feeling and desire to fact, and not unnaturally is closely connected with the brutal and anti-Christian views of nature in the minds of Helvétius and d'Holbach, and with the endeavor towards practical betterment of the physical being of the masses, as is seen in the Utilitarians. All alike are either hostile or indifferent to art and poetry, the hostility of Malebranche in his long list of the errors into which Imagination has led mankind being re-echoed in Locke's disparagement of poets and poetry, and in Hume's charge that the poet's art is similar to those of priests and politicians.[7] Those who were not hostile held poetry and art in strict subordination to intellectual and moral interests; and all alike maintained the supremacy of reason, as distinguished from those blinder and more obscure forces of the world which they called "nature." On the whole, their "mechanical" view of life and the world did not cause them to take a melancholy view of life, rather it seemed to have given them, if not a "cheerful godliness," yet a cheerful, if grim, acceptance of things as they are, and a philosophically calm faith that man can know all that is really necessary to his essential well-being if he but governs his lives and desires by the rules of "right reason."[8]

[7] Malebranche, *Recherche de la vérité*, Livre Deuxième; Locke, *Thoughts Concerning Education*; Hume, *Concerning Human Understanding*, Sect. XII.
[8] For this attitude, see Locke's *Essay on the Human Understanding*; especially for a formal statement of this attitude, the *Epistle to the Reader*.

There is a second attitude to Nature which is almost the exact opposite of the one which we have been considering. In general it is the attitude which is associated with the phrase "the return to Nature," and most persistently with its chief apostle Rousseau. This attitude is marked by a few leading characteristics which we shall note briefly. The first is the meaning of "nature," and its allied phrases "natural," and "the state of Nature." With this school of thought Nature is opposed to man, in that it is always good, while man as he is in society is evil. Thus the "natural" is the good, and the "state of Nature" is the state of felicity, because man with his contaminating thoughts has not broken in upon the harmony of things as they are in their pristine, natural state. Thus the "state of nature" is identified with the supposed reality which "romantic" travellers had reported as actually existing among savages: hence the "noble savage" is held up for the admiration of sophisticated, civilized society. This is nothing other than Arcadia; and it is towards this ideal that the Rousseauist looks for the realization of his hopes. In literature this aspect of Nature-worship came into florescence in the "Rousseauists," Bernardin de Ste. Pierre in his *Etudes, Harmonies, Paul et Virginie;* and in Chateaubriand in his *Atala, René,* and *Génie du Christianisme.*

This Arcadia is not one founded on the reason or on fact; but one which was based solely on sentiment; and this is a second important characteristic—the glorification of the sentiments and the feelings at the expense of intellect. "Man is a child when he reasons," says the Savoyard vicar;[9] and even the subtle and complex Pascal expresses the inmost soul of this attitude when he tells us that our reason in its last essence is but our giving way to our sentiment. Thus the tables were turned on those who had exalted the intellect, and sentiment and emotion were identified with all that is highest and most desirable in the individual and society.

With this sentimentality there went an undoubted moral flaccidity and a lack of the sterner virtues. The Spartan morals of a Hobbes and a Locke have no counterpart in Rousseau; for in Rousseau, in his later developments at least, and

---

[9] J. J. Rousseau, *Émile, Profession de foi d'un Vicaire Savoyard.*

in even the *Savoyard Vicar,* it is hard to see what essential differentiation he makes between the Man and the God in nature. He rather identifies the two; and so removes all need or possibility of redemption or repentance, or of personal ethical problems. He is thus not only anti-Christian but in logical results anti-ethical as well.[10]

With these characteristics went another, which, while it is not confined to the Rousseauists, is yet a marked one: melancholy. This is so obvious that it may be only noted here; but we should remember that its development and aesthetic expansion is a most striking fact in the Rousseauistic tradition in Bernardin de Ste. Pierre and Chateaubriand. All alike strove to express the very ecstasy of Melancholy.[11]

In differentiating these two attitudes to nature we must not forget that they have much in common when they make application of ideas to particular things. Thus we must not be surprised that Rousseau claimed Locke as one of his teachers, for it is only one of the many signs of the interrelations of these two apparently utterly antagonistic theories. Nevertheless, while the theories have much in common, and while both are not always self-consistent, it remains true that they are clearly distinguishable in essential principles.

Now, to which one of these attitudes does Wordsworth adhere? In answering this question, we must bear in mind what has just been said of the lack of consistency in both theories concerning an extremely complicated problem; and so we shall be prepared to find extreme complexity in the poet. With this reservation, and having in mind his characteristic and mature attitude, we can unhesitatingly say that he adhered to the rationalistic, intellectual, and anti-sentimental party. We shall present the reasons for this opinion in the poet's own words and according to his own method. If this process is long and involved, it should be remembered that the poet is attempting no easy thing, but nothing less than the problem of the relations of the individual man to his whole world of experience and knowledge. For the problem is no other than the growth

---

[10] P. M. Masson, *La formation religieuse de J. J. Rousseau,* II (1916), 278-294.

[11] See G. Méra, *L'Esthétique de Chateaubriand,* Paris, 1913, 45 ff.

of the active mind in knowledge and its intricate relationships to the "external World," to which it is "fitted" by the inevitable processes of life which bring about not only growth and inner development but also a series of adjustments of the mind to the world of reality which is external to it, yet "wedded" to it by the strange processes of the "glorious universe." It is again the method of the three ages of Man.

In his description of the three periods of man's life Wordsworth habitually regards the first two as being most closely related to external nature and to each other, as has been noted in the previous chapter. They are both marked by a lack of self-consciousness and by absorption in sensation. They are differentiated, however, in that the child is wholly unconscious and passive, and of the child it is especially and characteristically true that

> The eye it cannot chuse but see,
> We cannot bid the ear be still;
> Our bodies feel, where'er we be,
> Against, or with our will.[12]

All unknown to the infant, the education of the senses proceeds, and through those "blind impulses of deeper birth" and those "dumb yearnings, hidden appetites" which are characteristic of childhood, and which "must have their food" the soul is impelled towards physical and mental connections with the world of sense and experience. But there is no conscious reaction to this world, and the soul is passive to life, so far as the active soul of man can be such.

As has already been stated, the first two books of *The Prelude* are a detailed account of Childhood; and anyone who would know the "visionary" quality which dwelt upon all those "hallowed and pure motions of the sense," must study these books in detail.

Youth is closely related to external nature, but in an entirely different way. At this period the soul becomes active in its relationships with the world of sense in a great variety of ways, some of which the poet describes in considerable detail. First, in the poet's own case, from the age of ten to the age of

---

[12] *Expostulation and Reply.*

twenty-three, he developed the capacity for describing and noting with accuracy "the infinite variety of natural appearances which had not been noticed by the poets of any age or country," so far as he was acquainted with them; and so he developed a power to see and to note. This power was developed especially toward the latter period of youth, when he was an undergraduate at St. John's College, Cambridge, as he makes clear to us in his account of the ivy-clad ash tree in the college garden:

> A single tree
> With sinuous trunk, boughs exquisitely wreathed,
> Grew there; an ash which Winter for himself
> Decked as in pride, and with outlandish grace:
> Up from the ground, and almost to the top,
> The trunk and every master branch were green
> With clustering ivy, and the lightsome twigs
> And outer spray profusely tipped with seeds
> That hung in yellow tassels, while the air
> Stirred them, not voiceless.[13]

He often observed objects such as this and learned to observe with accuracy. Like George Meredith, he was acquiring the "disciplined habit to see,"[14] a habit which he never lost in his later years, the habit of writing "with his eye on the object," and stating the simple truth; a habit which gives to all his poetry the characteristics noted by Coleridge in the early poem, *The Female Vagrant:* "the fine balance of truth in observing, with the imaginative faculty in modifying the objects observed."[15] With this power of observation went a love for observing places famous for their natural beauty and picturesqueness, and in response to this impulse he visited many places in the north of England, in Wales, and in France and Switzerland.[16]

This power of observation and this desire to see had one great defect in the period of youth: the poet's world was one in which all things were in disunity. He was under the domination of the senses, and of those less "pure" forms of mental activity which are related to the immediate sensations, and the

---

[13] *The Prelude,* VI, 76-85.
[14] In *A Faith on Trial.*
[15] *Biographia Literaria,* Ch. IV.
[16] *The Prelude,* VI, 190-726.

only unity of his world was that which is supplied by the "eye":

> the bodily eye
> Amid my strongest workings evermore
> Was searching out the lines of difference
> As they lie hid in all external forms,
> Near or remote, minute or vast; an eye
> Which, from a tree, a stone, a withered leaf,
> To the broad ocean and the azure heavens
> Spangled with kindred multitudes of stars,
> Could find no surface where its powers might sleep;
> Which spake perpetual logic to my soul,
> And by an unrelenting agency
> Did bind my feelings even as in a chain.[17]

But this disconnection in his world was not accepted as a matter of course, for the poet felt the need of unity. This unity he found in one department of his knowledge—in geometry, for he tells us that here he first found relief for a mind "beset with images," that is, with particular experiences. It was his first insight into the ordered world of intelligence and imagination:

> Mighty is the charm
> Of those abstractions to a mind beset
> With images, and haunted by herself,
> And specially delightful unto me
> Was that clear synthesis built up aloft
> So gracefully; even then when it appeared
> Not more than a mere plaything, or a toy
> To sense embodied: not the thing it is
> In verity, an independent world,
> Created out of pure intelligence.[18]

This was the first means of producing unity in his disrupted world; but another more important one existed in the very constitution of his youthful mind. He tells us that when he attained maturity he discovered that he had "two natures," which he had learned "to keep in wholesome separation," the one that feels and the other that observes.[19] This important fact he did not know in youth; and he mingled objective and

---

[17] *The Prelude*, III. 155-166.
[18] *Op. cit.*, VI, 158-167.
[19] *Op. cit.*, XIV, 344-347.

subjective, transferring his own feelings to the objects of nature and making his feelings a part of them.

> To every natural form, rock, fruit, or flower,
> Even the loose stones that cover the highway,
> I gave a moral life: I saw them feel,
> Or linked them to some feeling: the great mass
> Lay bedded in a quickening soul, and all
> That I beheld respired with inward meaning.
> Add that whate'er of Terror or of Love
> Or Beauty, Nature's daily face put on
> From transitory passion, unto this
> I was as sensitive as waters are
> To the sky's influence in a kindred mood
> Of passion; was obedient as a lute
> That waits upon the touches of the wind.
> Unknown, unthought of, yet I was most rich—
> I had a world about me—'twas my own;
> I made it, for it only lived to me,
> And to the God who sees into the heart.[20]

It was his own world, for he had made it; and he himself was in all he saw. It was a deeply-seated habit; and from this habit "nothing was safe":

> the elder tree that grew
> Beside the well-known charnel-house had then
> A dismal look; the yew-tree had its ghost,
> That took his station there for ornament:
> The dignities of plain occurrence then
> Were tasteless, and truth's golden mean, a point
> Where no sufficient pleasure could be found.
> Then if a widow, staggering with the blow
> Of her distress, was known to have turned her steps
> To the cold grave in which her husband slept,
> One night, or haply more than one, through pain
> Or half-insensate impotence of mind,
> The fact was caught at greedily, and there
> She must be visitant the whole year through,
> Wetting the turf with never-ending tears.[21]

These "cravings" led him to compare the fox-glove, dismantled of all its flowers but one, to some vagrant mother; and to imagine the glistening rock to be the shield suspended over the tomb of some ancient knight, or the entrance to some

---

[20] *The Prelude*, III. 127-143.
[21] *Op. cit.*, VIII. 377-391.

magic cave, built by the fairies of the rock, and to fancy that the woodman, dying of disease, was suffering from the pangs of disappointed love, while the smoke from the charcoal pile was feigned to be the image of his ghost or spirit about to take its flight.[22]

This was "the wilfulness of fancy and conceit," which "beautified Nature and her objects" by "fictions,"[23] very frequently of a melancholy nature. As he says, "understanding sleeps in order that the fancy may dream";[24] for this was the period of youth, and the understanding and the imagination "slept," waking but fitfully from time to time:

> Imagination slept,
> And yet not utterly.[25]

Thus the mind in its activity of youth asserts its independence and active power, rising superior to mere sense-impressions, even though the world which it creates is not a true one. For Fancy deals only with the superficialities of things and with mere "extrinsic" passion and feelings. But, none the less, amid this world, which is not based on truth but on fancy, he was

> mounting now
> To such community with highest truth[26]

by the natural means afforded to youth, that is, by analogies; and through these he is on the way to Truth by the shortest route allowed to youth. He was mounting; but he had not attained in the season of youth. Reason and imagination slept as yet; but their slumbers became less deep; and their awakening became more frequent as he approached his wonderful twenty-third year. He was becoming human-hearted, his reason was developing, life was schooling him by sending him to France,[27] by detaining him in London,[28] until the time came for Reason and Imagination to exert their full directive power. His world

---

[22] *The Prelude*, VIII. 392-458.
[23] *Op. cit.*, VIII, 370-375.
[24] *Letter* to "Mathetes."
[25] *The Prelude*, III, 257-258.
[26] *Op. cit.*, III, 122-123.
[27] *Op. cit.*, VI. IX, X, XI.
[28] *Op. cit.*, VII.

9

was his own, but not one which conformed to objective reality;
yet it stood as proof of his own self-activity and superiority to
Nature. But the time was soon to arrive when his world becomes the real world of all of us, being founded on simple
Truth, when Nature, Reason, and Imagination are one. Then
his world was harmonized and unified: then and not till then
could he "see into the life of things."[29]

The transition in the life of man from youth to maturity is
signalized in the sub-title of the eighth book of *The Prelude:*
"Love of Nature leading to Love of Man"; and the processes
by which this is accomplished are detailed in this and the succeeding books of this poem. In childhood, nature was "secondary" to his "own pursuits and animal activities, and all
their trivial pleasures." Then, with youth, Nature became
prized "for her own sake" and became his joy, to the ex-
clusion of man, "until two-and-twenty summers had been
told," "his hour being not yet come."[30] At the end of the
book he tells Coleridge that he has brought the story of his life
down to the beginning of Maturity, and that he will narrate
the consummation of maturity in the books that are to follow.[31] This promise he proceeds to keep; and in the twelfth
book he expounds at some length the peculiarities of the third
age, as contrasted with those of youth. Youth is marked by
great activity:

> enough that my delights
> (Such as they were) were sought insatiably.
> Vivid the transport, vivid though not profound;
> I roamed from hill to hill, from rock to rock,
> Still craving combinations of new forms,
> New pleasures, wider empire for the sight,
> Proud of her own endowments, and rejoiced
> To lay the inner faculties asleep.[32]

Youth was the time,

> When the bodily eye, in every stage of life
> The most despotic of the senses, gained
> Such strength in *me* as often held my mind
> In absolute dominion.[33]

---

[29] *Tintern Abbey*, 50.
[30] *The Prelude*, VIII, 340-356. "His," of course, refers to "man."
[31] Lines 676-686.
[32] *The Prelude*, XII, 140-147.
[33] *Op. cit.*, XII, 128-131.

But this thraldom was to be changed. By those abstruse operations of life, Liberty and Power were achieved by the mind through the means employed by Nature, to cause the senses each to counteract the other and themselves. Nature no longer was the prime mover of the soul. Imagination and Intellect became the guiding forces, and he now stood in nature's presence, contemplating her, and knowing himself distinct from her and•above her, a sensitive being, a creative soul.[34] Now it was that Nature, which had been destined to remain so long foremost in his affections,—that is, up to his twenty-third year,—fell back into the second place, pleased to become a handmaid to a nobler than herself:[35] that is, to Imagination,

> which in truth,
> Is but another name for absolute power
> And clearest insight, amplitude of mind,
> And Reason in her most exalted mood.[36]

To this conclusion he came at maturity, by "the progressive powers" of life, through which the mind is fitted to the World.

It follows logically from this that Wordsworth should hold the opinion that the love of Nature is an intermediate step, and a necessary one, if the individual is to attain the "purer mind" of maturity. Thus in maturity the emotions are intellectualized and rationalized. It follows that in Wordsworth there is not that dwelling upon the sentiments and emotions, such as we find in Rousseau; nor that worship of "The Lady Sorrow,"[37] such as we find in Bernardin de Ste. Pierre and Chateaubriand, with their exaltation of melancholy into a chief source of poetry— "the delectable melancholy of the memorials of infancy." Nor is there in Wordsworth any of that distrust of intellect which we find in the Rousseauists. The passages which have been so interpreted clearly show that he has in mind false knowledge, or reasonings which are based on unreal knowledge, as can be seen in his criticism of the "false secondary power by which we multiply distinctions";[38] for the poet explains that

---

[34] *The Prelude*, XII. 205-207.

[35] *Op. cit.*, XIV, 256-260.

[36] *Op. cit.*, XIV, 189-192.

[37] *Op. cit.*, VI, 555. Wordsworth expressly assigns his devotion to melancholy to the period of his youth.

[38] *Op. cit.*, II, 215-219.

such false knowledge breaks up the unity of reality, and establishes "puny boundaries" and multiplies "distinctions," not in accordance with observed realities, but out of unreal knowledge which in no way corresponds to external truth.   Such a procedure comes from deficiency of reason or imagination, which is "duped by shows, enslaved by words, corrupted by mistaken delicacy and false refinement," "not having even attended with care to the reports of the senses, and therefore deficient grossly in the rudiments of its own power," and so takes its departure from the side of "Truth, its original parent."[39]   To truth, which gave him a universe of knowledge based on higher activities than those of sense, he had been brought, and his was the universe of mind, including the activities of sense, but transcending and regulating them.   This higher universe is apprehended by the reason and by the imagination; and it sees the "active principle" which at once makes up the unity of the universe and assures to the mind that sees it, unity with itself, the freedom of the universe,

> Perfect contentment, Unity entire.[40]

Unlike the Rousseauist, Wordsworth views this universe not as Utopia, not as Arcadia, where we can hide from the crude facts of life.   We live here, in this world,

> Not in Utopia,—subterranean fields,—
> Or some secreted island, Heaven knows where!
> But in the very world, which is the world
> Of all of us,—the place where, in the end,
> We find our happiness, or not at all![41]

This he learned early, and all his development was away from fanciful Utopias, and to the end he

> sought
> For present good in life's familiar face,
> And built thereon [his] hopes of good to come.[42]

This is re-enforced in his prose statement: "Our eyes have

---

[39] *Letter* to "Mathetes."
[40] *The Excursion*, IX, 1-26 ; *The Recluse*, 142-151.
[41] *The Prelude*, XI, 140-144.
[42] *Op. cit.*, XIII, 61-63.

not been fixed upon virtue which lies apart from human nature, or transcends it.   In fact there is no such virtue."[43]

And herein is another way in which he differentiates himself from the Rousseauists and identifies himself with the line of Bacon and Locke, namely his love of man and humankind. To him man is not alien: on the contrary, his whole development from childhood to maturity is towards man:

> Thus from a very early age, O Friend!
> My thoughts by slow gradations had been drawn
> To human-kind, and to the good and ill
> Of human life.[44]

This statement is substantiated by his declaration that man was his last and ultimate discovery; when his hour was at length come,[45] man was elevated to the central place:

> In the midst stood Man,
> Outwardly, inwardly contemplated,
> As, of all visible natures, crown, though born
> Of dust, and kindred to the worm; a Being,
> Both in perception and discernment, first
> In every capability of rapture,
> Through the divine effect of power and love;
> As, more than anything we know, instinct
> With godhead, and, by reason and by will,
> Acknowledging dependency sublime.[46]

This is confirmed by the account of his attaining to his final outlook on life, when he

> found
> Once more in Man an object of delight,
> Of pure imagination and of love.[47]

This is the same attitude as in the *Elegiac Stanzas on Peele Castle;* in which he declares his attitude of maturity, as contrasted with that of youth.   In his youth he would have had his ideal in Elysium:

---

[43] *Letter* to "Mathetes."
[44] *The Prelude*, VIII, 676-679.
[45] *Op. cit.*, VIII, 356.
[46] *Op. cit.*, VIII, 485-494.
[47] *Op. cit.*, XIII, 48-50.

Ah! THEN, if mine had been the painter's hand,
    To express what then I saw; and add the gleam,
The light that never was, on sea or land,
    The consecration, and the Poet's dream;[48]

I would have planted thee, thou hoary Pile,
    Amid a world how different from this!
Beside a sea that could not cease to smile;
    On tranquil land, beneath a sky of bliss.

        .   .   .   .   .

A Picture had it been of lasting ease,
    Elysian quiet, without toil or strife;
No motion but the moving tide, a breeze,
    Or merely silent Nature's breathing life.

Such, in the fond illusion[49] of my heart,
    Such picture would I at that time have made;
And seen the soul of truth in every part,
    A steadfast peace that might not be betrayed.

But it would have been a false picture, the poet says; for in this world Elysiums and Arcadias do not exist. This is the wisdom of maturity. And so he continues:

So once it would have been—'tis so no more;
    I have submitted to a new control:
A power is gone, which nothing can restore;
    A deep distress hath humanized my soul.

        .   .   .   .   .

Farewell, farewell the heart that lives alone,
    Housed in a dream, at distance from the Kind!
Such happiness, wherever it is known,
    Is to be pitied; for 'tis surely blind.

The date of this poem is 1805, and the attitude is the same as in the *Lines Composed a Few Miles above Tintern Abbey,* 1798, and as in the *Ode. Intimations of Immortality,* composed

[48] In spite of the fact that this stanza is frequently quoted as an expression of Wordsworth's final attitude, it is not. He attempted to make it clear by a new reading in 1820:
        "and add a gleam,
    Of lustre, known to neither sea or land,
    But borrowed from the Youthful Poet's dream."
But the old reading was known and admired by friends; and in reply to protests it was restored in 1827, with the slight change, "the gleam, The lustre."
From the context, even as the lines now stand, the idea of lack of truth in his youthful interpretation of life is clear. The reading of 1820 is a complete commentary on them. It should be noted that this reading is cast in terms of the "three ages"—*youthful.*
[49] "delusion," 1807.

1802-1806. All alike identify complete attainment and unity, with complete identification of the individual with his kind: "the still, sad music of humanity"[50] is the ultimate human note; and the "eye that hath kept watch o'er man's mortality"[51] catches the gleam of ultimate human truth. This he did not forget in his theories concerning his art; for in the *Advertisement* to the *Lyrical Ballads* in 1798, he threw over all aesthetic theories and based the merits of his poetry on the sole merit of a "natural delineation of *human* passions, *human* characters, and *human* incidents," a position which he never abandoned, but held tenaciously in all the succeeding prefaces.

It follows as a matter of course that the "noble savage" of the Rousseau tradition never appears in Wordsworth. Man, as he is, not "ideal" man, is his theme. This is constantly implied; and it is rather fully developed in the third book of *The Excursion*. The Solitary hoped that he might find in the savage the type of perfect man which he had failed to find both in the European in Europe and the European in America:

> So, westward, tow'rd the unviolated woods
> I bent my way; and roaming far and wide,
> Failed not to greet the merry Mockingbird;
> And, while the melancholy Muccawiss
> (The sportive bird's companion in the grove)
> Repeated o'er and o'er his plaintive cry,
> I sympathised at leisure with the sound;
> But that pure archetype of human greatness,
> I found him not. There, in his stead, appeared
> A creature, squalid, vengeful, and impure;
> Remorseless, and submissive to no law
> But superstitious fear, and abject sloth.[52]

This is certainly no Arcadian picture of the Rousseauistic savage, but a picture of the real savage as he existed in the books of travel which Wordsworth had read, such as Hearne's *Journey to the Northern Ocean*,[53] which gives no flattering picture of the savage; Shelvocke's *Voyage;* Carver's *Travels;* Bryan Edwards' *History of the West Indies,* with its account

---

[50] *Lines Composed a few Miles above Tintern Abbey.*
[51] *Ode. Intimations of Immortality,* 201-202.
[52] *The Excursion,* III, 944-955.
[53] Hearne does give us an account of Matonabbee, who "had benevolence and universal humanity to all the human race"; but avowedly as an exception.

of *obi* magic; Bartram's *Travels;* and other books which in no way idealized the Indian, but made him a creature of quite another sort than the "savages" of Bernardin de Ste. Pierre and Chateaubriand.[54]

Again, Wordsworth differs from the Rousseauists in that he does not exalt melancholy. This is so palpably clear that not much need be said about it. As we have already noted in this chapter, melancholy is an attribute of youth, according to Wordsworth, and passes away with the other weaknesses of youth on the arrival of maturity. Wordsworth's guiding star is Hope, and Aspiration. This he discovered early, first by dim glimpses,[55] and later by clear demonstration; as in *The Excursion,* whose whole burden is "the sanity of Hope."[56]

Thus the function of Nature is to furnish us with the materials of a true knowledge, and the education of man is to adjust his relations to her so that she becomes the helper, and not the usurper, of a power and place which she should not possess. But she is the necessary aid to the attainment of Imagination and right reason; and the function of Imagination and right reason, when they are attained, is to view her in due proportion to the whole of life and knowledge. The nature of reason and imagination, those regulating principles of the mind, and their relations to fancy, we shall consider in the next two chapters.

---

[54] See Lane Cooper, "A Glance at Wordsworth's Reading," in *Modern Language Notes,* XXII, 83-88; 110-117. Reprinted in *Methods and Aims in the Study of Literature,* 1915. pp. 96-132, with many alterations.

[55] As in *The Prelude,* VI, 592-608.

[56] *The Excursion,* IV-V, especially.

CHAPTER VIII

THE ACTIVE PRINCIPLE: DERIVATION OF THE IMAGINATION

> To every Form of being is assigned, . . .
> An *active* Principle.
>> William Wordsworth, *The Excursion*, IX, 1814.

> TASTE . . . is a metaphor taken from a *passive* sense of the human body, and transferred to things which are in their essence *not* passive,—to intellectual *acts* and *operations*. . . . The word Taste has been stretched to the sense which it bears in modern Europe,—inducing that inversion in the order of things whereby a passive faculty is made paramount among the faculties conversant with the fine arts.
>> William Wordsworth, *Essay, Supplementary to the Preface*, 1815.

In our exposition of Wordsworth's account of the formation of the mind and its connection with the principles of Locke, Berkeley, Hume, and Hartley, we have said but little of the activity of the mind in this process; that is, of the self-activity which assures the mind of its own integrity and unity in all its changes and mutations. We have deferred speaking of this, not because we regard this aspect of the problem as unimportant, but because we regard it as so important that it deserves separate treatment.

It has been a popular notion that Wordsworth was a complacent person, passive, non-resistant, acquiescent; a mild youth who quite naturally developed into a conservative office-holder and admirer of quiet, picturesque, natural scenes, and who rather accidentally and quite inexplicably wrote a goodly number of poems, by virtue of the good fortune that attends some of the children of this earth. How grotesquely false this is can easily be shown. He himself tells us that as a child he was of anything but a tractable disposition. In his *Autobiographical Memoranda,* he says:

An intimate friend of hers [his mother's], Miss Hamilton by name, who was used to visiting her at Cockermouth, told me that she once said to her, that the only one of her five children about whose future life she was anxious, was William; and he, she said, would be remarkable either for good or evil. The cause of this was that I was of a stiff, moody, and violent temper; so much so that I remember going once into the attic of my grandfather's house at Penrith, upon some indignity having been put upon me, with an intention of destroying myself with one of the foils which I knew was kept there. I took the foil in hand, but my heart failed. Upon another occasion, while I was at my grandfather's house at Penrith, along with my eldest brother Richard, we were whipping tops together in the large drawing-room, on which the carpet was only laid down upon particular occasions. The walls were hung round with family pictures, and I said to my brother, "Dare you strike your whip through that old lady's petticoat?" He replied, "No, I won't." "Then," said I, "here goes"; and I struck my lash through her hooped petticoat, for which, no doubt, though I have forgotten it, I was properly punished. But possibly, from some want of judgment in punishments inflicted, I have become perverse and obstinate in defying chastisement, and rather proud of it than otherwise.[1]

In *The Recluse* he likewise records his obstinacy and activity:

> While yet an innocent little one, with a heart
> That doubtless wanted not its tender moods,
> I breathed (for this I better recollect)
> Among wild appetites and blind desires,
> Motions of savage instinct my delight
> And exaltation. Nothing at that time
> So welcome, no temptation half so dear
> As that which urged me to a daring feat,
> Deep pools, tall trees, black chasms, and dizzy crags,
> And tottering towers: I loved to stand and read
> Their looks forbidding, read and disobey,
> Sometimes in act and evermore in thought.[2]

These characteristics survived childhood, and remained with him throughout life; and impulse and independence in thinking and acting were always justified in his theories and were his rule in practice. He was irregular in school and college, he refused to settle down to any regular calling after graduating, sailing off to France more to satisfy the desire "for to admire

---

[1] Christopher Wordsworth, *Memoirs of William Wordsworth*, I, 9.
[2] *The Recluse*, 704-714.

and for to see" than to fulfill any calculated plan. In France he underwent heart-shaking experiences, but they did not wean him from his rule of life by impulse. He joined himself to the revolutionaries in France, and when he returned to London it was not to adopt any profession, but to consort with agitators and revolutionists whose aim was to overthrow the existing government and all governments. This is scarcely the career of a quiet contemplator of life; and, while Wordsworth changed his opinions, and characterized many of his youthful acts and opinions as "juvenile errors,"[3] he never repudiated impulse as a habit of life. Rather, this quality of mind is exalted as the normal in his theory of the mind's development, not so much by exalting the importance of emotion and passion, as by noting the activity of the mind in those processes by which its very being is maintained as an integral whole. The independence of the mind is marked not merely by emotion, but also by the primary forms of sensation and intellection as well.

This activity of the mind is insisted upon by the English philosophers, whom we have shown to be related to Wordsworth, and whom he no doubt follows in this regard. Locke rejects the notion of innate ideas, arguing that such ideas are mere myths which cannot make good their claim to be truths by any appeal to the intellectual faculties of the individual. Knowledge, he insists, if it is to be real knowledge, must be won in only one way—by the active employment of our faculties in "the consideration of things, themselves." *"Men must think and know for themselves"* is the heading of the section in his *Essay on the Human Understanding*[4] from which this phrase is quoted; and in this section he says:

Not that I want a due respect to other men's opinions; but after all, the greatest reverence is due to truth; and I hope it will not be thought arrogance to say that perhaps we should make greater progress in the discovery of rational and contemplative knowledge, if we caught it in the fountain, in the consideration of things themselves, and make use rather of our own thoughts than other men's to find it; for I think we may as rationally hope to see with other men's eyes, as to know by other men's understandings. So much as

---

[3] *The Prelude*, XI, 54.
[4] Book I, Ch. IV, Sect. 23.

we ourselves consider and comprehend of truth and reason, so much we possess of real and true knowledge. The floating of other men's opinions in our brains, makes us not one jot the more knowing, though they happen to be true. What in them was science, is in us but opiniatrety; whilst we give up our assent only to reverenced names, and do not, as they did, employ our own reason to understand those truths which gave them reputation. . . . In the sciences everyone has so much as he really knows and comprehends. What he believes only, and takes upon trust, are but shreds, which, however well in the whole piece, make no considerable addition to his stock who gathers them. Such borrowed wealth, like fairy money, though it were gold in the hand from which he received it, will be but leaves and dust when it comes to us.

In like manner, Hartley insists upon the principle that all real knowledge is the product of the activity of the mind in accordance with the principle of association; for the mind has the power to create ideas and judgments by its own inherent power. This he held as true, even though he was a necessitarian, for his necessitarianism was never of the sort which prevented him from giving the highest place to sympathy, theopathy, and the moral sense.[5]

No one has interpreted Hartley more truly and clearly regarding his opinions of the activity of the mind in all the processes in the attainment of knowledge than Coleridge in his *Dejection: An Ode*. Addressing his friend, he says:

> O Wordsworth; we receive but what we give,
> And in *our* life alone doth Nature live!
> Ours is her wedding-garment, ours her shroud!
> And would we aught behold, of higher worth,
> Than that inanimate cold world, *allow'd*
> To the poor loveless, ever-anxious crowd,
> Ah! from the soul itself must issue forth,
> A light, a glory, a fair luminous cloud
> Enveloping the earth—
> And from the soul itself must there be sent
> A sweet and potent voice, of its own birth,
> Of all sweet sounds the life and element.[6]

Wordsworth seizes upon this activity of the mind, which resolves all things to itself, as we have already seen in our chapter on his conception of the relations between nature and the

[5] See Chapter VI.
[6] *Dejection: An Ode* (1802), lines 47-58. I quote from the earliest MS text.

mind of man. Mind is the ultimate and primary fact of the world, and determines man's relations to the rest of the sum of things, in Wordsworth's view; and the particular aspect of mind to which he devotes special attention is its activity, accepting all the notions of Locke and the associationists concerning this aspect of the mind and carrying his analysis deeper and his deductions farther than they dreamed of doing.

In the first place, Wordsworth conceives, not only an active mind, but an active universe. The Wanderer, in *The Excursion,* lays down an important principle, which is also a fundamental one in Berkeley; namely, that there is in the universe "an *active* principle":

> To every Form of being is assigned . . .
> An *active* Principle:—howe'er removed
> From sense and observation, it subsists
> In all things, in all natures; in the stars
> Of azure heaven, the unenduring clouds,
> In flower and tree, in every pebbly stone
> That paves the brooks, the stationary rocks,
> The moving waters, and the invisible air.[7]

This activity is not found in the external world only. It is also a characteristic of the mind:

> What'er exists hath properties that spread
> Beyond itself, communicating good,
> A simple blessing, or with evil mixed;
> Spirit that knows no insulated spot,
> No chasm, no solitude; from link to link
> It circulates, the Soul of all the worlds.
> That is the freedom of the Universe;
> Unfolded still the more, more visible,
> The more we know; and yet is reverenced least,
> And least respected in the human Mind,
> Its most apparent home.[8]

He then proceeds in this passage to illustrate the necessity of activity to the mind, if true life is to be realized:

> The food of hope
> Is meditated action; robbed of this
> Her sole support, she languishes and dies.
> We perish also; for we live by hope

---

[7] *The Excursion,* IX, 1-9.
[8] *Op. cit.,* IX, 10-20.

> And by desire; we see by the glad light
> And breathe the sweet air of futurity;
> And so we live, or else we have no life.[9]

The importance which he attached to the relationships between the active mind and the active universe is shown by the fact that he proclaims them as the main theme of his poetry, in an important statement of his programme as an artist:

> How exquisitely the individual Mind
> (And the progressive powers perhaps no less
> Of the whole species) to the external World
> Is fitted:—and how exquisitely, too—
> Theme this but little heard of among men—
> The external World is fitted to the Mind;
> And the creation (by no lower name
> Can it be called) which they with blended might
> Accomplish:—this is our high argument.[10]

A second characteristic of consciousness which is stressed by Wordsworth is its essential unity. He accepts fully the associationistic method of explaining the growth of the mind as the transmutation of sensations into higher knowledge and the sublimation of emotion from its lower forms into the purer forms of mentality. While he adopts this associationism as his own, he lays stress on unity of consciousness as a fact of transcending importance, and proclaims that the result of all the processes of life which blend all the disparate experiences into the thing which we call experience is a real unity:

> Dust as we are, the immortal spirit grows
> Like harmony in music; there is a dark
> Inscrutable workmanship that reconciles
> Discordant elements, makes them cling together
> In one society. How strange that all
> The terrors, pains, and early miseries,
> Regrets, vexations, lassitudes interfused
> Within my mind, should e'er have borne a part,
> And that a needful part, in making up
> The calm existence that is mine when I
> Am worthy of myself! Praise to the end!
> Thanks to the means which Nature deigned to employ;
> Whether her fearless visitings, or those

[9] *The Excursion.* IX. 20-26.
[10] *The Recluse,* 1816-1824. First published in the *Preface* of *The Excursion,* 1814.

> That came with soft alarm, like hurtless light
> Opening the peaceful clouds; or she may use
> Severer interventions, ministry
> More palpable, as best might suit her aim.[11]

However, with Wordsworth this Unity is not a simple one, but is cut across by another and almost contradictory consciousness. For with him consciousness is not merely a realization of what we are, but also a realization of what we have been, both consciousnesses being held together by the unity of our whole present mature consciousness. This thought he expresses in more than one place, and it is in intimate association with his whole idea of mental unity:

> One is there, though the wisest and the best
> Of all mankind, who covets not at times
> Union that cannot be;—who would not give,
> If so he might, to duty and to truth
> The eagerness of infantine desire?
> A tranquillising spirit presses now
> On my corporeal frame, so wide appears
> The vacancy between me and those days
> Which yet have such self-presence in my mind,
> That, musing on them, often do I seem
> Two consciousnesses, conscious of myself
> And of some other Being.[12]

This multiple consciousness is bound up with another fundamental fact in the history of consciousness, namely, the fact that the mind develops in each individual. We have already noted that the three ages of man is in the associationistic philosophers, and even in Locke and Berkeley; it takes on a particular form in Hartley and Darwin; that is, with them the analysis of mind into (1) simple sensations, (2) ideas of sensation, and (3) ideas of reflection, is not merely a description of the facts of mature consciousness, but is an indication of growth and development. This is clearly seen in Hartley's insistence on the idea that the mind has its first individual life in its earliest sensations, and draws upon them and rests upon these lower forms of mentality even in its highest and purest development:

[11] *The Prelude*, I, 340-356.
[12] *Op. cit.*, II, 22-33. Compare *The Prelude*, III, 121-126; *Memorials of a Tour on the Continent, 1820*. No. XXXIV, 9-14. All such passages refer to his present consciousness and earlier ones. They are not mystical.

In adults, the pleasures of mere colours are very languid in comparison with their present aggregates of pleasure, formed by association. And thus the eye approaches more and more, as we advance in spirituality and perfection, to an inlet for mental pleasure, and an organ suited to the exigencies of a being, whose happiness consists in the improvement of his understanding and affections. However, the original pleasures of mere colours remain, in a small degree, to the last, and those transferred upon them by association with other pleasures (for the influence is in these things reciprocal, without limits) in a considerable one. So that our intellectual pleasures are not only at first generated, but afterwards supported and recruited, in part from the pleasures affecting the eye; which holds particularly in respect of the pleasures afforded by the beauties of nature, and by the imitations of them, which the arts of poetry and painting furnish us with.[13]

So clear is the process of mental growth to Hartley, that he asserts the possibility of using it as a powerful instrument for the betterment of the individual and the race:

It is of the utmost consequence to morality and religion, that the affections and passions should be analysed into their simple compounding parts, by reversing the steps of the associations which concur to form them. For thus we may learn how to cherish and improve good ones, check and root out such as are mischievous and immoral, and how to suit our manner of life, in some tolerable measure, to our intellectual and religious wants. And as this holds, in respect to persons of all ages, so it is particularly true, and worthy of consideration, in respect to children and youth. The world is, indeed, sufficiently stocked with general precepts for this purpose, grounded on experience; and whosoever will follow these faithfully, may expect good general success. However, the doctrine of association, when traced up to the first rudiments of understanding and affection, unfolds such a scene as cannot fail both to instruct and alarm all such as have any degree of interested concern for themselves, or of a benevolent one for others. It ought to be added here, that the doctrine of association explains also the rise and progress of those voluntary and semivoluntary powers which we exert over our ideas, affections, and bodily motions, and by doing this, teaches us how to regulate and improve these powers. . . . We must therefore estimate all our pleasures equally, by their magnitude, permanency, and tendency to procure others; and our pains in like manner.[14]

It should be noted, by the way, that this statement of Hartley on education is far removed from that of Rousseau, who

---

[13] *Observations on Man*, I, 208. (Proposition LX).

[14] *Op. cit.*, I, 80-84 (Proposition XIV). Hartley's specific mention of "children" and "youth" is to be noted.

regarded education as merely negative. That Wordsworth accepted the positive notion of education is shown very clearly from his tributes to his teachers,[15] and his acknowledgments to poets,[16] books,[17] and science,[18] and, most clearly of all, by his passionate advocacy of popular education and eager looking forward to a time when England would admit

> An obligation, on her part, to *teach*
> Them who are born to serve her and obey.[19]

Wordsworth also fully agreed with Hartley in his belief that this fluidity of the living mind is an all-important instrument for possible good. This is abundantly shown by his use of the principle in his poetry. He makes use of this principle to show how health of mind may be assured in childhood, youth, and maturity, as in *The Prelude*. He shows how minds that have been developed in wrong directions, or not developed at all, may be corrected and restored by being given the necessary aid to enable them to assume their healthy, normal activity, as in *Peter Bell* and some of the stories in *The Excursion*. These stories illustrate Wordsworth's belief that, where the mind retains sufficient activity, it may be cured of its lassitude by being given the power to assert its natural position as "lord and master," and so become assured of unity and harmony in itself.

But how can this aid be given and this activity and power be exerted? To answer this, we may begin by summarizing: Wordsworth holds that the Mind is characterized, (1) by activity; (2) by unity; (3) by development. In the previous chapter we have noted that emotion is regarded as "factitious," or derived and "extrinsic." In this last-named aspect of the mind—that is, emotion as "extrinsic"—lies a large part of Wordsworth's doctrine both of consciousness and of art, and the key to his theory of the derivation of the imagination.

---

[15] *Matthew, Two April Mornings, The Fountain.*
[16] *The Prelude*, III.
[17] *Op. cit.*, V.
[18] *Op. cit.*, VI, 115-167.
[19] *The Excursion*, IX, 297-298. The whole passage, lines 293-475, is a notable passage on education as the mainstay of the nation. It is best known, perhaps, because it is the object of Matthew Arnold's uncomplimentary remarks in his essay on Wordsworth, in *Selections from Wordsworth*, Golden Treasury Series, 1879.

The association theory of mind regards emotion as derived, or "extrinsic." Hartley, as we have seen in the previous chapter, holds this view regarding the "passions" or "affections" as nothing more than "aggregates of simple ideas united by association," and "aggregates of the ideas, or traces of the sensible pleasures and pains, which ideas make up by their numbers, and mutual influence upon one another."[20] In similar manner, Alison derives the aesthetic emotions of beauty and sublimity from association of ideas, especially by "the relation of resemblance." He illustrates this by several examples: Spring, by suggesting "analogies with the life of man," brings before us "those images of hope or fear," which, "according to our peculiar situations," have the dominion of our hearts; autumn impresses the mind "with a sentiment of melancholy," and leads on "to the solemn imagination of that inevitable fate which is to bring on alike the decay of life, of empire, and of nature itself"; and so on. On the simple emotions of fear, cheerfulness, elevation, etc., the emotions of beauty and sublimity are based, there being no case where emotions of taste are felt, "without the production of some such simple emotion." The emotions of taste based on the simple emotions, which are themselves derived from ideas are "ideas of emotion."[21]

Wordsworth closely resembles both of these associationists, with the important difference that he places very much greater importance on the activity of the mind in the process of growth. The mind has a marvelous absorbing power and very early transforms the "extrinsic" emotion which is given it by the "analogies" and "relations of resemblance" described by Alison, into "intrinsic" emotions, and unifies it with the whole of the mind. This is the problem which he sets himself in *The Prelude,* especially in the first two books, in which the early experiences of the child are shown as being transmuted into the purer forms of the understanding and becoming an integral part of the unified consciousness. This is clearly enunciated in a passage in the first book of *The Prelude,* already quoted in

[20] *Observations on Man,* I, 368.
[21] *Essays on Taste,* Essay I, Ch. I.

Chapter VI,[22] in which he states the associationistic principle of the change of "collateral," or "extrinsic" emotion into "intrinsic"; the passing of sensations into the "purer" forms of mind; and the constant interplay of past sensations, "representative of things forgotten," and transformed into ideas, with recent sensations which are too fresh to be so transmuted.

How can we see the working of this power of the mind? Wordsworth's answer is simple. He holds that mind develops, and by reminiscence and introspection he observes that emotion is the mark of the mind's activity. Hence those moments of emotional stress, in which hope, fear, disappointment, terror,[23] and similar emotions, are the points in our development which denote the highest self-activity of the mind, and therefore the highest self-development. This theory he designates as "spots of time," and "ties that bind," and calls them the revealers of the "hiding places of man's power." These are "unremembered," but "rememberable," sensations and feelings, which "sleep until maturer seasons" awake them to coalesce in forming the integrity and unity of the mind, thus indicating its development:

> There are in our existence spots of time,
> That with distinct pre-eminence maintain
> A renovating virtue, whence, depressed
> By false opinion and contentious thought,
> On aught of heavier or more deadly weight
> In trivial occupations, and the round
> Of ordinary intercourse, our minds
> Are nourished and invisibly repaired;
> A virtue, by which pleasure is enhanced,
> That penetrates, enables us to mount,
> When high, more high, and lifts us up when fallen.
> This efficacious spirit chiefly lurks
> Among those passages of life that give
> Profoundest knowledge to what point, and how,
> The mind is lord and master—outward sense
> The obedient servant of her will. Such moments
> Are scattered everywhere, taking their first date[24]
> From our first childhood.[25]

[22] *The Prelude*, I, 581-612.
[23] As in the notable instance of the stolen boat, I, 357-400.
[24] That is "origin," or "beginning."
[25] *The Prelude*, XII, 208-225.

That is, these "spots of time," appear as early as our child-hood, and are to be found in the course of our subsequent experiences. The passage quoted proceeds to illustrate the principle by certain selected instances. In early childhood, the poet when riding on the Border Beacon, near Penrith, became separated from his companion, an ancient servant; dismayed, he dismounted and led his horse to the valley. His natural perturbation was added to by the wild scenery, the sight of a gibbet, and the visionary dreariness of the landscape. The re-sult was a state of mental terror, which was not allayed by the sight of a girl who bore a pitcher on her head and forced her way against the blowing wind. This very place in later years,[26] was the scene of his roving with his sweetheart, and the ob-jects affected him all the more powerfully because he had once been terrified by them. His pleasure was the greater because of his childish terror:

> Upon the naked pool and the dreary crags,
> And on the melancholy beacon, fell
> A spirit of pleasure and youth's golden gleam;
> And think ye not with radiance more sublime
> For these remembrances, and for the power
> They had left behind? So feeling comes in aid
> Of feeling, and diversity of strength
> Attends us, if but once we have been strong.
> Oh! mystery of man, from what a depth
> Proceed thy honours. I am lost, but see
> In simple childhood something of the base
> On which thy greatness stands; but this I feel,
> That from thyself it comes, that thou must give,
> Else never canst receive.[27]

The last lines are of great importance, for they reiterate the principle that these "spots of time" are all marked by the initial activity of the mind. The lines are an echo of the fa-mous lines from Coleridge's *Dejection*, which we have just quoted. On these notable occasions the mind in its workings is plainly displayed; and these "spots of time" are a revela-tion of the "hiding-places of man's power."[28]

---

[26] See Legouis, *The Early Life of William Wordsworth*, 105-106.
[27] *The Prelude*, XII, 264-277.
[28] *Op. cit.*, XII, 279.

The principle of man's power is again illustrated by another incident. The poet, aged thirteen, and his brothers were returning home at Christmas from the school at Hawkshead. The palfreys which were to meet them at a crossroads were late, and the boy was impatient. He ascended a crag, and in the intensity of his emotions, as he sat by a naked wall he noted a single sheep, a blasted hawthorn, and the wind whistling through the wall. He had not been home ten days before he was following his father's body to the grave. As he remembered the scene at the crossroads, he thought that his father's death was a punishment for his impatience. As an adult the poet knows this was not true; but none the less scenes such as this have the power to stir deepest thoughts and feelings; and "restore" and "repair" his mind.[29] His mind once was strong, and "gave"; so that ever after it "received." It attained "diversity of strength," because it had "once been strong."

This is the answer to our question of how *Peter Bell* and sundry characters in *The Excursion* are corrected and restored. They receive a shock, or impulse which awakens in their minds the latent powers, and so opens up the avenue of association, so that the belated processes by which the mature mind is built up out of sensations are begun. To use Wordsworth's own term, they are restored to "a healthful state of association." We must take note, however, that not all Wordsworth's characters are restored to such a healthful state. The husband of Ruth, the Luke of *Michael,* and, notably, the Solitary of *The Excursion* are instances of characters who are dismissed by the poet with their minds unawakened and their hearts untouched. The principle is true nevertheless, and *may* work a transformation in any soul, the poet would say; for we see it operate in the extreme cases of Peter Bell, of the unamiable woman in *The Excursion,* and of many others.

This is the law of life; and the unconscious child follows it, and gains real sensations, feelings, and knowledge; for by the natural strength and activity of its mind it supplies the energy to stir matter which otherwise would be inert, and so to gain reality. Hence the insistence upon "activity" or "feeling" in

---

[29] *The Prelude,* XII, 287-335.

certain poems which have been interpreted as mystical or fanciful:

> No joyless forms shall regulate
>   Our living Calendar:
> We from to-day, my friend, will date
>   The opening of the year.
>
> Love, now an universal birth,
>   From heart to heart is stealing,
> From earth to man, from man to earth,
>   —It is the hour of feeling.
>
> One moment now may give us more
>   Than fifty years of reason;
> Our minds shall drink at every pore
>   The spirit of the season.
>
> Some silent laws our hearts may make,
>   Which they shall long obey;
> We for the year to come may take
>   Our temper from to-day.[30]

That is to say, real knowledge begins only with real mental activity and emotion; and if we can as adults have these direct experiences it is a sign that we are "in a healthy state of association."[31] It is a sign that we have the mental activity and life that should be ours, in that we have kept open the passages that connect the days of our childhood with those of our maturity, that we observe

> The ties
> That bind the perishable hours of life
> Each to the other, and the curious props
> By which the world of memory and thought
> Exists and is sustained.[32]

We thus preserve our mental health, for we approach sensations with all the directness of the child and the youth, but interpret our experiences in the light of thought. Our thoughts generate emotions, but they are intellectual emotions, far removed from the sensuous; they are thoughts that lie "too deep for tears."

---

[30] *Lines Written at a Small Distance from my House (To my Sister).*
[31] *Preface* of 1800.
[32] *The Prelude,* VII, 461-465.

Coleridge thus interprets Wordsworth's thought:

If men laugh at the falsehoods that were imposed on themselves during their childhood, it is because they are not good and wise enough to contemplate the Past in the Present, and so to produce by a virtuous and thoughtful sensibility that continuity in their self-consciousness, which nature has made the law of their animal life. Ingratitude, sensuality, and hardness of heart all flow from this source. Men are ungrateful to others only when they have ceased to look back on their former selves with joy and tenderness. They exist in fragments, annihilated as to the Past, they are dead to the Future, or seek for the proofs of it everywhere, only not (where alone they can be found) in themselves. A contemporary poet has exprest and illustrated this sentiment with equal fineness of thought and feeling;[33]

and he quotes the familiar poem, *My heart leaps up*.

"The Child is father of the Man"; this is to say that all the powers grow more purely intellectual and spiritual with maturity; and the power that binds our mental life in one also is transformed to higher and "purer" forms. And so it is that the spontaneous, instinctive urge of the child becomes the "feeling intellect" of maturity. It becomes that which

> Is but another name for absolute power
> And clearest insight, amplitude of mind,
> And Reason in her most exalted mood.[34]

This faculty is the Imagination, the natural product of the mind in its growth, appearing first as Fancy in Youth, and only in Maturity assuming its authentic shape and its true function as the presiding genius of art and poetry, by virtue of its being the emanation of the "creative soul," humanized and intellectualized by the inevitable processes of a normal life.

From this conception of mental processes as an activity, and his consequent belief that poetry and art are produced by an active power, came his quarrel with the school of Taste.

The word has been stretched to the sense which it bears in Modern Europe by habits of self-conceit, including that inversion in the order of things, whereby a passive faculty is made paramount among the faculties conversant with the fine arts. Proportion and congruity, the requisite knowledge being supposed, are

[33] *The Friend*, No. 3, August 10, 1809.
[34] *The Prelude*, XIV, 190-192.

subjects upon which taste may be trusted; it is competent to this office;—for in its intercourse with these the mind is *passive*, and is affected painfully or pleasurably as by an instinct. But the profound and the exquisite in feeling, the lofty and universal in thought and imagination; or, in ordinary language, the pathetic and the sublime;—are neither of them, accurately speaking, objects of a faculty which could never without a sinking in the spirit of Nations have been designated by the metaphor—Taste. And why? Because without the exertion of a co-operating *power* in the mind of the Reader, there can be no adequate sympathy with either of these emotions: without this auxiliary impulse, elevated or profound passion cannot exist.[35]

Imagination is activity, and its creations are at once the products of activity; and objects that can be appreciated only by the active mind. Art, like life and the universe, is pervaded by an *"active Principle."*[36]

---

[35] *Essay, Supplementary to the Preface*, 1815.

[36] Joseph Priestley's theory of the Imagination, in his *Course of Lectures on Oratory and Criticism*, London, 1777, is an excellent example of a theory which is avowedly and patently based on Hartley, using the same terms and discussing many of the same problems as Wordsworth, and yet remaining unprogressive in theory. His discussion of reminiscence, and imagination, and diction may well have been at once a stimulant and irritant to Wordsworth. His identification of Imagination and Taste is indicated in the title of Lecture Seventeen of the book to which we refer, *Of the Pleasures of Imagination in General, and of the Standard of Good Taste*, XXIII, 350, in Rutt's Complete Edition.

CHAPTER IX

FANCY AND IMAGINATION: THEORY OF POETRY

For all good poetry is the spontaneous overflow of powerful feelings; but though this be true, poems to which any value can be attached, were never produced on any variety of subjects but by a man who, being possessed of more than usual organic sensibility, had also thought long and deeply. For our continued influxes of feeling are modified and directed by our thoughts. . . . That sane state of feeling which arises out of thought.

William Wordsworth, *Preface* of 1800.

From the preceding chapters the connection of Wordsworth's theory of Fancy and Imagination with the three stages in man's development should be clear. The mind in its development moves on from the control of sensation to the sway and direction of an activity and power which is within the mind alone, in accordance with which the world of experience is built up into the judgments and sentiments of the growing mind. That power, as we have seen, is the principle of association, and it asserts itself in two distinct forms, the one following the other in chronological sequence; the earliest form being that developed in Youth, which Wordsworth calls *Fancy;* and the latest, that which he calls *Imagination.* He has devoted considerable space to differentiating these two terms, and we must understand his differentiation of them if we are to understand his theory of poetry.

In the eighth book of *The Prelude,* in which he explains the transition from love of nature to love of man, that is, from youth to maturity, he discusses the origin and nature of Fancy. Up through late youth, until "not less than two and twenty summers had been told," nature held the first place in his affections and regards, man being "only a delight occasional and an accidental grace, his hour being not yet come." This was also the time of Fancy, against the strength of which the "plain Imagination and severe" was powerless. From this "new power nothing was safe," for it so dominated the mind that all the poet's youthful perceptions were colored by it. This "power" had two striking characteristics; it was untrue to fact and it was melancholy. In youth, "Imagination slept" as yet, and so was powerless to combat the untruths of the Fancy. The youthful poet "was mounting to highest truth"; but he had not yet attained, for under the domination of Fancy he saw the world of reality only through "analogies" which were supplied by his own thought:

> To every natural form, rock, fruit, or flower,
> Even the loose stones that cover the highway,
> I gave a moral life: I saw them feel,
> Or linked them to some feeling: the great mass
> Lay bedded in a quickening soul, and all
> That I beheld respired with inward meaning.[1]

This was the sole power of unifying his world of perceptions; for he saw no connections in the objects of his knowledge:

> The bodily eye
> Amid my strongest workings evermore
> Was searching out the lines of difference
> As they lie hid in all external forms,
> Near or remote, minute or vast, an eye
> Which, from a tree, a stone, a withered leaf,
> To the broad ocean and the azure heavens
> Spangled with kindred multitudes of stars,
> Could find no surface where its power might sleep.[2]

But the impulse towards unifying his world was such that even though he could not see that unity in the things of real knowledge, he subdued all things to himself:

> There came
> Among the simple shapes of human life
> A wilfulness of fancy and conceit:
> And Nature and her objects beautified
> These fictions, as in some sort, in their turn,
> They burnished her. From touch of this new power
> Nothing was safe: the elder-tree that grew
> Beside the well-known charnel-house had then
> A dismal look; the yew-tree had its ghost,
> That took his station there for ornament:
> The dignities of plain occurrence then
> Were tasteless, and truth's golden mean, a point

---

[1] *The Prelude*, III, 127-132.
[2] *Op. cit.*, III, 155-163.

> Where no sufficient pleasure could be found.
> Then if a widow, staggering with the blow
> Of her distress, was known to have turned her steps,
> To the cold grave in which her husband slept,
> One night, or haply more than one, through pain
> Or half-insensate impotence of mind,
> The fact was caught at greedily, and there
> She must be visitant the whole year through,
> Wetting the turf with never-ending tears.[3]

So too, beside the last bell on the fox-glove Fancy loved to seat

> Some vagrant mother, whose arch little ones,
> All unconcerned by her dejected plight,
> Laughed as with rival eagerness their hands
> Gathered the purple cups that round them lay,
> Strewing the turf's green slope.[4]

A diamond light smiting a wet rock set his restless fancy to work, and it became now a burnished silver shield suspended over the tomb of a knight who lay inglorious, buried in the dusky wood; now the entrance of a magic cave. Thus "wilful Fancy," "busy power," "engrafted far-fetched shapes on feelings bred by pure Imagination"; and a world was created in Fancy's own image:

> I had a world about me—'twas my own;
> I made it, for it only lived to me.[5]

"Imagination slept,"[6] the understanding slept, that fancy might "dream,"[7] but their slumbers became less deep as he approached the years of maturity, as we have already noted in the fifth chapter. This untrue world of Fancy was but a point in the "winding, excursive and often retrograde course" along which his intellect passed. It was appropriate to the age of youth, and was to be transmuted and to put on the nobler form and higher faculties of Imagination, which is appropriate to maturity.[8] The Fancy of youth was melancholy, but

---

[3] *The Prelude*, VIII, 371-391.
[4] *Op. cit.*, VIII, 402-406.
[5] *Op. cit.*, III, 141-142.
[6] *Op. cit.*, III, 257.
[7] *Letter* to "Mathetes."
[8] *Op. cit.* It may be noted that Hartley, too, connected Youth and Fancy (what he calls imagination). Proposition XCVIII, Vol. I, 486-492.

the growing Imagination had Hope as its ideal. This he felt
obscurely as early as 1790 in his tour on the continent, when
he reached the summit of the Alps without realizing it:

> Imagination—here the Power so called
> Through sad incompetence of human speech,
> That awful Power rose from the Mind's abyss
> Like an unfathered vapour that enwraps,
> At once, some lonely traveller . . . in such strength
> Of usurpation, when the light of sense
> Goes out, but with a flash that has revealed
> The invisible world, doth greatness make abode,
> There harbours; whether we be young or old,
> Our destiny, our being's heart and home,
> Is with infinitude, and only there;
> With hope it is, hope that can never die,
> Effort, and expectation, and desire,
> And something evermore about to be.[9]

This discovery made in his early youth, then only dimly
realized, became one of the great truths of his maturity. The
melancholy of Fancy and Youth became the Hope of Imagination and Maturity:

> For we live by hope
> And by desire; we see by the glad light
> And breathe the sweet air of futurity;
> And so we live, or else we have no life.[10]

With maturity he came under the control of "plain Imagination and severe," through which he saw the truth of fact and of
life. In youth he was under the "tyranny of the eye" and of
the senses, as yet unprovided with a regulative faculty which
summoned all the senses to a higher tribunal, and so ordered
the content of the mind into an organized system which is at
one with Truth and Reason. With Maturity this tyranny of
sense ceases; for the Imagination and Reason assert themselves, and constitute a power which

> Summons all the senses each
> To counteract the other, and themselves,
> And makes them all, and the objects with which all
> Are conversant, subservient in their turn
> To the great ends of Liberty and Power.[11]

---

[9] *The Prelude*, VI, 592-608.
[10] *The Excursion*, IX, 23-26.
[11] *The Prelude*, XII, 135-139.

Imagination freed him, and in his maturity he stood in Nature's presence, superior to her and not dominated by her,

> A sensitive being, a *creative* soul.[12]

He was now *free*, standing above Nature, capable of recombining her into the free forms of creative art in accordance with Truth and right Reason. This is the full development of Imagination,

> Which in truth,
> Is but another name for absolute power
> And clearest insight, amplitude of mind,
> And Reason in her most exalted mood.[13]

This is the culmination of man's mental development, from its first faint beginnings in sense, through the more complex forms of experience, up to God:

> This faculty hath been the feeding source
> Of our long labour: we have traced the stream
> From the blind cavern whence is faintly heard
> Its natal murmur; followed it to light
> And open day; accompanied its course
> Among the ways of Nature, for a time
> Lost sight of it bewildered and engulphed;
> Then given it greeting as it rose once more
> In strength, reflecting from its placid breast
> The works of man and face of human life;
> And lastly, from its progress have we drawn
> Faith in life endless, the sustaining thought
> Of human Being, Eternity, and God.[14]

Thus we have the ultimate Imagination, the result of the development of all men, through the processes of life; by the power of association. As Hartley says, in terms almost identical:

> And thus we may perceive, that all the pleasures and pains of sensation, imagination, ambition, self-interest, sympathy, and theopathy, as far as they are consistent with one another, with the frame of our natures, and with the course of the world, beget in us a moral sense, and lead us to the love and approbation of virtue, and to the fear, hatred, and abhorrence of vice. . . . It appears also, that the moral sense carries us perpetually to the pure love of

---

[12] *The Prelude*, XII, 206-207.
[13] *Op. cit.*, XIV, 189-192.
[14] *Op. cit.*, XIV, 193-205.

God, as our highest and ultimate perfection, our end, centre, and only resting-place to which we can ever attain.[15]

We must clearly grasp Wordsworth's identification of Imagination and Reason, or Truth, in order to understand the basis of his defence of his own poetry, and his resultant theories of the poetic art. We must also remember that this identification is the result of his explaining the Imagination by associationistic principles, especially by the system of Hartley, and that consequently we cannot explain his theories by reference to Coleridge's theory of the Imagination or to those of any transcendental philosophy.

Wordsworth's discussion of poetry takes the form of two main questions: 1st, that of the language of poetry, and, 2nd, that of the matter of poetry. We have considered the first in the chapter on Poetic Diction; and shall proceed to consider the second in connection with his theory of Imagination.

In the *Advertisement* to the *Lyrical Ballads* of 1798 he asks his readers to judge the poems by just one standard. They must not be repelled by strangeness and awkwardness in the book; they must "ask themselves if it contains a *natural* delineation of *human passions, human characters,* and *human incidents."* If they find this true, then "they should consent to be pleased in spite of that most dreadful enemy to our pleasures, our own pre-established codes of decision." This is a bold challenge, for Wordsworth knew very well that the prevailing judgments in poetry were based on taste, which placed the emphasis on devices of vocabulary and figures of speech, rather than on truth of content. In order to realize the revolutionary nature of Wordsworth's principles, we must note the nature of the theory of poetry and imagination to which he was opposed. Two aspects of this we shall note in particular— (1) his conception of imagination and, (2) his theory of the origin and purpose of poetry.

The common attitude to the imagination is given by Richard Price in his statement that imagination is "a faculty nearly allied to sense."[16] Thus it is opposed to reason; a conception which is explicitly expressed by Hume:

---

[15] *Observations on Man,* I, 497.
[16] *Review of the Principal Questions in Morals,* 1758.

The *Imagination* of man is naturally sublime, delighted with whatever is remote and extraordinary, and running, without control, into the most distant parts of space and time in order to avoid the objects which custom has rendered too familiar to us. A correct *judgment* observes a contrary method, and avoiding all distant and high inquiries, confines itself to common life, and to such objects as fall under daily practice and experience, leaving the more sublime topics to the embellishment of poets and orators, or to the arts of priests and politicians.[17]

This is in the full tradition of Malebranche, who waged such bitter war on the imagination because he regarded it as the origin of human error.[18] While Hartley is not hostile to the imagination, he is distrustful of it, and gives it no commanding position:

It is evident that the pleasures of the imagination were not intended for our primary pursuit, because they are, in general, the first of our intellectual pleasures, which are generated from the sensible ones by association, come to their height early in life, and decline in old age.[19]

None of these definitions of imagination was found satisfactory by Wordsworth, as they all connected the faculty with the lower and less intellectual processes of the mind, and opposed it to the rational. Knowing in his own heart the power of poetry, and at the same time, feeling that he had arrived at the stage of reason, he steadfastly refused to recognize any power of the mind as the source of poetry any less regal than reason itself. Hence his insistence on the *purpose* of poetry as the presentation of the incidents of common life, showing "the manner in which our feelings and ideas are associated in a state of excitement." And what are the sources of "excitement?" They are "the great and simple affections of our nature"—the maternal and paternal passion, death, the fraternal passion, and some of the "less impassioned feelings."[20] This is illustrated by Wordsworth when he says that "poetry is the history, or science, of the feelings."[21]

---

[17] *An Enquiry Concerning Human Understanding,* 1748, Sect. XII, Part III.
[18] *De la recherche de la vérité,* 1674, 1675.
[19] *Observations on Man,* II, 244, Propositions LV, LVI.
[20] *Preface* of 1800-1805.
[21] Note to *The Thorn,* 1800.

The relations between feeling and thought we have already explained ;[22] so it will be necessary only to mention that, in accordance with the associationistic philosophy of Hartley, the feelings which are worthy of a history or of being the object of science are those feelings which are derived from thought. It is important to remember this, and to realize that Wordsworth does not speak of feeling as being opposed to thought and the intellect, when he speaks of the proper subject of poetry.[22]

All good poetry is the spontaneous overflow of powerful feelings; but though this be true, Poems to which any value can be attached, were never produced on any variety of subjects but by a man who being possessed of more than usual organic sensibility had also thought long and deeply. For our continual influxes of feeling are modified and directed by our thoughts.[23]

And, since this is true, the power which produces poetry can be no lower power than the intellect, for though it deals with feeling, these influxes of feelings are a product of thought and the intellect. Hence Imagination is the counterpart of Intellect, the other side of the shield. The two powers are partners, but the Imagination is the dominant one, for it represents the life of thought; it represents life in being; it "is the breath and finer spirit of all knowledge; it is the impassioned expression which is in the countenance of all Science. It is the first and last of all knowledge; it is as immortal as the heart of man."[24] Imagination is "Reason in her most exalted mood."[25]

Such being the case, how is poetry produced? This he answers in the *Preface* of 1800. "The grand elementary principle of pleasure" must always be kept in mind by the poet, for this is the ultimate end of poetry and of life, and cannot be neglected by the poet. With this caution, Wordsworth proceeds to lay down the method of poetry. Taking for granted that the only feeling, or emotion, that is worthy of being presented aesthetically, or capable of being so presented, is "the feeling which arises out of thought," he deals with the problem of

[22] Chapter VI.
[23] *Preface*, 1800-1805.
[24] *Preface*, 1802-1805.
[25] *The Prelude*, XIV, 193.

connecting the thought and its associated feeling in a poem. According to his explanation of the working of association, we can begin either with the feeling and so evoke its associated thought, or we can begin with the thought, and evoke its associated feeling. In poetry, the first processes are always followed. At this point his statement begins:

I have said that Poetry is the spontaneous overflow of powerful feelings: it takes its origin from emotion recollected in tranquillity: the emotion is contemplated till by a species of reaction the tranquillity gradually disappears, and an emotion, similar to that which was before the subject of contemplation, is gradually produced, and does itself actually exist in the mind. In this mood successful composition generally begins, and in a mood similar to this it is carried on; but the emotion, of whatever kind and in whatever degree, from various causes is qualified by various pleasures, so that in describing any passions whatsoever, which are voluntarily described, the mind will upon the whole be in a state of enjoyment. Now if Nature be thus cautious in preserving in a state of enjoyment a being thus employed, the poet ought to profit by the lesson thus held forth to him, and ought especially to take care, that whatever passions he communicates to his Reader, those passions, if his Reader's mind be sound and vigorous, should always be accompanied with an overbalance of pleasure.

Thus poetry is a union of feeling and reason, working in harmony with the chief end of man, pleasure and well-being: in other words, poetry is the result of the activity of the imagination. Surely Wordsworth's own theory as shown by a careful study of his very words in this *Preface* of 1800 ought to dispel the popular notion, only too prevalently held even by serious students of literature, that Wordsworth disparaged intellect and reason, and glorified feeling and emotion at their expense. No critic has been more careful to explain the fine balance between these two aspects of mind, and to give to each its due in the production of poetry.

This brings his discussion of the Imagination up to 1805, and it seems plain that his notion of it is associationistic, even though he assigns a much higher place to it than Hartley allows it. Here he goes beyond his master by giving a new interpretation to the facts of the mind as he knew them. We have noted that he found the unifying principle of mind in the associationistic doctrine, in accordance with which he represented the mind as a self-active unit, in which sensations, ideas, thoughts, and feelings all react the one upon the other, and so insure the continuity of the mental life of the individual from age to age. But this theory, as developed by Hartley, could not be fully accepted by Wordsworth, for by it the Imagination is given a very subordinate part to play in the mental life. He knew from his own experience that the poet's art is no mean one; hence he exalted the Imagination to the highest place. In Wordsworth's thought it takes the place of the law of association in the system of Hartley. Hence with him we do not hear of "Fancy *or* Imagination" but of "Fancy *and* Imagination"; they are regarded as two distinct things.

This was his position in the year 1805, and it is his final position in all essentials, for in the succeeding years, up to 1815, he developed his theory in the direction of analyzing the term and disclosing its complex nature and manifestations, but without altering his general conception of the activity for which it stood. This analysis and exposition is found in the *Preface* of 1815, a large part of which is taken up with the differentiation between Fancy and Imagination. He begins by making it clear that Imagination, as he uses the term, "has no reference to images that are merely a faithful copy, existing in the mind, of absent external objects; but is a word of higher import, denoting operations of the mind upon those objects, and processes of creation or of composition governed by certain fixed laws." It is thus regarded as quite distinct from memory, in contrast to the opinion of Hobbes,[26] and the sensationalist school, of which Condillac is a representative,[27] and a function of the mind which shows the fullest activity and power of which the individual mind is capable. This power operates by, 1st, conferring, 2nd, abstracting, and, 3rd, modifying the images which are made use of as the stuff of creative activity. This conferring, abstracting, and modifying power may be shown in two typical cases; either, 1st, upon single images,

[26] *Leviathan,* Ch. II. "So that imagination and memory are but one thing, which for diverse considerations hath diverse names."

[27] Condillac, *Treatise on the Sensations,* Ch. I, Section 29. "Imagination is memory itself, which has attained the fullest power of which it is susceptible."

or, 2nd, upon several images in a conjunction. In the case
of the single image the power operates "by conferring additional properties upon an object, or abstracting from it some of
those which it actually possesses, and thus enabling it to re-act
upon the mind which has performed the process, like a new existence."[28]   This conferring and abstracting he illustrates for
both *sight* and *sound,* from passages in Virgil, Shakespeare,
and Milton, as well as from his own poems, to show the processes by which images are "immediately endowed by the mind
with properties that do not inhere in them, upon an incitement
from properties and qualities the existence of which is inherent
and obvious."   For example:

> Shall I call thee Bird
> Or but a wandering Voice?

This concise interrogation characterizes the seeming ubiquity of
the voice of the cuckoo, and dispossesses the creature almost of a
corporeal existence; the Imagination being tempted to this exertion
of her power by a consciousness in the memory that the cuckoo is
almost perpetually heard throughout the season of spring, but seldom becomes an object of sight.[29]

The second way in which the powers of imagination are exerted is on images in a conjunction, by which the images modify each other. This Wordsworth illustrates from his *Resolution and Independence:*

> As a huge stone is sometimes seen to lie
> Couched on the bald top of an eminence,
> Wonder to all who do the same espy
> By what means it could thither come, and whence,
> So that it seems a thing endued with sense,
> Like a sea-beast crawled forth, which on a shelf
> Of rock or sand reposeth, there to sun himself.
>
> Such seemed this Man; not all alive or dead
> Nor all asleep, in his extreme old age.
>
> .   .   .   .
>
> Motionless as a cloud the old Man stood,
> That heareth not the loud winds when they call,
> And moveth altogether if it move at all.

In these images, the conferring, the abstracting, and the modifying powers of the Imagination, immediately and mediately

[28] *Preface* to the *Poems* of 1815.
[29] *Preface* to the *Poems* of 1815.

acting, are all brought into conjunction. The stone is endowed with something of the power of life to approximate it to the sea-beast; and the sea-beast stripped of some of its vital qualities to assimilate it to the stone; which intermediate image is thus treated for the purpose of bringing the original image, that of the stone, to a nearer resemblance to the figure and condition of the aged Man; who is divested of so much of the indications of life and motion as to bring him to the point where the two objects unite and coalesce in just comparison. After what has been said, the image of the cloud need not be commented upon.[30]

A third form of this activity of the imagination not only endows and modifies; it also shapes and *creates*. This it does in many ways;

and in none does it more delight than in that of consolidating numbers into unity, and dissolving and separating unity into number, —alterations proceeding from, and governed by a sublime consciousness of the soul in her own mighty and almost divine powers.[31]

> As when far off at sea a fleet descried
> *Hangs* in the clouds, by equinoctial winds
> Close sailing from Bengala, or the isles
> Of Ternate or Tidore, whence merchants bring
> Their spicy drugs; they on the trading flood
> Through the wide Ethiopian to the Cape
> Ply, stemming nightly toward the Pole: so seemed
> Far off the flying Fiend.

In this passage from Milton,

When the compact Fleet, as one Person, has been introduced "sailing from Bengala" "They," *i. e.* the "merchants," representing the fleet resolved into a multitude of ships, "ply" their voyage towards the extremities of the earth; "So," (referring to the word "As" in the commencement) "seemed the flying Fiend"; the image of his Person acting to recombine the multitude of ships into one body,— the point from which the comparison set out. "So seemed," and to whom seemed? To the heavenly Muse who dictates the poem, to the eye of the Poet's mind, and to that of the Reader, present at one moment in the wide Ethiopian, and the next in the solitudes, then first broken in upon, of the infernal regions! . . . Hear again this mighty Poet,—speaking of the Messiah going forth to expel from heaven the rebellious angels,

> "Attended by ten thousand thousand Saints
> He onward came: far off his coming shone,"—

---

[30] *Preface* to the *Poems* of 1815.
[31] *Op. cit.*

the retinue of Saints, and the Person of the Messiah himself, lost almost and merged in the splendour of that indefinite abstraction, "His coming!"[32]

The analysis of the Imagination is carried no further by Wordsworth; but he concludes by pointing to the prophetic and lyrical parts of Holy Scripture, Milton, and Spenser as the grand storehouse of the enthusiastic and meditative Imagination; and to the works of Shakespeare as an inexhaustible source of the human and dramatic Imagination.

The Fancy is contrasted with the Imagination in that she does not *shape* or *create*.

Fancy does not require that the materials which she makes use of should be susceptible of change in their constitution, from her touch; and, where they admit of modification, it is enough for her purpose if it be slight, limited, and evanescent. Directly the reverse of these, are the desires and demands of the Imagination. She recoils from everything but the plastic, the pliant, and the indefinite. She leaves it to Fancy to describe Queen Mab as coming

> "In shape no bigger than an agate-stone
> On the fore-finger of an alderman."

. . . When the Imagination frames a comparison, if it does not strike on the first presentation, a sense of the truth of the likeness, from the moment that it is perceived, grows—and continues to grow—upon the mind; the resemblance depending less upon outline of form and feature, than upon expression and effect; less upon casual and outstanding, than upon inherent and internal properties; moreover, the images invariably modify each other.—The law under accidents of things, and the effects are surprising, playful, ludicrous, amusing, tender, or pathetic, as the objects happen to be appositely produced or fortunately combined.

Fancy moulds the conceit,

> The dews of the evening most carefully shun,
> They are tears of the sky for the loss of the sun;

and Imagination the following,

> Sky lowered, and, muttering thunder, some sad drops
> Wept at completion of the mortal sin.

The associating link is the same in each instance: Dew and Rain, not distinguishable from the liquid substance of tears, are employed as indications of sorrow. A flash of surprise is the effect in

---

[32] *Preface* to the *Poems* of 1815.

the former case; a flash of surprise, and nothing more; for the nature of things does not sustain the combination. In the latter, the effects from the act, of which there is this immediate consequence and visible sign, are so momentous, that the mind acknowledges the justice and reasonableness of the sympathy in nature so manifested; and the sky weeps drops of water as if with human eyes, as "Earth had before trembled from her entrails, and Nature given a second groan."[33]

The analysis of Imagination furnished us by Wordsworth in this *Preface* of 1815 is clearly a more explicit form of his opinions in 1805. The imagination is still identified with Reason, as in *The Prelude:* it is still "Reason in her most exalted mood," it is still "feeling intellect," and "intellectual Love";[34] and all the directive and analytic power of the intellect is claimed for it. The analysis brings this out very clearly by its form; and it is a curious coincidence that the three-fold forms by which the imagination manifests itself in the single image, in the conjoined images, and in the creative activity, together with the importance assigned to abstraction, shows that his mind was still running in the channels of English eighteenth-century thought; for it has a remarkable likeness to Locke's account of the formation of complex ideas. The general method and spirit of Wordsworth in this analysis seem to be borrowed from Locke, especially in his insistence that this activity is proof positive of the freedom of the mind as a self-directed thing, above Nature and using her for its own purposes. It is in terms similar to these that Locke declares that as the mind is wholly passive in the reception of simple ideas, so it exerts several acts of its own when it forms complex ideas;[35] and he goes on to discuss Abstraction, Pleasure, Number, Infinity, Liberty, and Power. Wordsworth too lays it down as a fundamental principle that all the varied elements of mind must be made

> subservient in their turn
> To the great ends of Liberty and Power.[36]

---

[33] *Preface* to the *Poems* of 1815.
[34] *The Prelude*, XIV, 192, 207, 226.
[35] Locke, *Essay on the Human Understanding*, Book II, Ch. XII. Compare J. Harris, *Hermes: or a Philosophical Inquiry Concerning Language and Universal Grammar*, 1751, Book III, Ch. IV.
[36] *The Prelude*, XII, 139.

From this analysis it is also easy to see how far Wordsworth agrees with Coleridge and how fundamentally he differs from him in his conception of Fancy, and, consequently, of Imagination. Coleridge speaks of Imagination as the "shaping and modifying power," and of Fancy as the "aggregative and associative power."[37] Now, as we have seen, Wordsworth cannot allow any such power as aggregation and association to an inferior faculty such as Fancy; for these powers are given to the superior imagination in their superior forms, though they may exist in their more lowly forms as Fancy. But Fancy and Imagination are different in a fundamental way, for they operate "under a different law," and they work "for a different purpose."[38] The law under which Imagination works is clearly the law of Intellect, the manifest proof of the independence of the mind and of its freedom to work changes in objects of its perception so as to change, modify, and re-shape them to a new creation. Fancy, the main activity of youth, has no such power; it is not guided by thought, and so it cannot shape. Hence comes Wordsworth's refusal to grant associative power to it; and hence his disagreement with Coleridge— a disagreement which is not explained by Coleridge's criticism of Wordsworth

that he has mistaken the co-presence of fancy and imagination for the operation of the latter singly. A man may work with two very different tools at the same moment; each has its share in the work, but the work effected by each is distinct and different.[39]

If Coleridge had but remembered Wordsworth's plain statement, he would not have made this charge; for in the *Preface* which he is criticising, Wordsworth very explicitly says that Imagination and Fancy *may* cooperate in the production of a poem. Speaking of the classification of the poems in the edition of 1815, he says:

Certain poems are placed according to the powers of mind, in the Author's conception, predominant in the production of them; *predominant*, which implies the exertion of other faculties in less degree. Where there is more imagination than fancy in a poem, it is placed under the head of Imagination, and *vice versa*.

[37] *Biographia Literaria*, Ch. XII.
[38] *Preface* to the *Poems* of 1815.
[39] *Biographia Literaria*, Ch. XII.

Wordsworth was perfectly clear in his conception of the terms, and his differences with Coleridge must be explained on grounds other than those which Coleridge suggests. These differences rest on a much more fundamental disagreement than a mistake or a misunderstanding concerning the meaning of a term. They result from an almost opposite outlook on the whole problem involved. By 1815 Coleridge had repudiated everything like associationism as a source of infidelity and atheism, and was a full believer in transcendentalism. Hence his conception of the imagination is that of a transcendentalist and similar to that of Kant. With him it is a power of the mind which mediates between sensuous knowledge and the higher and more purely mental forms of the understanding. It is an "intermediate faculty"; a description which applies to the fancy; for, though they are distinct, they are rather clearly allied as mediate faculties. Wordsworth, on the other hand, was in all essentials an associationist, "compounding a mind out of the senses" in the old heroically associationistic way. Now, as we have seen, to him the fancy and the imagination are of a different order, the fancy being the faculty of the lower powers, and the imagination the possession of only those persons who have attained to the purer mature understanding. Hence his refusal to grant to the fancy functions which Coleridge accords it.

In this associationistic belief Wordsworth had written *The Prelude* and *The Excursion,* and they stood as a record of the development of the individual and the race. They represented the realities of experience to him, and he would not yield one jot even to Coleridge, when he was warned that he should take the transcendental turn, and attempt to "inform the senses from the mind." That way of German transcendentalism he never trod. This position was surely justified by him as an artist; for it is in English associationism that all the poems by which his fame endures are conceived. Hence results his final artistic and theoretical position: that imagination is simple truth to experience, to the real experience which we all know; not to some transcendental, far-away, or Utopian, or supposedly ideal truth, but to the truth of the world in which we live. He knows no higher aesthetic, no purer ethics, than that. In his own words:

> Our eyes have not been fixed upon virtue which lies apart from human nature, or transcends it. In fact, there is no such virtue.[40]

So, too, he never fixed his eyes on poetry which lies apart from human nature; to him there is no such poetry: Imagination is simple truth.[41]

---

[40] *Letter* to "Mathetes."

[41] We may realize how far apart the two friends had drifted by 1814, when we note that Coleridge defines taste as "the intermediate faculty which connects the active with the passive powers of our nature, the intellect and the senses," in his *Essays on the Principles of Genial Criticism, Miscellanies,* Ashe's edition, p. 14. This is the faculty which he calls Imagination, in the *Biographia Literaria.* It is interesting to observe how the earlier nomenclature persists, even when the meaning of the terms is utterly changed by him.

PART III

WORDSWORTH'S POETRY

"It only remains to be added once more that Wordsworth's poetry derives its power from the same source as his philosophy. It speaks to our strongest feelings because his speculation rests upon our deepest thoughts. His singular capacity for investing all objects with a glow derived from early associations; his keen sympathy with natural and simple emotions; his sense of the sanctifying influences which can be extracted from sorrow, are of equal value to his power over our intellects and our imaginations. His psychology, stated systematically, is rational; and, when expressed passionately, turns into poetry."

Leslie Stephen, 1874.

CHAPTER X

THE SHORTER POEMS

The principal object then which I proposed to myself in these Poems was to make the incidents of common life interesting by tracing in them, truly though not ostentatiously, the primary laws of our nature: chiefly as far as regards the manner in which we associate ideas in a state of excitement. . . . But speaking in less general language, it is to follow the fluxes and refluxes of the mind when agitated by the great and simple affections of our nature.

William Wordsworth, *Preface* to *Lyrical Ballads*, 1800.

The preparatory poem is biographical, and conducts the history of the Author's mind to the point when he was emboldened to hope that his faculties were sufficiently matured for entering upon the arduous labour which he had proposed to himself; and the two Works have the same kind of relation to each other, if he may so express himself, as the ante-chapel has to the body of a gothic church. Continuing this allusion, he may be permitted to add, that his minor Pieces, which have been long before the Public, when they shall be properly arranged, will be found by the attentive Reader to have such connection with the main Work as may give them claim to be likened to the little cells, oratories, and sepulchral recesses, ordinarily included in those edifices.

William Wordsworth, *Preface* to *The Excursion*, 1814.

The two quotations which stand at the head of this chapter sum up rather completely what can be said regarding the shorter poems, if we confine ourselves to the method of discussion adopted by the author himself. This I shall do; dealing with representative poems according as they illustrate (1) the primary laws of our nature, and the association of ideas in connection therewith; (2) the relationship of the individual poem, or series of poems, to the main theme of the philosophical poem—the relation of "the little cells, oratories, and sepulchral recesses" to the "body of the gothic church"; and (3) the relation of the poem to the classification of the shorter poems adopted in the edition of 1815. But first and as a preliminary step to the discussion of the poems, it will be useful to discuss

the history and the leading purposes which govern the classification of the minor poems, and to indicate its relation to the
general body of Wordsworth's doctrine.

We commonly speak of the classification of the poems in the
edition of 1815 as if a scheme of classification were something new in Wordsworth at that time. But, as a matter of
fact, this opinion is quite erroneous; for the idea of classifying
and arranging his poems is present, in germ at least, as early
as the first edition of the *Lyrical Ballads* in 1798. The title
page makes two quite distinct classes: (1) the lyrical ballads,
and (2) the "few other poems"; a classification which, in the
title-page of the edition of 1802 becomes (1) the lyrical ballads, (2) the pastorals, and (3) the "other poems." If we
attach no importance to the title pages, we may consider the
prefaces and the tables of contents. In the *Advertisement* to
the edition of 1798 Wordsworth speaks of his "experiments"
as being natural representations of (1) human passions, (2) human characters, and (3) human incidents, and asks the reader
to accept these attempts as poetry if they succeed in what they
attempt. In the *Preface* to the second edition of 1800, the attention of the poet is fixed upon the first aspect of reality; that
is, upon the natural delineation of human passion, since character and incident are to be understood through the passion,
or emotion, which is represented as dominant, and since the
feeling which is developed in the poem gives importance to the
action and situation and not the action and situation to the feeling. Hence in this *Preface* he speaks of the main purpose of
poetry as that of making the incidents of common life interesting by tracing in them the primary laws of our nature; that is,
by following the fluxes and refluxes of the mind when agitated
by the great and simple affections, or passions, or emotions, of
our nature. He then proceeds to explain what these passions
are: (1) the maternal passion; that is, maternal love; (2)
death, as contemplated by the adult and by the child; (3)
the fraternal passion; that is, fraternal love; (4) moral passion, variously viewed; and (5) the less impassioned feelings
which are aroused by the contemplation of old age and childhood. The poems are not classified in their arrangement in the
volume.

In the *Poems in two Volumes,* 1807, the contents are partially classified and arranged in seven classes as follows:

1. A class without any name, comprising seventeen poems, among which are *The Happy Warrior, The Affliction of Margaret,* and the *Ode to Duty.*

2. Poems composed during a tour, chiefly on foot, comprising five poems, among which is *Resolution and Independence.*

3. Sonnets: Part the First—Miscellaneous Sonnets; Part the Second—Sonnets Dedicated to Liberty; This section contains forty-seven sonnets, twenty-six of which belong to the second part.

4. Poems written during a tour in Scotland. Nine poems.

5. Moods of my own mind. Thirteen poems.

6. *The Blind Highland Boy;* with other poems. This class contains twenty-three poems, five of which are sonnets.

7. Ode.

This classification is of an extremely miscellaneous sort, sometimes based on psychology, like section 5; and, in less measure, sections 2 and 4; sometimes on the form of the poems, as in sections 3 and 7; and again on purely accidental grounds, like sections 1 and 6.

The earliest reasoned classification which we find is given in an important letter written to Coleridge early in May, 1809.[1] He here gives the arrangement in which he meant to place his published poems if they should ever be republished during his lifetime:

1. Poems relating to childhood, and such feelings as rise in the mind in after-life in direct contemplation of that state. To these I should prefix the motto, "The child is father of the man, etc." The class would begin with the simplest dawn of the affections or faculties, as *Foresight, or Children gathering Flowers*, the *Pet Lamb*, etc.; and would ascend in a gradual scale of imagination to *Hartley*, "There was a boy," and it would conclude with the Ode, "There was a time," which might be preceded by *We are Seven*, if it were not advisable to place that earlier . . .

2. The second class would relate to the fraternal affections, to friendship, to love, and to all those emotions which follow after

---

[1] *Letters of the Wordsworth Family*, III, 468-474. Only pages 471-474 have any bearing on the classification.

childhood, in youth and early manhood. . . . This class to ascend, in a scale of imagination or interest, through " 'T is said that some have died for love," *Ellen Irwin*, and to conclude with *Ruth* or *the Brothers* printed as an adjunct. . . .

3. The third class, poems relating to natural objects and their influence on the Mind, either as growing or in an advanced state; to begin with the simply human and conclude with the highly imaginative, as *Tintern Abbey;* to be immediately preceded by the Cuckoo poems, and *Nutting*, after having passed through all stages from objects as they affect a human being from properties with which they are endowed, and as they affect the mind by properties conferred; by the life found in them, or their life given. . . .[2] The above class would be numerous, and conclude in the manner mentioned above, with *Tintern Abbey*.

4. Next might come the "Poems on the Naming of Places."

5. Those relating to human life, which might be connected . . . to ascend, through a regular scale of imagination, to *The Thorn, The Highland Girl, The Leech-gatherer, Hartleap Well*. This class of poems I suppose to consist chiefly of objects most interesting to the mind, not by its personal feelings or a strong appeal to the instincts or natural affections, but to be interesting to a meditative or imaginative mind, either from the moral importance of the pictures, or from the employment they give to the understanding affected through the imagination, and to the higher faculties.

6. Then might come perhaps those relating to the social and civic duties, chiefly interesting to the imagination through the understanding, and not to the understanding through the imagination, as the "Political Sonnets," *The Character of the Happy Warrior, Rob Roy's Grave, Personal Talk, Poet's Epitaph, Ode to Duty, To Burns's Sons*, etc.

7. Those relating to maternal feeling, connubial or parental, the maternal to ascend from *The Sailor's Mother* through *The Emigrant Mother, Affliction of M— of M—*, to the *Mad Mother*, to conclude with *The Idiot Boy*.

8. Finally, the class of poems on old age . . . to conclude perhaps with *Michael*, which might conclude the whole.

The letter concludes:

The principle of the arrangement is that there should be a scale in each class, and in the whole; and that each poem should be so placed as to direct the reader's attention by its position to its primary interest.

---

[2] Compare *The Prelude*, I, 581-612, and the explanation of this and similar passages in Chapter VIII, especially pages 145-152. On the "Conferring" power of the Imagination see pages 162-166.

The next statement of the poet comes some years later, on the occasion to which he refers in this letter, namely the reissue of his published poems in two volumes in 1815. It is important to note that the elaborate classification of his poems there made public for the first time, was no sudden whim on the part of the poet, but little more than the enlargement of a plan roughly sketched out ten years before. It is to be noted that the classification denoted more clearly the importance of imagination as a distinct element and power in poetry, in harmony with the detailed consideration which is given to it in the *Preface* specially written for this, the first collected edition of his poems.[3]   The poems are divided into fourteen classes, as follows:

1. Poems Referring to the Period of Childhood.
2. Juvenile Pieces.
3. Poems Founded on the Affections.
4. Poems of the Fancy.
5. Poems of the Imagination.
6. Poems Proceeding from Sentiment and Reflection.
7. Miscellaneous Sonnets.
8. Sonnets Dedicated to Liberty.   First Part, Published in 1807.
9. Sonnets Dedicated to Liberty.   Second Part, From the Year 1807 to 1813.
10. Poems on the Naming of Places.
11. Inscriptions.
12. Poems Referring to the Period of Old Age.
13. Epitaphs and Elegiac Poems.
14. Ode—Intimations, etc.

This classification is Wordsworth's final one; the poet's later editions increasing the number of classes without introducing any new principles.   One other edition, however, is very important, that edited by Professor Henry Reed and published at Philadelphia in 1837.   This edition, by greatly extending the classification of Imagination, arranges the contents under only twelve main heads.   This classification I shall deal with in con-

---

[3] The *Poems* of 1815 did not include *The Excursion,* which had been published just one year before.

nection with the *Preface* which accompanies the poems of 1815,
but for convenience of reference I shall present Professor
Reed's Table of General Titles at this point:

1. Poems Written in Youth.
2. Poems Referring to the Period of Childhood.
3. Poems Founded on the Affections.
4. Poems on the Naming of Places.
5. Poems of the Fancy.
6. Poems of the Imagination.
7. Poems of Sentiment and Reflection.
8. Miscellaneous Poems.
9. Selections from Chaucer Modernized.
10. Inscriptions.
11. Poems Referring to the Period of Old Age.
12. Epitaphs and Elegiac Pieces.

The *Preface* opens with a summary statement of the function of the various powers of the mind which are requisite for
the production of poetry: (1) Observation and Description,
(2) Sensibility, (3) Reflection, (4) Imagination and Fancy,
(5) Invention, and (6) Judgment. Each of these terms is
briefly defined, and two, Imagination and Fancy, are marked
out for that fuller discussion which occupies the greater part of
the *Preface*. Next are considered the various moulds into
which the materials of poetry are cast: (1) The Narrative,
(2) The Dramatic, (3) The Lyrical, (4) Idyllium, (5) The
Didactic, and (6) Philosophical Satire, each dealing with its
appropriate subject according to its own method. From these
considerations Wordsworth deduces the conclusion that poems
which are apparently of a miscellaneous character may with
propriety be arranged in accordance with three different principles: (1) with reference to the powers of the mind *predominant* in the production of them, (2) with reference to the
mould in which they are cast, and (3) with reference to the
subjects to which they relate.

All these three methods are used in the classification of the
poems, which classes have their order determined by another
principle; that of the development of the individual in an order
of time, "commencing with Childhood, and terminating with
Old Age, Death, and Immortality." By this arrangement it

was Wordsworth's wish, first, that the poems might show "the three requisites of a legitimate whole, a beginning, a middle, and an end;" and, second, that they might show clearly that as a whole they are "adjuncts to the Philosophical Poem, *The Recluse*." It is thus perfectly clear that Wordsworth looked upon his minor poems as one whole, each one contributing its share toward the development of his general theme of human life; or, in other words, that he looked upon his poems as dealing with the main period of man's life, from Childhood to Old Age. That is to say, in these shorter poems, he deals with human life just as he deals with it in the philosophical poem, and that is why he wishes them to be thought of as an "adjunct" to it. Now, if we keep in mind Wordsworth's definition of Fancy and Imagination, we can see why the poems of Fancy are placed before the poems of Imagination; for, as Fancy is the power of youth and youth comes before maturity; so poems which are primarily the product of Fancy should precede those which are primarily the product of maturity. With this classification solely in mind, we might expect the poems of the Imagination to be very much more numerous than those of Fancy; that is, to include all those which were not expressly excluded as being more strongly marked by subject-matter or by form. This was the interpretation placed on the term Imagination by Professor Henry Reed in the edition to which I have referred. He preserves the main outlines of Wordsworth's own classification; but among the Poems of the Imagination he includes nearly all the mature minor poems, including all the sonnets. That he properly interpreted Wordsworth's mind is made clear by the letter written to Professor Reed, September 27, 1845, in which Wordsworth discusses this point:

I do not remember whether I have mentioned to you, that, following your example, I have greatly extended the class entitled "Poems of the Imagination," thinking as you must have done that, if Imagination were predominant in the class, it was not indispensable that it should pervade every poem which it contained. Limiting the class as I had done before, seemed to imply, and to the uncandid and observing did so, that the faculty, which is the *primum mobile* in poetry, had little to do, in the estimation of the author, with pieces not arranged under that head. I therefore feel much obliged to you for suggesting by your practice the plan which I have adopted.[4]

This letter shows very clearly the way in which Wordsworth's conception of imagination grew, as a method of explaining the origin of poetry. The term first appears in the note to *The Thorn,* in 1800, and is there contrasted with fancy. The terms are not used in any aesthetic sense; but are used to explain the peculiarities of the mentality of the superstitious, who are credited with the power of imagination. In the second edition of the *Preface* to the *Lyrical Ballads,* 1802, the term is used in an aesthetic sense for the first time, and is used by Wordsworth to express the way in which the poet presents "ordinary things" in "an unusual way," and thereby supplements his main task, namely, the presentation of "the primary laws of our nature." Thus his analysis of poetry is still made in terms of subject rather than of method in the presentation of incidents which illustrate the working of the primary laws of our nature. By 1815, though he did not then or at any later date abandon this position, he shifted from subject-matter to method, and so laid more and more stress on Imagination and its more humble companion Fancy. By this enlarged interpretation of Imagination the classification of the poems is very much simplified; and the importance of the faculty of imagination is visibly shown by the fact that the poems coming under the enlarged classification amount to over half of the minor poems, and to about one-third of all the poet's work, including *The Prelude* and *The Excursion.* It is a great pity that modern editors have not conformed to Wordsworth's own interpretation and application of the term, and his declaration of policy, for by his definition of imagination, the classification is much simplified and clarified. The great majority of the minor poems fall under the two classes of Fancy and Imagination, thus indicating the same importance in the classification as that which the poet attached to these faculties in this *Preface.* They

[4] In the *Preface* to Professor Reed's edition of 1851. This letter is not included in Knight's *Letters of the Wordsworth Family.* Compare another letter of July 31 of the same year. The salient passage is omitted by Knight. *Letters of the Wordsworth Family,* III, 139. The omitted passage reads: "In the heading of the pages I have followed the example of your Edition, by extending the classification of Imagination far beyond what it has hitherto been, except in your Edition."

form the main classes, and are the centre of the poet's work, so far as it is represented by the minor poems; with the other classes supplementing them, that is, the class based on subject-matter, and the class based on form, the most important of which is the first. Preceding the central group of Fancy and Imagination come two main classes, (1) that referring to the period of childhood, and (2) that founded on the affections. Immediately after the poems of Imagination comes the related group, poems of sentiment and reflection, followed by the poems referring to old age. The class based on form is represented by Inscriptions, and by the Epitaphs and Elegiac Pieces, which is the concluding group and rounds out the account of the story of human life.

Thus there are three main aspects according to which each short poem may be considered, as I have stated at the beginning of this chapter: (1) as illustrating the primary laws of our nature, in the phraseology of 1800; that is, according to the classification of 1815, (a) as referring to the period of childhood, (b) as founded on the affections, or (c) as referring to the period of old age; (2) as having its origin in (a) fancy, or (b) imagination, or (c) in sentiment and reflection; or (3) as having a relationship with the main theme of the philosophic poem. This scheme of classification is thus seen to be closely connected with Wordsworth's thought, and is not by any means so "ingenious" and "far-fetched" as Matthew Arnold thinks,[5] however unsatisfactory it may be, and however inconsistently it is carried out. Each poem fills a definite place in connection with some aspect of the general scheme of human life as Wordsworth conceived it, and so each poem must be read and studied with the general plan in view if we are to give to the poem Wordsworth's own interpretation. This is true, even in face of the fact that the poet frequently changed his mind as to the class to which certain poems belonged. He himself stated very clearly that he had in mind the progressive powers of man and the individual, beginning with the early and simple, and proceeding to the later and complex. These

---

[5] *Preface* to his *Poems of Wordsworth*, 1879.

are his own words in explanation of his arrangement of the
poems in the class of Poems of the Imagination:

In the series of Poems, placed under the head of Imagination, I
have begun with one of the earliest processes of Nature in the development of this faculty. Guided by one of my own primary consciousnesses, I have represented a commutation and transfer of internal feelings, co-operating with external accidents to plant, for
immortality, images of sound and sight, in the celestial soil of the
Imagination. The Boy, ("There was a Boy") there introduced, is
listening, with something of a feverish and restless anxiety, for the
recurrence of the riotous sounds which he had previously excited;
and, at the moment when the intenseness of his mind is beginning
to remit, he is surprised into a perception of the solemn and tranquillizing images which the Poem describes.—The Poems next in
succession exhibit the faculty exerting itself upon various objects
of the external universe; then follow others, where it is employed
upon feelings, characters, and actions: and the Class is concluded
with imaginative pictures of moral, political, and religious sentiments.[6]

That he clearly regarded Fancy as being transformed into
Imagination, in exact accord with the theory developed in *The
Prelude* and *The Excursion,* is shown by a paragraph which
was later suppressed:

Awe-stricken as I am by contemplating the operations of the mind
of this truly divine Poet (Milton), I scarcely dare venture to add
that, "An Address to an Infant," which the Reader will find under
the class of Fancy in the present Volumes, exhibits something of this
communion and interchange of instruments and functions between
the two powers (of Fancy and Imagination); and is, accordingly,
placed last in the class, as a preparation for that of Imagination
which follows.[7]

It must constantly be remembered that Wordsworth explicitly says that his classification is made on the basis not of the
power which exclusively produces the poems, but which is predominant:

As I wish to guard against the possibility of misleading by this
classification, it is proper first to remind the Reader, that certain
poems are placed according to the powers of mind, in the Author's
conception, predominant in the production of them; *predominant,*

---

    [6] In 1815 edition. It is, perhaps, unnecessary to remind the reader that
this is thoroughly Hartleian, the last three categories corresponding to
Hartley's culminating classes of pleasures and pains. See p. 102.
    [7] Edition of 1815.

which implies the exertion of other faculties in less degree. Where there is more imagination than fancy in a poem, it is placed under the head of imagination, and *vice versa*. Both the above classes might without impropriety have been enlarged from that consisting of "Poems founded on the Affections"; as might this latter from those, and from the class "proceeding from Sentiment and Reflection." The most striking characteristics of each piece, mutual illustration, variety, and proportion, have governed me throughout.[8]

These statements very clearly indicate that Wordsworth's primary thought in the classification of his poems was exactly what he says, namely, to present them as a whole and as an adjunct to the philosophical poem; that is to present them as a statement of the development of man from childhood to age; and thus he considers all the subdivisions of his classification to be subordinate to this general idea, even to the extent of a redistribution of the poems in the most important categories. His ultimate purpose was so to arrange his minor poems that they should produce the effect which is made by one artistic whole, with a beginning, a middle, and an end, and to indicate clearly that they deal as a whole with the same topic as that of the philosophic poem. All other purposes were subordinate to this: hence the shifting of poems from one class to the other, which he practiced in every subsequent edition, is to be explained not by attributing to him inconsistency, but by remembering this larger purpose—a purpose which was not derived from any sudden impulse but one which had long presented itself habitually to his mind,[9] and thus was of as early a date as the plan of the philosophical poem itself. This plan, as I shall explain in the next succeeding chapters, is none other than that of a study of man's mind as he acquires knowledge by direct contact with reality and thus feels and acknowledges the vividness of the sensation and emotion which accompany that vital knowledge that alone leads to wisdom, and so to the retention of hope by the individual, and its recovery by all who have been misled by sham, second-hand knowledge and are willing to walk the way of Truth and Wisdom. This is the theme of the great philosophic poem, as represented by *The*

---

[8] *Preface* of 1815. Compare pp. 167-168.
[9] *Preface* of 1815.

Prelude and *The Excursion:* it is also the theme of the shorter poems, where it is more miscellaneously and variously treated.

I shall now study certain of these poems, taking them up, as a rule, in chronological order, and interpreting them in the light of Wordsworth's own explanations, and always with reference to the general categories which the poet makes use of in classifying them.

As we have seen, the poet asserts in 1800 that the poems of 1798 and 1800 have as a purpose the illustration of "the manner in which our feelings and ideas are associated in a state of excitement," which purpose he defines as following "the fluxes and refluxes of the mind when agitated by the great and simple affections of our nature."[10] This purpose is expressed in another way; to give "the history or science of the feelings."[11] By "feelings" here, he means those feelings which, according to Wordsworth's associationistic philosophy, arise out of thought, as he explains in this *Preface,* and as we have already sufficiently indicated.[12]

Among "the great and simple affections of our nature" is mother love, spoken of by Wordsworth as the "maternal passion." On this the *Lyrical Ballads* has four poems—*The Thorn, The Mad Mother, The Idiot Boy* and *The Complaint of a Forsaken Indian Woman.* Of this group not much need be said, with the exception of *The Idiot Boy.* This poem has been made the jest of many a critic; but many are deceived by the title, not seeing that the subject is mother-love in its most absolute form, asking no return, poured out not upon a brilliant child but on an idiot, unaware of the pathos or ridiculousness of itself, and claiming no reward. Thus the mother is the centre of the story: and we do injustice to the poet when we lay undue stress upon the object of the mother's love. If we but keep in mind that she is the incarnation, in its purest and most absolute form, of one of the greatest passions of human nature, the poem will not appear ridiculous, as some have made it out to be.

---

[10] *Preface* of 1800.
[11] Note to *The Thorn,* 1800.
[12] Chs. VI, pp. 104-107 ; IX, pp. 160-161.

To the corresponding passion, paternal love, he has devoted a pair of poems concerning an idealization of Wordsworth's former teacher, *Two April Mornings* and *The Fountain*. The narrator is a mature man who tells of an incident which happened to him in his childhood. The old man tells the child, with whom he is out walking, that thirty years ago he visited his daughter's grave on just such a morning in April as that on which he is relating the incident. His daughter had died at nine years of age. He stopped beside her grave:

> Six feet in earth my Emma lay;
> And yet I loved her more,
> For so it seemed, than till that day,
> I e'er had loved before.

He turned from the grave, and he met a beautiful young girl,— and he did not wish her his! The narrator remembers this surprising ending to the old man's story: he did not then know the strange facts of parental love—that a child who is one's own can never be replaced by one who is not. Almost the same idea is expressed in *The Fountain*. The old man is sad, and bewails the loss of kindred; and the boy exclaims that he could be a son to him. But the old man knows better than that, and says, "Alas! that cannot be." It would be very pretty, very sentimental, if it could be, but the facts of human nature make such a cheap solution of life's difficulties a mere Utopian dream. *The Childless Father* is the picture of the father who cannot grow accustomed to the fact that his daughter is dead. When he goes to the chase, he says to himself, as if to remind himself, "This key I must take, for my Ellen is dead." Simple indeed, but elemental in truth to human fact—"a natural delineation of human passions."

Fraternal love has its representative in *The Brothers*, a story of the love between brothers which has withstood years of separation and burns all the more brightly in the hour when Leonard hears the story of his brother's death and realizes the tragedy which had been enacted in his absence.

Love between the sexes is displayed in various forms: self-imposed death, in *Ellen Irwin;* the strange thoughts of the lover, who fears that his sweetheart may die before he reaches her home, in *Strange Fits of Passion*—a strange bit of human psychology not understood by everyone; perhaps only by lovers, as the poet intimates:

> Strange fits of passion I have known:
> And I will dare to tell,
> But in the Lover's ear alone,
> What once to me befel.

Counter pictures of the reality of death are given in *She Dwelt among the Untrodden Ways,* and *A Slumber did my Spirit Seal,* culminating in the last, with its resolute facing of the inevitable:

> No motion has she now, no force;
> She neither hears nor sees,
> Rolled round in earth's diurnal course
> With rocks and stones and trees!

The "passion of death" is displayed by two contrasting pictures; the adult and the child. *The Complaint of a Forsaken Indian Woman* belongs in this class, for it is the account of a mother in the presence of death—the account is actually given in Hearne's *Voyage to the Northern Ocean.* The child's notion of death is presented in *We Are Seven.* This is a much disputed poem, but one which seems perfectly simple if we keep the theme in mind. In the first place, the poem is anti-Rousseauistic. The Savoyard Vicar in *Emile* holds that the fear of death is innate: but Wordsworth met this little unedu- cated, unsophisticated girl, and he discovered that Rousseau's principle is not true, for she made no distinction between the living and the dead. This is a thoroughly associationistic poem, for the child's insensibility to death is accounted for by the life that is in her limbs. She has not yet received even such an elementary lesson in feeling for others as is given by the expiring candle, in the *Letter* to "Mathetes." She has the utter self-concentration, and insensibility of the child. Pro- fessor A. C. Bradley argues that the child has not the idea of death because she has a feeling for immortality. But the idea of immortality is just as far removed from the child as is the fear of death; that is, immortality as a judgment and ap- plicable to others. To explain one by the other is therefore the principle of *ignotum per ignotius;* besides there is in the child mind no necessary connection between the two. Wordsworth is perfectly explicit on this point in the Fenwick note on the *Ode:*

Nothing was more difficult for me in childhood than to admit the notion of death as a state applicable to my own being. I have said elsewhere—

> "A simple child,
> That lightly draws its breath,
> And feels its life in every limb,
> What should it know of death!"—

But it was not so much from feelings of animal vivacity that *my* difficulty came as from a sense of the indomitableness of the Spirit within me. I used to brood over the stories of Enoch and Elijah, and almost to persuade myself that, whatever might become of others, I should be translated, in something of the same way, to heaven. With a feeling congenial to this, I was often unable to think of external things as having external existence, and I communed with all that I saw as something not apart from, but inherent in, my own immaterial nature. Many times while going to school I have grasped at a wall or a tree to recall myself from this abyss of idealism to the reality. . . . To that dream-like vividness and splendour which invest objects of sight in childhood, every one, I believe, if he would look back, could bear testimony, and I need not dwell upon it here.

Wordsworth here expressly states that it is because of "feelings of animal vivacity" that the little girl cannot admit the notion of death, at the same time distinguishing his own case from hers, as he could not admit such a notion because of his "sense of the indomitableness of the Spirit" within him. The result of either of these feelings is a sense of personal identity, and the consequent impossibility on the part of the child to admit the idea of personal annihilation, and so of the annihilation of others. That is to say, the child has no general notion of death, as its mind is not sufficiently developed to entertain such a general judgment. But the germs are there, and, in accordance with associationistic principles these will develop into a judgment which will include not only the idea of death but the belief in immortality. But such a judgment or belief is beyond the child; it will arrive only with maturity.

Professor Bradley uses as a proof of the correctness of his interpretation of the poem a passage from the *Essay upon Epitaphs:*

Forlorn, and cut off from communication with the best part of his nature must that man be, who should derive the sense of immortality, as it exists in the mind of a child, from the same unthinking gaiety or liveliness of animal spirits with which the lamb in the meadow, or any other irrational creature is endowed; who should ascribe it, in short, to blank ignorance in the child; to an inability arising from the imperfect state of his faculties to come, in any point of his being, into contact with a notion of death; or to an unreflecting acquiescence in what had been instilled into him!

But this "sense of immortality" is not a judgment on the part of the child; it is an unconscious feeling arising from the assurance of self-identity so characteristic of childhood, and so any child would have answered as the little girl did, and denied the thought that the departed are annihilated. It is true that Wordsworth speaks of the child meditating upon death and immortality, but we should note that they meditate "feelingly." That is to say, they do not employ the judgments of maturity, but of childhood, which are rather impressions, sensations, and feelings than thoughts. To connect such ideas as death and immortality in a single idea is beyond the child, and all children would make an answer similar to that of the little maid. Therefore, despite Professor Bradley's doubts, the thought of the poem is expressed in the opening stanza, if we give it the proper Wordsworthian interpretation in terms of associationism.[13]

There are a number of anti-Godwinian poems in the *Lyrical Ballads: Anecdote for Fathers, Lines Written at a Small Distance (To My Sister), The Last of the Flock, Expostulation and Reply, The Tables Turned,* and *Michael,* each one directed toward the assertion of some human affection or passion, or an all-important thing in actual humanity, which has its proper place in the scheme of things, and which cannot be displaced by reason in the abstract, as conceived by Godwin. In the *Anecdote for Fathers* we observe the vagrant wish of the child to be in a place which is not the place he is in, when questioned by

---

[13] Professor Bradley's stimulating doubts are expressed in *Oxford Lectures on Poetry,* 146-148. The *Essay upon Epitaphs* belongs to the years 1809-1810, being published in *The Friend,* Feb. 22, 1810.

the father, and this thoughtless wish in turn bolstered up by still another vagrant statement, which is a lie. It is an example of the intrusion of the adult mind with its reasons and its ideas of cause and effect, into the unthinking mind of the child. This is the wisdom which the poet learned from his "dearest boy." No wonder he was thankful; for it is a confirmation of the fundamentals of associationism. *The Last of the Flock* and *Michael* are poems based on the "passion of property," of ownership, and are a counterblast to Godwin's attack on property as the great evil of society. The first is a very simple case: the man has fallen into poverty and has lost his manliness— he "weeps on the public roads alone!" *Michael* is a much more complicated case, because the property involved is landed property, and because with this love of property is united love for his son; the two loves strengthening each other, and the love of property sustaining him after the son disappears. That this was the intention of the poet is made perfectly clear by his letter to Tom Poole:

I have attempted to give a picture of a man, of strong mind and lively sensibility, agitated by two of the most powerful affections of the human heart—the parental affection, and the love of property, *landed* property, including the feelings of inheritance, home and personal and family independence.[14]

This declaration of his purpose is confirmed by the long letter which he wrote to Charles James Fox, January 14, 1801, in which he explains that in *The Brothers* and *Michael* he attempts "to draw a picture of the domestic affections," as he knows them to exist among the farmers of the north of England, proprietors of estates which have descended to them by inheritance, and so the highest type of men.[15] By all the Godwinian reasoning these ought to be the worst of men; but they develop Michaels and Leonards instead.[16]

The poems, *Lines Written at a Small Distance (To My Sister), Expostulation and Reply, The Tables Turned,* and

---

[14] Mrs. Henry Sandford, *Thomas Poole and his Friends*, 2 vols., 1888, II, 54-56.

[15] *Letters of the Wordsworth Family*, I, 137-139.

[16] Compare Southey in *The Doctor:* "To have held these small patrimonies, as well as enlarged, through so many generations, implies more contentment, more happiness, and a more uniform course of steadiness and good conduct, than could be found in the proudest genealogies."

Lines Written in Early Spring form a group which deals with primary sensations and the emotional reactions which accompany them. They are thus a discussion of one of Wordsworth's favorite subjects, and of one of the central doctrines of associationism. What is the origin of the guide of life? What is real knowledge and whence does it come? Surely, from experience. Hence we must keep our senses open; for we do not know when the decisive experience may come. It may not seem important at the time, but the processes of life will make it known. This is another form of the principle of the "ties that bind," of the "spots of time," which at once constitute the unity of our consciousness and determine its quality.[17] Thus interpreted in the light of Wordsworth's whole doctrine, these poems, which lay such stress on immediate experience and the real knowledge and morals developed from it, are not mystical, or playful sallies, but brief, unguarded statements of principles which he stated more carefully and precisely later. They are expressed with the "first fine, careless rapture" of a new discoverer, without the saving clauses which would have been added in a more prosaic statement of them and a more careful definition of the terms. With these saving clauses and definitions, the poems contrast false, secondary reason, taken on mere faith, with the warm, immediate experience of sensation, the very vividness and visionary quality of which is a guarantee that it will develop into real knowledge, because it is based on both inner and outer reality. Hence it is not "mystical and idle" to say:

> One moment now may give us more
> Than fifty years of reason,[18]

or that

> One impulse from a vernal wood
>   May teach you more of man;
> Of moral evil and of good,
>   Than all the sages can,[19]

especially if it is kept in mind that these last lines are the reply to a strong statement regarding the value of just those "sages"

[17] See the whole of Chapter VIII, *The Active Principle.*
[18] *Lines Written at a Small Distance (To My Sister).*
[19] *The Tables Turned.*

—the "philosophes" of the French Revolution—who had brought the world to such a pass, and against whom he warned the young William Hazlitt.[20]

The "passiveness" advocated in *Expostulation and Reply* need not give us so much difficulty as it has caused some critics if we interpret it in connection with the general problem of knowledge as Wordsworth conceives it. As we have explained,[21] the mind must be passive in all simple sensations; therefore if the adult is to obtain such fresh sensations as can be assimilated by the principle of association, he must allow his senses to operate. Our senses are alive at all times:

> The eye it cannot chuse but see,
>   We cannot bid the ear be still;
> Our bodies feel, where'er they be,
>   Against, or with our will;

therefore let us profit by this, and allow new impressions to come in upon us. Our knowledge is always in the making, if we have that activity which we ought to have. Let us therefore be passive *wisely:*

> Nor less I deem that there are powers,
>   Which of themselves our minds impress,
> That we can feed this mind of ours,
>   In a wise passiveness.

But this does not mean permanent passiveness and lethargy: it means the passiveness of the active will to suit its own purposes, the passiveness of the creative poet, which is the preliminary to the activity of the *creative* faculty, in order that he may be certain that his creations are made up of the facts and realities of the real world.[22]

Those who regard Wordsworth as a preacher of the doctrine that Nature is the cure-all of human ills, should ponder *Ruth.* Ruth's husband lived in the open air, in England, in Georgia, and on the ocean; but he got nothing but evil. Why is this? Because he *gave* nothing in the way of feeling,

---

[20] See the *Advertisement* of 1798, in which he gives the origin of *Expostulation and Reply* and *The Tables Turned.* Hazlitt's *My First Acquaintance with Poets,* indicates that he was the person so warned.

[21] Chapter VIII, *The Active Principle.*

[22] *Preface* to the *Poems* of 1815. See pages 115; 140-142.

so that his mind had nothing to transmute into the higher forms of feeling, and he developed into a savage and never reached the moral heights of a man. In contrast stands the little lyric, *Three Years She Grew,* an ideal picture of what normal human development might be, in which both the law and the impulse, the kindling and restraining power of nature lead to the perfect development of beauty and grace. But the child dies and leaves only the memory of herself. The poem is the poignant regret of a parent's heart, and the thought of what might have been.

In the second edition of the *Ballads* there are two extracts from the philosophical poem, *There Was a Boy* and *Nutting,* both of which are studies of the strange yet familiar workings of the mind in its early contact with "this visible universe." These poems represent the first elemental reactions of the mind to its perceptions, those faint beginnings of reason and imagination. Wordsworth himself has fully explained both in the paragraph noted in this chapter from the first edition of the *Preface* of 1815, in terms which show clearly that neither is meant in a "mystical and idle sense," but as a picture of the first beginnings of that mutation of mental contents into the higher and "purer" forms of mind, in accordance with associationism.

Ruth's husband is left in his hardness of heart and abandonment, as if there were nothing more to tell of him. Is there any possibility of such a man as he attaining to wisdom? As if to answer that question, Wordsworth writes *Peter Bell.*[23] This poem has been the centre of controversy from its first composition, and has continued to be so up to the present time. I shall not attempt even to summarize this discussion, but shall study the poem from what I conceive to be Wordsworth's point of view.[24] Like Ruth's husband, Peter was immoral, cruel, unsocial, living in the open air, and travelling in sight of the grand, the fair, and the beautiful. But he might as well have been closely confined in the Fleet prison; for to all that he saw and experienced he had no reactions—neither heart nor head was the better. Nature never found her way to his cen-

[23] Written, 1798; published, 1819.

[24] A brief review of the unfavorable criticisms is given in Edmund Gosse's essay, "Peter Bell and His Tormentors," in *Gossip in a Library,* 215-224.

tral consciousness; that is to say, his experiences never made an impression, because he gave nothing of himself and so never furnished any materials for his mind to transmute into the higher forms of thought and affection. Hence, according to the famous stanza,

> In vain, through every changeful year,
> Did Nature lead him as before;
> A primrose by a river's brim
> A yellow primrose was to him,
> And it was nothing more.

How can such a person begin the way to wisdom and love of man? In *The Prelude* Wordsworth discusses the ways in which the immortal spirit of man grows, and makes special mention of the "severer interventions," "more palpable" than the usual experience, as best might suit Nature's own aims.[25] Here we have the clue to *Peter Bell:* no ordinary experience will do. It must be a unique one, with moonlight, death, sorrow of child, of son, of mother and wife, of religion, of explosion in the mine beneath the terrified man's feet, of the ass with its strange ways and unaccountable devotion, of Methodist preacher striking fear into the heart, of ruins, of hills, of vales, of river-depths and retired meadow, all mingled into one combined terror, which, by its sheer impelling force beats its way into Peter's stubborn heart. The opening made, all follows according to system, one might say, as expounded in *The Excursion.*[26] The emotion aroused will develop into the higher forms of feeling—sympathy, theopathy, and the moral sense. He thinks of his past, he experiences remorse, and then a new feeling comes to him:

> He feels what he for human-kind
> Has never felt before,

that is Sympathy. He has made the discovery "That man's heart is a holy thing," and feels sympathy for it. He has undergone the new birth; he forsakes his folly; and, "remanded back to nature," according to the principle laid down in the *Letter* to "Mathetes" and *The Excursion,* he passes

---

[25] *The Prelude*, I, 340-356.
[26] Chapters VI and XII.

13

through the stage of youth in his belated development, and suffers youth's pains of melancholy for ten months, and ultimately becomes "a good and honest man." The poem is a very bold experiment, for one would expect a serious subject, such as the correct way of life and how to begin it treated with a greater dignity;[27] and it is small wonder that the poem has appeared ridiculous to many. The poet composed the poem "under a belief that the Imagination does not require for its exercise the intervention of supernatural agency, but that, though such agency be excluded, the faculty may be called forth as imperiously, and for kindred results of pleasure, by incidents within the compass of poetic probability, in the humblest departments of daily life.[28] This may be true; but Wordsworth should have known that a low pedlar and an ass may easily spoil any poem for the average reader; for it is a very easy matter to turn them into a jest. It is probably only too true that if he had used Richardson's Lovelace and Androcles' lion as the leading characters of his poem, the story would have been found edifying by many who now know it only as a thing to be treated with contempt.[29]

The *Poems in Two Volumes,* 1807, continued the work of the *Lyrical Ballads* in many particulars; but some new and important tendencies made themselves felt, especially *Duty and Patriotism.* The *Ode to Duty* is the expression of the ethical aspect of the problems of knowledge, which make up the subjects of such poems as *Tintern Abbey* and the *Ode.* Growth of the individual mind implies a growth toward sympathy, theopathy, and the moral sense; and nothing is higher in this development than duty, which is the ethical expression of the law of reason; and so he prays for this consummation:

> I myself commend
> Unto thy guidance from this hour
> Oh! let my weakness have an end!
> Give unto me, made lowly wise,
> The spirit of self-sacrifice;

---

[27] This is how the problem is put in *The Excursion,* IV. See Chapter XII.

[28] Dedication of *Peter Bell,* 1819.

[29] The most complete interpretation of the poem so far published is to be found in O. J. Campbell, *Sentimental Morality in Wordsworth's Narrative Poems,* University of Wisconsin Studies in Language and Literature, No. 11.

The confidence of reason give;
And in the light of truth thy Bondman let me live![30]

This poem is his earliest statement of the ethical law of Duty, which he afterwards develops at length in the fourth book of *The Excursion*.[31]

The subject of patriotism is much more fully expressed, especially in the "Sonnets dedicated to Liberty." This topic is one immediately connected with duty, and grows out of it. The French Revolution had failed because it was based on a false ideal, and Napoleon had made himself the representative of the results of that false thought. Hence, Wordsworth, who believes that the hopes of man had been absurdly raised and as basely lowered by that false knowledge which was behind the revolution, is the enemy of Napoleon; and as England is the special object of Napoleon's attack, Wordsworth is all the more an enemy of Napoleon. For England, as Wordsworth believes, with all her faults, is the hope of the world, as she alone gives liberty to those within her borders. From this source springs that magnificent series of Sonnets, in which high-souled patriotism is mingled with the most sublime ethical love of the high and scorn of the low, so absolutely unique that in 1914, when the world was falling, Englishmen turned to him as the sole English poet who had shown that duty and patriotism can be one.[32]

Meanwhile the method of *Tintern Abbey* was being continued; for Wordsworth was always the explorer, and never took the attitude of having discovered all. This is seen in three poems; *To the Cuckoo, Peele Castle,* and the *Ode. To the Cuckoo* is regarded by many as Wordsworth's most characteristically successful poem; and they are right, in so far as they

---

[30] The *Ode to Duty* was composed in 1805, probably before the drowning of Wordsworth's brother John. At least he says he was "untried" as yet.

[31] See Chapter XII. For Wordsworth's thoroughly associationistic account of the development of the sense of Duty, see also the *Letter* to "Mathetes" and the *Essay upon Epitaphs*.

[32] For example see *Wordsworth's Patriotic Poetry*, edited by the Right Honorable Arthur H. D. Acland, and dedicated to Viscount Grey of Falloden, Oxford, 1915. The volume has a worthy introduction, and reprints *The Happy Warrior* and thirty-five sonnets, with useful notes. For an excellent discussion of Wordsworth's patriotism, see A. V. Dicey, *The Statesmanship of Wordsworth, An Essay*, 1917. See also Wordsworth's *Tract on the Convention of Cintra*, with an introduction by A. V. Dicey, 1915.

claim that the poem is characteristic in method. It will be worth while to consider some details in connection with it. The poem is very clearly modelled upon an *Ode to the Cuckoo*, written by John Logan (1748-1788), or by Michael Bruce (1746-1767), and found by Wordsworth in Anderson's *Poets*. In order to discuss Wordsworth's poem it will be necessary to have its progenitor before us:

ODE

TO THE CUCKOO

1. Hail, beauteous stranger of the grove!
     Thou messenger of Spring!
   Now Heaven repairs thy rural seat,
     And woods thy welcome ring.

2. What time the daisy decks the green,
     Thy certain voice we hear;
   Hast thou a star to guide thy path,
     Or mark the rolling year?

3. Delightful visitant! with thee
     I hail the time of flowers,
   And hear the sounds of music sweet
     From birds among the bowers.

4. The school-boy wandering thro' the woods
     To pull the primrose gay,
   Starts, the new voice of Spring to hear,
     And imitates thy lay.

5. What time the pea puts on the bloom
     Thou fliest thy vocal vale,
   An annual guest in other lands,
     Another Spring to hail.

6. Sweet bird! thy bower is ever green,
     Thy sky is ever clear;
   Thou hast no sorrow in thy song,
     No winter in thy year!

7. O could I fly, I'd fly with thee!
     We'd make, with joyful wing,
   Our annual visit o'er the globe,
     Companions of the Spring.

This is a very charming account of the habits of the bird, with emphasis on the fact that it is migratory, and so enjoys eternal summer. With Wordsworth, on the other hand, the bird becomes a symbol around which his reminiscence gathers, the image of all the "visionary" hours of school-boy days, of those "glad animal" feelings so vivid and so evanescent. The poem is thus the opening movement, as it were, of an Ode on the Three Ages, and is the thought actually expressed in *Tintern Abbey,* the *Ode,* and the first two books of *The Prelude.* It differs from these only in the fact that for one fleeting moment the world seems to the adult the "unsubstantial, faery place" which it is to the child in his "golden prime." But only for a moment; for with the fading of the cuckoo's note the stern realities will again assert themselves.

The White Doe of Rylstone is one of the longest of Wordsworth's shorter poems. It was composed from 1807 to 1810, and was no doubt given some attention up to the year of its publication, in 1815. It is an interpretation of a tradition connected with Bolton Priory, in Yorkshire, which Wordsworth had learned locally, and of the ballad in Percy's *Reliques of Ancient English Poetry,* entitled *The Rising of the North.* It is the story of the Catholic Nortons, who rise against Queen Elizabeth, contrary to the advice of Francis, one of the sons of the house. They offer battle, and meet with defeat and death. The sole sister of the house, Emily, a Protestant like Francis, remains at home, and Francis will not fight on either side. He too is slain; and Emily is left alone, apparently without hope. But such is the strength of her mind that she conquers sorrow and wins peace:

> Her soul doth in itself stand fast,
> Sustained by memory of the past
> And strength of Reason; held above
> The infirmities of mortal love.

Of this peace obtained through suffering the white doe of the legend is the symbol. Wordsworth's purpose is to represent "the subduing of the will, and the inferior fancies, to the perfect purifying and spiritualising of the intellectual nature."[33] The poem represents the fullest spirituality possible to man, the sublimation of the love of God (theopathy) and the moral

[33] *Memoirs of Wordsworth,* II, 311.

sense. The language of Hartley expresses the spirit of the poem exactly:

Since God is the source of all good, and consequently must at last appear to be so, *i. e.* be associated with all our pleasures, it seems to follow, even from this proposition, that the idea of God, and of the ways by which his goodness and happiness are made manifest, must at last, take place of, and absorb all other ideas, and HE himself become, according to the language of the scriptures, all in all.[34]

Our eighth chapter develops Wordsworth's conception of the unity of the mind of the individual, despite its disparate experiences; and attempts to explain his application of it to the solution of the problems arising out of the peculiarities of human consciousness and development. In our discussion of *The Excursion* we shall see how this idea is applied to the problems of life. Fortunately for us, if we wish to study this important subject farther, and in a form which is quite distinct from that of *The Excursion,* we have at hand a poem of quite another sort, which deals with this same problem. This is that sonnet sequence entitled *The River Duddon: A Series of Sonnets,* composed between the years 1806 and 1820, the last date being their year of publication as a series. In the valuable introductory note to the collection Wordsworth gives us an explanation of the actual experiences which lie back of the poems. He became acquainted with the river Duddon in early boyhood, on one occasion undergoing an experience which was peculiarly distressing. In his college vacation he again had intimate experiences in connection with it, and in his mature years he had affecting experiences on its banks as late as 1811. The river was thus an object of long and familiar acquaintance, and was an excellent object to illustrate how one experience in childhood will lend deeper significance to all other subsequent ones "if once we have been strong." In a note we learn that as early as 1798 Coleridge had spoken of writing a rural poem

[34] *Observations on Man,* I, 114.

The Brook,[35] and for many years Wordsworth had developed the same idea, quite unconscious that he was trespassing on his friend's ground.

On reflection, however, Wordsworth decided that a particular poem such as Coleridge planned could hardly much interfere with a general one as he himself had composed. Thus the river long known merged with the symbol long held in the poet's mind in expressing an idea which was constantly before his mind, and the result is this sequence of sonnets. The symbol is the river traced from its home among the clouds and hills with its prehistoric and its human associations, a child of the mists at last mingling with the great ocean; an image of the soul of man traced from its first faint beginnings, through its growth, to its final mingling with Eternity. But the symbol is not general only; it is not *any* river, but the Duddon, long and lovingly known and the symbol of the harmonizing powers of human life. In the introductory note he says; "Little did I think then (in boyhood) it would be my lot to celebrate, in a strain of love and admiration, the stream which for many years I never thought of without recollections of disappointment and distress"; and in the poem he echoes,

> Return, Content! for fondly I pursued,
> Even when a child, the Streams—unheard, unseen;
> Through tangled woods, impending rocks between;
> Or, free as air, with flying inquest viewed
> The sullen reservoirs whence their bold brood—
> Pure as the morning, fretful, boisterous, keen,
> Green as the salt-sea billows, white and green—
> Poured down the hills, a choral multitude!
> Nor have I traced their course for scanty gains;
> They taught me random cares and truant joys,

---

[35] Coleridge's account of his plan is to be found in *Biographia Literaria*, Ch. X: "I sought for a subject, that should give equal room and freedom for description, incident. and impassioned reflections on men, nature, and society. yet supply in itself a natural connection to the parts, and unity to the whole. Such a subject I conceived myself to have found in a stream, traced from its source in the hills among the yellow-red moss and conical glass-shaped tufts of bent, to the first break or fall. where its drop becomes audible, and it begins to form a channel; thence to the peat and turf barn, itself built of the same dark squares as it sheltered; to the sheepfold; to the first cultivated plot of ground; to the lonely cottage and its bleak garden won from the heath; to the hamlet, the villages, the market-town, the manufactures. and the seaport."

Wordsworth makes reference to this statement in his note, and may have been stimulated by it to bring his long drawn out labor to a conclusion.

That shield from mischief and preserve from stains
Vague minds, while men are growing out of boys;
Maturer Fancy owes to their rough noise
Impetuous thoughts that brook not servile reins.[36]

But the poet does not forget the universal. The thought of the course of man in the race as well as in the individual is clearly expressed throughout the series. In the concluding sonnet, *After-Thought,* the symbol is made still more clear. The ever-gliding stream is a type of the ever-vanishing, yet ever developing race of man, who lives "by Admiration, Hope and Love," and "breathes the sweet air of futurity." Here this sequence of sonnets identifies itself with the great philosophic poem: as a worthy "adjunct," in accordance with the poet's complete design of his work as a poet. In this characteristic it is a type and consummation of the minor poems as a whole, which Wordsworth designed to form an essential part of his message, and which he earnestly strove to classify and arrange so as to show as clearly as might be the various contributions which each of them makes towards the solution of the deep mysteries of man, and nature and human life, which are more systematically discussed in the great philosophic poem:

AFTER-THOUGHT

I thought of Thee, my partner and my guide,
As being past away.—Vain sympathies!
For, backward, Duddon! as I cast my eyes,
I see what was, and is, and will abide;
Still glides the Stream, and shall for ever glide;
The Form remains, the Function never dies;
While we, the brave, the mighty, and the wise,
We Men, who in our morn of youth defied
The elements, must vanish;—be it so!
Enough, if something from our hands have power
To live, and act, and serve the future hour;
And if, as toward the silent tomb we go,
Through love, through hope, and faith's transcendent dower,
We feel that we are greater than we know.

---

[36] No. XXVI.

CHAPTER XI

THE PHILOSOPHIC POEM: *THE PRELUDE* AND PERSONAL READJUSTMENT

> O Friend! O Teacher! God's great Gift to me!
> Into my heart I have receiv'd that Lay,
> More than historic, that prophetic Lay,
> Wherein (high theme by Thee first sung aright)
> Of the Foundations and the Building up
> Of thy own Spirit, thou hast lov'd to tell
> What may be told, to th' understanding mind
> Revealable; and what within the mind
> May rise enkindled. Theme as hard as high!
> . . . . An Orphic Tale indeed,
> A Tale divine of high and passionate Thoughts
> To their own music chaunted!
>
> Samuel Taylor Coleridge,
> *To W. Wordsworth*, 1807.

We have presented evidence in the fifth chapter that the plan of a philosophical poem was formed by Wordsworth not long after 1795, and so it may be held as certain that the plan of a long poem was in his mind earlier than the plan of a series of short lyrics or ballads. Thus, if we are to study Wordsworth from the point of view of his intentions, we cannot ignore this "great philosophic poem" in its development towards such degree of completion as it ever attained. In this and the succeeding chapter we shall deal with specific problems of theme and method in *The Prelude* and *The Excursion*.

As we have seen, the earliest mention by Wordsworth himself of the philosophical poem is in a letter dated March 6, 1798, written to James Tobin:

I have written 1300 lines of a poem in which I contrive to convey most of the knowledge of which I am possessed. My object is to give pictures of Nature, Man, and Society. Indeed, I know not anything which will not come within the scope of my plan.[1]

---

[1] *Letters of the Wordsworth Family*, I, 115.

A few days later, March 11, 1798, he writes to James Losh:

I have written 706 lines of a poem which I hope to make of considerable utility. Its title will be *The Recluse; or, Views of Nature, Man, and Society.*[2]

Coleridge shows his great interest in the poem, on which he had obviously been consulted, by writing to Wordsworth in the summer of 1799: "I am anxiously eager to have you steadily employed on *The Recluse*,"[3] and on October 12 of the same year he urges Wordsworth to proceed with his poem:

I long to see what you have been doing. O let it be the tail-piece of *The Recluse!* for of nothing but The Recluse can I hear patiently. That it is to be addressed to me makes me more desirous that it should not be a poem of itself. To be addressed, as a beloved man, by a thinker, at the close of such a poem as "The Recluse," a poem *non unius populi*, is the only event, I believe, capable of inciting in me an hour's vanity—vanity, nay, it is too good a feeling to be so called; it would indeed be a self-elevation produced *ab extra.*[4]

The Wordsworth correspondence does not make specific mention of any poem which can be identified as *The Prelude*[5] earlier than the beginning of 1804, but within the poem itself we have positive information that it was begun in the spring of 1795, the preamble being written then,[6] after which "short-lived transport," "a less impetuous stream" flowed awhile; that is, during 1799-1800; then ceased until the summer of 1804, and continued with few interruptions until its completion in June 1805.[7] The first two books were probably written in 1799-1800, and the poem was taken up again early in 1804. In a letter written to Francis Wrangham at this time Wordsworth speaks of *The Prelude,* and mentions the other two parts of the philosophical poem:

[2] *Letters of the Wordsworth Family,* III, 359.
[3] *Memoirs of Wordsworth,* I, 159.
[4] *Op. cit.,* I, 159.
[5] I use this title for convenience. Wordsworth never gave the poem a specific title, but refers to it as "the poem on my early life," "the poem on my life," etc.
[6] That is, lines 1-45 of Book I. I am aware that the *Memoirs,* I, 143, gives this date as 1799. But Goslar is not "the vast city." Besides, London was "the City" to Wordsworth. Dorothy Wordsworth's letter to Mrs. Marshall, September 2, 1795, gives the very spirit of this passage. His going from London to Racedown was a veritable escape to liberty. *Letters of the Wordsworth Family,* I, 85-87.
[7] *The Prelude,* VII, 1-12.

At present I am engaged in a poem on my own earlier life, which will take five parts, or books, to complete, three of which are nearly finished. My other meditated works are a philosophical poem and a narrative one.[8]

As I have said, he here speaks of the plan of his complete philosophical poem of which *The Prelude* is to be a part—either an introduction, or a conclusion, "tail-piece," or "appendix"; (1) the poem on his own earlier life, (2) a philosophical poem, and (3) a narrative poem.

Very shortly after this date Dorothy writes to Mrs. Clarkson, February 13, 1804, announcing that she and William are well and that "he is writing the poem on his own early life, which is to be an appendix to *The Recluse*."[9]   That the poem was going forward with considerable rapidity is seen from Wordsworth's letter to De Quincey, March 6, 1804, in which he gives a number of details concerning the poem "on his own earlier life" and its connection with the greater poem:

I am now writing a poem on my own earlier life; I have just finished that part in which I speak of my residence at the University;[10] it would give me a great pleasure to read this work to you at this time, as I am sure, from the interest you have taken in the L[yrical] B[allads], that it would please you, and might also be of service to you. This poem will not be published these many years, and never during my lifetime, till I have finished a larger and more important work to which it is tributary. Of this larger work I have written one book[11] and several scattered fragments: it is a moral and philosophical poem; the subject whatever I find most interesting in Nature, Man, and Society, and most adapted to poetic illustration. To this work I mean to devote the prime of my life, and the chief force of my mind. I have also arranged the plan of a narrative poem; and if I live to finish these three principal works I shall be content. That on my own life, the least important of the three, is better than half complete, viz., four books, amounting to about 2500 lines. They are all to be in blank verse.[12]

This very important letter makes clear two things: first, the relation of "the poem on his own earlier life" to the other two

[8] *Letters of the Wordsworth Family*, I, 156.

[9] *Op. cit.*, I, 158.

[10] Book III. *Residence at Cambridge,* according to the arrangement of the materials as published in 1850. At the end of the letter he says that four books are complete, which denotes a different distribution.

[11] *Home at Grasmere,* first published 1888; or perhaps *Margaret,* now in Book I of *The Excursion.*

[12] *Letters of the Wordsworth Family*, I, 161-162.

parts of the complete poem; and, secondly, the proportions of "the poem on his earlier life," in itself. As he says in the letter to Wrangham, there are three parts in the great poem; but in this letter he gives the additional information that "the poem on his own earlier life" is "better than half complete"; that is, "four books," and so it is clear that at this date he had in mind a much shorter poem than *The Prelude* as we know it.

That the poem on his earlier life was to be comparatively brief is confirmed by the letter which he wrote to Coleridge on the same day, March 6, 1804:

> I finished five or six days ago another book of my poem amounting to six hundred and fifty lines. And now I am positively arrived at the subject I spoke of in my last. When this next book is done which I shall begin in two or three days' time, I shall consider the work as finished. Farewell. I am very anxious to have your notes for *The Recluse*. I cannot say how much importance I attach to this, if it should please God that I survive you. I should reproach myself forever in writing the work if I had neglected to procure this help.[13]

This "other book" would seem to be the book which he refers to in his letter to De Quincey; and so it seems that he means that he would regard the poem as finished with the completion of the fifth book. The writing of this fifth book is probably referred to in Dorothy's letter to Coleridge, March 29, 1804, in which she says that William had begun another part of "the poem addressed to Coleridge," and the same thing is spoken of in the addition which Wordsworth made to this letter: "I am now, after a halt of nearly three weeks, started again, and I hope to go forward rapidly."[14]

That the poem thus brought to a conclusion was regarded as a whole is indicated by the fact that when Coleridge went to Malta on April 2 of this year he took with him, copied out by the hands of Dorothy and Mary Wordsworth, these five books.

But the plan of the poem on his own life continued to grow, for on April 29, 1804, in a letter to Richard Sharp he thus gives an account of himself. In reading this passage we must remember that the first two books had been written in 1799-1800, so that the calculated three thousand lines are over and

[13] *Letters of the Wordsworth Family*, III, 459-460.
[14] *Op. cit.*, III, 462-463.

above these two books. Thus, he had written six books and a third of the seventh, which, apparently, he regards as the conclusion of the poem.

I have been very busy these last ten weeks, having written between two and three thousand lines—accurately near three thousand—in that time; namely, four books, and a third of another, of the poem which I believe I mentioned to you on my own early life. I am at present in the seventh book of this work, which will turn out far longer than I ever dreamed of. It seems a frightful deal to say about myself; and, of course, will never be published—during my lifetime, I mean—till another work has been written and published of sufficient importance to justify me in giving my own history to the world. I pray God to give me life to finish these works, which, I trust, will live, and do good; especially the one to which that, which I have been speaking of as far advanced, is only supplementary.[15]

There is not so great a discrepancy between this statement of the plan of *The Prelude* and the previous one, on March 6, 1804, as appears on the surface. It is true that on March 6, he believed that five books would complete the poem, and on April 29, he regarded seven as necessary; but this does not indicate any radical alteration of plan. It is to be noted that he usually does not speak of the poem as one which deals with his life, but with his "early," or "earlier," life. Wordsworth was thirty-four when he used these terms; and so he must mean to end the poem at a period considerably short of the age to which he had attained. Now, the fifth book brings the story of his life down to the beginning of his second year at Cambridge in 1788, when he was eighteen, and the seventh book continues it to the autumn of 1791, on the eve of his first visit to France, at the age of twenty-one. These two dates, as we have already noted in previous chapters, are of peculiar importance to Wordsworth in his explanation of his development. His seventeenth year and thereabout was the period when the peculiar activity of youth asserted itself, causing him to transfer to "unorganic natures" "his own enjoyments," and thus demonstrating that his mind has passed from the passivity of childhood to the activity of youth.[16] This period he has described at

---

[15] *Letters of the Wordsworth Family*, III, 380-382.
[16] *The Prelude*, I, 382-418. It is to be noted that the eighteenth year of The Wanderer is of great importance. At that age, Nature was paramount in his interests. *The Excursion*, I, 280-300.

length in the eighth book of the poem: the mind is active, but, being guided by Fancy, does not build its world of thought according to the truth of things, but only according to its own heart's desire, and so builds falsely.[17]   The year 1791 is also a very important date, for in January of that year he received the degree of B. A. from the University, and it was the year of his second visit to France.   That this summer was the last one marked by the capacities of youth as contrasted with those of maturity he has abundantly shown, making it clear that man held a place in his mind subordinate to nature, which was "prized for her own sake" "until not less than two and twenty summers had been told."[18]   His experiences in France, which began in this year, were to turn him into a man; and as he looks back in retrospect he views this summer as the end of youth, which was about to change to something else.   As his seventeenth year was the culmination, so his twenty-first was the end of youth, and both were notable points in his "earlier" life. Thus it is that both the fifth book and the seventh book form suitable conclusions of the poem, as it is obvious from his letters that he intended to write only on his earlier life.

His intention at this time is tolerably clear.   He proposed to write a long philosophical poem, of which the poem on his own earlier life was to be an introduction, or "portico."   Obviously, as the philosophical poem was to deal with "Man, Nature, and Society" it would be an expression of his present opinions. The poem on his own life would bring the history of his opinions up to the present, or rather, up through childhood and youth to the time of maturity.   Thus the philosophic and the narrative poems would give him ample opportunity to express his mature thoughts "on Man and Nature, and on Human Life."   These last poems were to be very much more important than the one on his early life, as it was to be merely introductory to the main poem—the portico of the cathedral, or the ante-chapel to the body of the gothic church.[19]   This is the early plan of the poem, as it was in his mind in 1798, or even earlier, and as its contents are summarized in *Tintern Abbey* in 1798.

---

[17] *The Prelude*, VIII, 340-502.
[18] *Op. cit.*, 340-355.
[19] *Preface* to *The Excursion*.

Just when he enlarged the plan of *The Prelude* so as to include within its scope the passage from youth to maturity with an elaborate presentation of his mature mind, we cannot be certain. On September 8, 1804, he writes as if the original plan was unchanged; for he tells Sir George Beaumont that he has been working on *The Recluse,* thus indicating that *The Prelude* had been laid aside as finished, having given way to the more important poem: "I wrote one book of The Recluse, nearly a thousand lines, then had to rest. Last week I began again, and have written three hundred more."[20]

But the next letter on the subject of his poetry announces a change of plan. On December 25, 1804, he tells Sir George Beaumont that he is advancing with his work, and that he has written upwards of two thousand verses during the last ten weeks. It will be noted that the verses referred to in this letter do not include the thirteen hundred odd lines mentioned in the last. Thus the change of plan in *The Prelude* which he announces in the present letter may be later than September 8, 1804. The letter continues:

I do not know if you are exactly acquainted with the plan of my poetical labour. It is two-fold—first, a poem, to be called *The Recluse:* in which will be my object to express in verse my most interesting feelings concerning Man, Nature, and Society; and next, a poem (in which I am at present chiefly engaged) on my earlier life, or the growth of my own mind, taken up upon a large scale. This latter work I expect to have finished before the month of May; and then I purpose to fall with all my might on the former, which is the chief object upon which my thoughts have been fixed these many years. Of this poem, that of The Pedlar, which Coleridge read you, is part, and I may have written of it about two thousand lines. It will consist, I hope, of ten or twelve thousand.[21]

This general plan is again referred to in a letter to Richard Sharp, written in February, 1805: "My poem advances, quick or slow as the fit comes; but I wish sadly to have it finished, in order that, after a reasonable respite, I may fall to my principal work."[22]

[20] *Letters of the Wordsworth Family,* I, 171.
[21] *Op. cit.,* I, 173.
[22] *Op. cit.,* I, 182.

We next hear of the poem on his own life "taken up upon a large scale," on May 1, 1805, in a letter to Sir George Beaumont:

Unable to proceed with this work,[23] I turned my thoughts again to the poem on my own life, and you will be glad to hear that I have added three hundred lines to it in the course of last week. Two books more will conclude it. It will be not much less than nine thousand lines,—not hundred but thousand lines long,—an alarming length! and a thing unprecedented in literary history that a man should talk so much about himself. It is not self-conceit, as you will know well, that has induced me to do this, but real humility. I began the work because I was unprepared to treat any more arduous subject, and diffident of my own powers. Here, at least, I hoped that to a certain degree I should be sure of succeeding, as I had nothing to do but describe what I had felt and thought; therefore could not easily be bewildered. This might certainly have been done in narrower compass by a man of more address; but I have done my best.[24]

The poet's hope that he might complete the poem on his life before May was fulfilled only half a month later than he expected, but the end was reached with little satisfaction to the author. On June 3, 1805, he writes to Sir George Beaumont:

I have the pleasure to say that I finished my poem about a fortnight ago. I had looked forward to the day as a most happy one; and I was indeed grateful to God for giving me life to complete the work, such as it is. But it was not a happy day for me; I was dejected on many accounts: when I looked back upon the performance it seemed to have a dead weight about it,—the reality so far short of the expectation. It was the first long labour that I had finished; and the doubt whether I should ever live to write *The Recluse*, and the sense which I had of this poem being so far below what I seemed capable of executing, depressed me much; above all, many heavy thoughts of my poor departed brother hung upon me, the joy which I should have had in showing him the manuscript, and a thousand other vain fancies and dreams. I have spoken of this because it was a state of feeling new to me, the occasion being new. This work may be considered as a sort of *portico* to *The Recluse*, part of the same building, which I hope to be able, ere long, to begin with in earnest; and if I am permitted to bring to a conclu-

---

[23] A poem in memory of his brother John, who was drowned in the wreck of his vessel, the *Abergavenny*, February 5, 1805. This poem was later finished in December, 1805, or January, 1806, and was entitled *Character of The Happy Warrior*.

[24] *Letters of the Wordsworth Family*, I, 185-186.

sion, and to write, further, a narrative poem of the epic kind, I shall consider the task of my life as over. I ought to add that I have the satisfaction of finding the present poem not quite of so alarming a length as I apprehended.[25]

The Prelude finished, the poet now turns again to the main poem, and we find him writing Sir George Beaumont on August 1, 1805, that all goes well:

Within this last month I have returned to *The Recluse*, and have written seven hundred additional lines. Should Coleridge return, so that I might have some conversation with him on the subject, I should go on swimmingly.[26]

Not long after this date other projects intervened, notably the publication of the minor poems which had collected since the second edition of the *Lyrical Ballads,* 1802, a project which was not completed until 1807.[27] *The Recluse* is not frequently mentioned after 1805, but in a letter of Dorothy's to Lady Beaumont, dated February 28 (1810), she says that after William completes certain essays for Coleridge's *Friend,* before he turns to any other labor, she hopes he will have finished three books of *The Recluse.*[28] Four years later (April 24, 1814), she announces that William is actually printing nine books of "his long poem," and expresses her thankfulness that he "has brought his mind to consent to printing so much of this work."[29]

Two days later, April 26, 1814, Wordsworth writes to his friend, Wrangham:

I am busy with the printers' devils. A portion of a long poem from me will see the light ere long. I hope it will give you pleasure. It is serious, and has been written with great labour.[30]

These "nine books" of the "long poem," thus published separately under the name of *The Excursion,* were to be the first of the philosophical poem to be published in the author's lifetime; and after this almost nothing was added to it, unless there are manuscripts in existence that are not generally

[25] *Letters of the Wordsworth Family,* I, 190.
[26] *Op. cit.,* I, 196.
[27] *Poems in Two Volumes,* 1807.
[28] *Letters of the Wordsworth Family,* I, 494.
[29] *Op. cit.,* II, 26.
[30] *Op. cit.,* II, 28.

14

known. We hear very little about it in the correspondence;
and that little indicates that the poet no longer feels able to
face the completion of the task so early undertaken and so difficult to accomplish. On April 20, 1822, Wordsworth writes
to Walter Savage Landor to this effect:

> The Recluse has had a long sleep, save in my thoughts; my MSS.
> are so ill-penned and blurred that they are useless to all but myself;
> and at present I cannot face them. But if my stomach can be pre-
> served in tolerable order, I hope you will hear of me again in the
> character chosen for the title of that poem.[31]

Dorothy, writing to Crabb Robinson, December 13, 1824,
gives small hope of the completion of the poem, in the following terms:

> My brother has not yet looked at The Recluse; he seems to feel
> the task so weighty that he shrinks from beginning with it, yet
> knows that he has now no time to loiter if another great work is to
> be accomplished by him. I say another, for I consider The Excur-
> sion as one work, though the title-page tells that it is but a part of
> one that has another title.[32]

At this point The Recluse passes out of the correspondence.
There was nothing more to tell, for apparently it was dropped
as a project, the various revisions of The Excursion, and the
final revisions of The Prelude commanding as much of the
poet's attention as he could give to the great poem.[33]

This lapse in the execution of the plan of the great poem has
commonly been attributed to failing poetic powers on the part
of Wordsworth; and there can be no doubt that this does
partly explain it. But there is a further reason. In the first
place, it is to be noted that the general plan was a very unde-
fined and mobile one—so much so that it is frequently very
difficult, or impossible to be certain which parts of the poem
are referred to. We have noted that we seem to have rather
clear evidence that The Prelude grew and grew until it attained
its present proportions, taking its beginning from a comparatively short poem. The same thing seems to have happened to

---

[31] Letters of the Wordsworth Family, II, 179.

[32] Op. cit., II. 237.

[33] There were numerous and important revisions of The Excursion in the
editions of 1827, 1832, 1837, and 1845. There are very few changes in the
1820 edition: the significant changes were made later. The Prelude received its final form in 1832.

The Excursion. We are to suppose that by *The Pedlar,* a name which occurs in the correspondence and especially in Dorothy's *Journals* from October 10, 1801, to July 8, 1802,[34] is indicated the poem which we now know by the name of *The Excursion;* but the poem of that name was finished on Friday, March 5, 1802.[35] Its length was something comparable to *The White Doe of Rylstone,* as Wordsworth was considering publishing the two together,[36] even if there is some error in Dorothy's statement that *The Pedlar* was only two hundred and eighty lines long when William arranged it and she wrote it out on July 8, 1802.[37] But when *The Excursion* appeared in print it was not a poem of two hundred and eighty lines nor one of nineteen hundred, like *The White Doe of Rylstone,* but one of eight thousand five hundred odd lines. Moreover, when it was published, it was made up of only nine books, which were extracted from the mass of manuscripts which had been written on the subject of Man, Nature, and Society.

Now, what happened is sufficiently clear. When *The Prelude* was completed in 1805 it occupied a much more important place in the general scheme than was at first intended; and in the same way the comparatively simple and brief *Pedlar* was united with the early poem *Margaret,* together with portions of the philosophical poem called *The Recluse,* the "long poem," or "views of Man, Nature, and Society." Thus it was that these two poems absorbed the matter which had been intended for *The Recluse:* and so, when the poet contemplated the main subject, he found he had already expressed his ideas on Man and Nature, and Human Life as completely as he found within himself the power and the impulse. Hence it is not strictly true to say that the parts which are spoken of as not

<hr/>

[34] *Journals of Dorothy Wordsworth,* edited by William Knight, 2 vols. 1910, I, 61-137.

[35] *Op. cit.,* I, 97.

[36] *Op. cit.,* I, 99. That is, if we can identify *The White Doe of Rylstone* with the *Yorkshire Wolds Poem* spoken of in the *Journal.* Wordsworth's *Advertisement* to *The White Doe of Rylstone* in the first edition, 1815, clearly implies that the poem was not begun before 1806. The "tale" which is referred to by Dorothy, December 6, 1807, as being not quite half done is probably *The White Doe.* But, whatever poem was meant by the title of the *Yorkshire Wolds Poem* must have been of considerable length, and no known poem of Wordsworth answers at once to this title and length except *The White Doe.*

[37] *Journals of Dorothy Wordsworth,* I, 136.

completed, were never written: they were written in large
measure, no doubt, and are to be found in the greatly enlarged
Excursion and in *The Prelude* which had been "taken up upon
a large scale" towards the end of 1804. This should be kept
in mind whenever we read any account of the changed plan of
"the great philosophical poem," even when the account is
Wordsworth's own. The facts are that while the poet did not
complete all the projected parts of the poem, he much more
than completed others. If we are to do justice to the completed parts of the poem and to the author we must remember
that the change in plan is very largely the redistribution of the
material, and not merely the failure to execute.

For the sake of definiteness it will be useful to note what the
plan of the whole "philosophical poem" was to be and in what
degree this proposed plan was completed, according to Wordsworth's own account of the matter as this is found in the letters and in the *Preface* to *The Excursion*. Both the plan and
the measure of completion may be represented in tabular form
as follows:

I. *THE PRELUDE.* (Introductory to *The Recluse,* Fourteen
Books, Published, 1850.)

II. *THE RECLUSE.* To Consist of *Three* Parts.

Part i. (One Book written. Published, 1888, with
title *Home at Grasmere.*)

Part ii. (*The Excursion.* Nine Books, Published,
1814.)

Part iii. ("Only planned." "The materials of which
it would have been formed have, however,
been incorporated for the most part, in the
Author's other Publications, written subse-
quently to *The Excursion.*") [38]

According to this outline plan the poem is about only half
finished; but we must interpret this in the light of what has
just been said concerning the vast increase in the length of Part
I *(The Prelude)* and Part II, ii *(The Excursion),* in virtue of
which parts of the poem which were thought of as occupying
a certain place in the plan when they were composed actually
found their position in quite another part of the structure.

---

[38] *Advertisement* to *The Prelude,* 1850.

Thus it is that the poem which was planned as a whole to present the views of the poet on Man, Nature, and Society preserves its unity of tone even in its unfinished state, both in style and in manner and method of treatment.   Thus it is too that *The Prelude, The Excursion,* and the fragments scattered here and there throughout his work but never gathered into the scheme of the poem, such as *Vaudracour and Julia,* as well as the one completed book of *The Recluse,* are all of a piece, philosophic in nature, developing in their individual ways aspects of the general philosophic questions raised by the poet concerning Man, Nature, and Society, and discussing and answering them from his point of view.   Thus, too, it follows that *The Prelude* must not be viewed as a biography and compared with the *Confessions* of Rousseau and such-like revelations.   Its structure is not at all chronological in the strict sense of the term, for the matter is arranged in accordance with a systematic explanation of the development of the mind of the individual. The material of the poem is in the general plan arranged in chronological order because the development of the mind proceeds from one period of life to another; but that the chronological idea is not the governing one is shown by the lack of chronological order in the appearance of incidents in his life to which he attaches the greatest importance.   That it is not different in method from *The Excursion* and *The Recluse* is shown by the fact that both these poems are in a large measure revelations of the growth of his mind and opinions.   They are in large measure autobiographical, but even *The Prelude* is at bottom philosophical in method.   It is a poem of the personal readjustment which was made necessary by a shift in opinion so radical that from a faith in the faith of the revolutionists he acquired a profound distrust of it as not being founded on real knowledge.   How he acquired this new faith in man as he really is and not as the Utopians dream he is, and how this faith is justified, is the theme of *The Prelude.*   Briefly, Wordsworth holds that it is the history of a mind passing from the shadows of sham knowledge to the light of true knowledge; and so inevitably the poem considers the history of his own development towards the goal to which he has attained—to reason, real knowledge of life and man, to imagination, as contrasted with unreal knowledge, secondary intellect, the opinions of others, and fancy. The material of the poem is thus handled in a philosophical manner and not in the manner of a narrative. If the poem is read as a narrative it is obscure, involved, ineffective; if it is read as an analytical poem it remains difficult, but it is clear enough in method, and as simple as the analysis of a profoundly complex thing can allow it to be. If we take this view of the poem we can see why the incidents of his life are introduced in such an apparently haphazard order. It is because he expounds certain fundamental principles and draws upon his own and others' experiences as a storehouse of illustration and examples of these principles.

We have very little first-hand evidence concerning the genesis either of the philosophical poem as a whole, or of *The Prelude,* and so we are fortunate to have so clear a statement of it as that given by Coleridge in the summer of 1799. It is so important that I quote it in full. Coleridge writes to Wordsworth in the following explicit terms:

My dear friend, I do entreat you to go on with "The Recluse," and I wish you would write a poem, in blank verse, addressed to those, who, in consequence of the complete failure of the French Revolution, have thrown up all hopes of the amelioration of mankind, and are sinking into an almost epicurean selfishness, disguising the same under the soft titles of domestic attachment and contempt for visionary *philosophes.* It would do great good, and might form a part of "The Recluse," for in my present mood I am wholly against the publication of any small poems.[39]

These words were obviously accepted by Wordsworth as expressive of his own desire, for he himself explicitly states his purpose in the following lines in which he exultingly claims true knowledge because he has gone to the source of all real knowledge, to first-hand impressions which cause the realities of life and the deeper impulses which give to life its urge and savor:

If in these times of fear,
This melancholy waste of hopes o'erthrown,
If, 'mid indifference and apathy,
And wicked exultation when good men

---

[39] *Memoirs of Wordsworth,* I, 159. Already partially quoted early in this chapter.

On every side fall off, we know not how,
To selfishness, disguised in gentle names
Of peace and quiet and domestic love,
Yet mingled not unwillingly with sneers
On visionary minds; if, in this time
Of dereliction and dismay, I yet
Despair not of our nature, but retain
A more than Roman confidence, a faith
That fails not, in all sorrow my support,
The blessing of my life; the gift is yours,
Ye winds and sounding cataracts! 't is yours,
Ye mountains! thine, O Nature; Thou hast fed
My lofty speculations; and in thee,
For this uneasy heart of ours, I find
A never-failing principle of joy
And purest passion.[40]

In this spirit then, the poet proceeds to his subject, by way of the three ages. The doctrinal skeleton of the poem appears in the fifth, eighth, and the twelfth, thirteenth, and fourteenth books, with autobiographical details arranged around them. Thus the plan in outline is as follows:

Part I—Books I, II, III, and IV. From infancy to youth and the verge of maturity.

Part II—Book V. Books and the development of the Imagination.

Part III—Books VI and VII. Graduation, and residence in London. The approach to maturity.

Part IV—Book VIII. The change from youth to man. An explanation of the processes involved.

Part V—Books IX, X, and XI. Residence in France. The final ushering in of the soul of Humanity.

Part VI—Books XII, XIII, and XIV. The development of the Imagination and Reason, and hence the grounds of Hope and Optimism.

But even in those books which are more exactly chronological we find long passages devoted to explanation of the principles of mental and spiritual expression, growth, or change, which make them much more closely resemble the more analytical books than our classification might seem to signify. Conversely, too, the books which I have designated as

[40] *The Prelude*, II, 432-451.

analytical are enlivened with autobiographical details as vivid as any that appear in the more purely narrative books.

Thus by the analysis of the principles underlying his mental development Wordsworth explains how he attained to the wisdom of maturity, which he designates as Hope. The basis of all Hope is reality, and such a hope can never be false, or cause the heart to fall into despair. By the inevitable processes of life, when the life of the mind draws its sustenance from reality, through childhood, youth, and maturity, the mind develops towards Truth and Reason and Imagination, as we have indicated in the previous chapters. Despair and loss of hope and faith in life come only to those who build upon the false foundations of other people's opinions, the truth or falsity of which they have no means of testing, and so fall back upon that "false *secondary* power, by which we multiply distinctions." The poem points out the path of reality, to all who would walk that way. And that way the world must walk, for it is the only path which leads to sanity and Hope. Any other way madness lies.

Here is the problem of the times as Wordsworth conceives it. His solution of it is two-fold. The personal account of the way in which one person attained to true knowledge is found in *The Prelude,* illustrated with an abundance of detail and a clearness and fullness of explanation that make the poem a unique document in literature. This I call personal readjustment. The more general aspect of the question is found in *The Excursion,* in the form of a discussion of the way in which the despondency of the age can be changed to hope, through the attainment of real knowledge. This I call reconstruction, social and political.

I have said that the poem is not primarily chronological; and to illustrate this I have made a tabulation of the greater number of specific incidents of which the poet makes use, with the appropriate date and reference in each case. In the tabulation are included references from the other parts of the philosophical poem, as a further piece of evidence that all the parts are conceived of as a whole, in the mind of the poet. With regard to *The Prelude* as a poem to be considered as a whole in itself, we must recognize that its unity does not come from the simple chronological sequence that results from the main stress being laid on the personal adventures of the leading character in the poem. The intention of the poem is quite otherwise; it is the report of a man who "wandered to eternal truth," and who indicates to us the way. It is the story of a soul's readjustment in a changing age, who like Hazlitt, "began with the French Revolution"—

> Bliss was it in that dawn to be alive,
> But to be young was very Heaven;—41

who recoiled from it when he saw where it led; and who had the singular fortune to be in France in those critical years 1790 and 1791-1792 and to become so deeply involved in it as to be a veritable part of it. Hence the interest is in the principles involved in the Revolution and the ideas which were offered by the Revolution; and so the poem becomes a great interpretative document of the age, beside which all other English accounts pale into insignificance. He never repudiates the Revolution—his experience has made it too much a part of his very self for that—even when he repudiates Napoleon; nor does he praise it. He lived it; and he records for us that tremendous experience. This gives the poem a quality and a value which make it absolutely unique. To perceive this quality we must not look upon it as a mere autobiography, but as a "philosophic" poem, which uses autobiographical facts as illustrations of philosophical principles.

The tabulation of the main incidents in the order mentioned in *The Prelude, The Recluse,* and *The Excursion,* together with the actual chronology and location, is now presented.

---

41 *The Prelude,* XI, 108-109.

CHRONOLOGY OF *THE PRELUDE* AND SYNCHRONIZATION OF
THE PRELUDE WITH *THE EXCURSION* AND *THE RECLUSE*

Date	Place	Reference	Incident
1770-1774	Cockermouth	*Prelude* I 269-300	Babyhood by the river Derwent.
		Prelude III 235-272	Development of his mind begins through "Mute intercourse of touch" by the infant "with his mother's heart."
1775	Cockermouth	*Prelude* I 288-300	The five years' child bathes, basks, and runs in the thunder shower.
1776	Penrith and the Border Beacon	*Prelude* XII 225-260	The lost child's adventure with the horse, the steep mountain, and the gallows, when his hand as yet could scarcely hold the bridle.
1770-1778	Cockermouth	*Recluse* 713-730	The child's love of a daring feat.
		Prelude I 301	Beauty and fear are the child's tutors.
		Prelude XII 174-190	The child loves whatever he sees, and most intensely.
1778	Penrith	*Prelude* II 276-288	Death of his mother when he is eight years of age.
		Prelude V 256-260	Death of his mother.
1778	Hawkshead	*Prelude* I 303-305	Wider range of his wanderings at school.
1778	Hawkshead	*Prelude* V 425-460	The incident of the drowned man—realities softened and spiritualized by books.
		Prelude V	Plans to buy complete edition of the *Arabian Nights*.

Date	Place	Reference	Incident
1778	Vacation at Hawkshead, Grasmere, and neighborhood	*Recluse* 1-13	First sight of Grasmere.
	Vacation at Cockermouth	*Prelude* II 477-490	Love of books and reading absorbs him.
1778-1780	Hawkshead	*Prelude* II 1-45	School games.
		Prelude II 47-137	Picnics, and rides to Furness Abbey. The wren sings in the Abbey.
		Prelude II 138	Excursions to The White Lion inn, on Lake Windermere. The boy becomes more nearly conscious of Nature.
1779-1780	Hawkshead	*Prelude* I 305-325	He steals the woodcock from another's snare. Awakening conscience.
1780	Hawkshead	*Prelude* I 558-566	At "twice five summers" the boy holds "unconscious intercourse with beauty."
1770-1778	Cockermouth and Hawkshead	*Prelude* VIII 159-172	Influences of Danger, Tragedies, Hazards, and Beauty on his Childhood. Stirrings of Imagination.
		Prelude VIII 109-154	His childhood and youthful knowledge of the people—shepherds and farmers,—and of rural customs. His love for man in general begins with his love for particular friends, kindred, and playmates.
1780	Hawkshead	*Prelude* V 552-583	At twice five years or less his mind first opens to the charm of words in tuneful order. He and his friends repeat favorite verses.

Date	Place	Reference	Incident
1778-1783	Hawkshead, Esthwaite Lake	*Prelude* I 357-400	The stolen boat. The sterner and severer means which Nature adopts to teach the boy.
		Prelude I 425-463	Skating on Esthwaite Lake. The glory of motion felt by the boy.
		Prelude I 479-485	Hazel-nutting.
		Prelude I 485-490	Fishing.
		Prelude I 491-498	Kite-flying.
		Prelude I 499-543	Evening pleasures: fox and goose, Loo, whist, the rain falling, or the ice on Esthwaite resounding in the keen frost.
1778-1783	Hawkshead	*Prelude* VII 90-97	The envied traveller who has been to London, and is looked upon by Wordsworth as one who has been to Fairy-Land.
		Prelude V 360-388	"There was a Boy"—the primary processes of experience which produce the Imagination. An experience that was not Wordsworth's own.
		Prelude VIII 255-280	As a rambling school-boy, his knowledge of the shepherds of the hills gave him a noble idea of man.
		Prelude VIII 632-664	The bare hills and valleys, rocks, caverns, lakes, waterfalls, crags, seclusions, and echoes, were congenial to his young Imagination.
		Prelude XIV 330-345	The hardy independence of his school life.

Date	Place	Reference	Incident
		Excursion I 56-76	Wordsworth's friendship with the Pedlar.
		Excursion VII 5-30	Memories of pastoral melody or warlike air heard in his school-days.
		Excursion IX 484-488	Rowing on Lake Windermere.
1782	Near Hawkshead	*Prelude* XII 286-304	The unreasonable yearning and impatience of childhood. Clear impressions of sense under the stress of feeling.
1782	Penrith	*Prelude* XII 304-335	Death of Wordsworth's father.
1786	Hawkshead	*Prelude* VIII 462-475	Composition of the poem, "Dear native regions."
1787	Hawkshead	*Prelude* II 386	His seventeenth year. Transfer of his own enjoyments to nature. That is, Youth has come.
1787	Cambridge	*Prelude* III 1-62	He enters St. John's College, Cambridge.
		Prelude III 106	He looks for "universal things."
		Prelude III 141-142	The first *activity* of his mind. He creates his world.
		Prelude III 256-321	Fancy dominant. Imagination slept, but not utterly, for he read the English poets.
		Prelude III 509-530	The "deep vacation" of his first year at college was not given up to utter waste, for he learned something of social life.
1788	Cambridge	*Prelude* III 629-631	After eight months of "submissive idleness" he returns

Date	Place	Reference	Incident
			to his native hills in the north.
1788 Summer	Rampside (?)	*Prelude* V 50-165	His dream of the Arab, based on his reading of Cervantes' *Don Quixote*.
1788 Summer vacation	Hawkshead	*Prelude* IV 1-469	Summer vacation at Hawkshead marked by two important incidents:
		Prelude IV 276-338	(1) He felt himself to be a "dedicated spirit."
		Prelude IV 370-469	(2) Meeting with the discharged soldier, when returning at night from the boat-races on Lake Windermere.
1787-1791	Cambridge	*Prelude* VI 20-25	Two winters passed without a separate notice.
		Prelude VI 42-46	The poet's soul with him at this time.
		Prelude VI 65-94	Thinks of writing a poem "which pure hearts should reverence."
		Prelude VI 66-94	Observation of the ash tree.
		Prelude VI 95-114	More interested in words than thoughts.
		Prelude VI 115-167	Geometry gives him the first insight into the world of ordered unity, by the dominance of intelligence.
1787-1791	Yorkshire and The Lakes	*Prelude* VI 190-223	Wanderings in the North.
1787-1791	Yorkshire	*Prelude* VI 224-251	Renewed union with his sister Dorothy and renewed ac-

Date	Place	Reference	Incident
			quaintance with Mary Hutchinson.
1788 Autumn	London	*Prelude* VII 52-57 *Prelude* VIII 540-559	First entry into London.
1788	London	*Prelude* VII 65-68	Feels the shock of the huge town's first presence.
		Prelude VII 382-391	He hears a woman swear for the first time in his life.
1789	Penrith	*Prelude* XIII 120-126	Life's prime, and youthful love: Mary Hutchinson.
1790	France and the Alps	*Prelude* VI 322-726	Continental tour with his friend Robert Jones.
	Calais	*Prelude* VI 345-346	Landed in Calais on the eve of July 14, 1790.
	Burgundy	*Prelude* VI 374-407	Under vine-clad hills of Burgundy on the River Saône.
	The Grande Chartreuse	*Prelude* VI 407-414	The "awful solitude" of the Grande Chartreuse.
	Mont Blanc and Chamouni	*Prelude* VI 522-528	First sight of Mont Blanc and the Vale of Chamouni.
	Simplon Pass	*Prelude* VI 557-639	The crossing of the Alps brought home to him the nature of Imagination.
	France	*Prelude* VI 765-769	He looks upon the events of the Revolution without concern: he has not been touched by humanity.
	France	*Prelude* X 490-498	"A youthful pilgrim" in France.
1791	Cambridge	*Prelude* VIII 365-390	Begins the *Descriptive Sketches*. Begins *Guilt and Sorrow*.

Date	Place	Reference	Incident
1791	Cambridge	*Prelude* VII 52-57	B. A. University of Cambridge. He pitches "a vagrant tent among the unfenced regions of society."
	London	*Prelude* VII 60-65	"To London first I turned."
		Prelude VII 512-543	Burke.
		Prelude VII 544-572	The Pulpit.
		Prelude VII 602-618	The father's love for his child.
		Prelude VII 637-649	The Beggar.
		Prelude VII 650-721	The confusion of the many scenes in London.
		Prelude VII 766-770	Nature, Beauty, Life, and Harmony were with him in London. He feels the unity of man even amid all the confusion.
		Prelude VIII 665-675	He feels the unity of man in the great city.
		Prelude IX 22-29	He ranges through London, free as a colt at pasture, month after month, living obscurely. This lasts for less than a year.
	North Wales	*Prelude* XIV 1-85	Sunrise from Snowdon—the emblem of a mind that feeds upon infinity.
	France	*Prelude* IX 33-80	Goes to France and Paris. Marvels at the various sights. Visits the ruins of the Bastile, and Le Brun's painting of the Magdalen.

Date	Place	Reference	Incident
1791-1792	Orleans and Blois	*Prelude* IX 81-552	Friendship with Michel Beaupuy. He learns to value "man as man."
		Prelude IX 552-585	*Vaudracour and Julia* a shadowing forth of his own love for Annette, and for their child Caroline.
1792 October— November	Paris	*Prelude* X 1-221	Returns to Paris where he sees the city in revolution at close vision.
1792	England	*Prelude* VIII 340-364	Two and twenty summers old. Man begins to take first place in his interests, and Nature second.
1792 December		*Prelude* X 221	In London.
1793		*Prelude* X 144-510	He is perplexed by the excesses of the revolutionists in France, and by the declaration of war against France by E n g l a n d, February, 1793. Takes refuge in his "own soul."
1793 February		*Prelude* XI 105-205	His hope in the Revolution until "with open war Britain opposed the l i b e r t i e s of France."
		Prelude XI 208-224	France declares war against England and Holland.
1793-1794		*Prelude* XI 206-222	Frenchmen become oppressors in their turn.
		Prelude XI 223-320	Perplexed by his study of the revolutionary theorists, he "yields up moral questions in despair."
		Prelude XI 321-333	Turns to abstract science.

Date	Place	Reference	Incident
1794 August	River Leven, Estuary of Morecambe Bay	*Prelude* X. 511-603	His joy at hearing of the death of Robespierre (guillotined July 28, 1794).
1794-1795	Penrith, Halifax, Racedown	*Prelude* XI 333-370	Re-union with his sister Dorothy. She preserves him still a poet.
1795 Spring	Racedown	*Prelude* XIV 348-369	Raisley Calvert dies, leaving to Wordsworth £900, which enables him to settle with Dorothy at Racedown in Dorsetshire.
1795 Autumn	London	*Prelude* I 1-45	Escape from London. See, on this disputed date, Dorothy's letter to Mrs. Marshall, Sept. 2, 1795. *Letters*, I, 85-87. This date is much more probable than 1799, authorized by the *Memoirs*, I, 143.
1795-6-7-8	Racedown and Alfoxden	*Prelude* XIII 48-50	Thus moderated and composed, he finds in Man an object of delight, of pure imagination, and of love.
		Prelude XIV 255-265	At this time Nature falls back into a second place.
1795-1797	Bristol	*Prelude* VI 253-259	Meeting with Coleridge—"we were friends, to bend at last to the same discipline, predestined to seek the same delights, and have one health, one happiness."
1798	London and the North	*Prelude* VII 1-12	Began to write *The Prelude*.
1798-1799 Winter of	Goslar	*Prelude* VIII 185-215	Shepherd life near Goslar described.
1799 December 17	Sockburn and Grasmere	*Prelude* I 59-113	Journey from Sockburn to Grasmere. Grasmere described in line 106.

Date	Place	Reference	Incident
1799 December 21	Grasmere	*Recluse* 165-170	Settlement at Dove Cottage, Grasmere.
1799-1800		*Recluse* 56-59	At Grasmere, "perchance for life."
1800 February		*Recluse* 180-182	Two months of storm at Grasmere.
1800 March, April		*Recluse* 189	The Gates of Spring are open.
1800		*Prelude* VII 8-10	Early part of *Prelude* written (Books I and II).
1802		*Recluse* 648-657	Visit of his brother John.
		Recluse 659-666	Ready to receive as visitors the Hutchinsons and Coleridge.
1800-1804		*Prelude* VII 11	Composition of *The Prelude,* "stopped for years."
1802 October 6	Dove Cottage	*Prelude* VI 224-230	Marries Mary Hutchinson.
		Prelude XIV 267-275	Tribute to his wife.
1804 April 7	Dove Cottage	*Prelude* VI 47-52	"Four years and thirty, told this very week, have I been now a sojourner on earth."
1804 Summer		*Prelude* VII	*The Prelude* begun anew.
1804 April 2		*Prelude* VII 11-15	Coleridge starts for Malta. The composition of *The Prelude* moves slowly; he has been doing nothing on it all summer.

Date	Place	Reference	Incident
1805 February 5		*Prelude* XIV 415-423	John Wordsworth drowned in the wreck of the *Abergavenny.*
1812 June and December	The Rectory, Grasmere	*Excursion* III 640-650	Death of two of Wordsworth's children.

CHAPTER XII

THE PHILOSOPHIC POEM: *THE EXCURSION* AND RECONSTRUCTION

> . . . By words
> Which speak of nothing more than what we are,
> Would I arouse the sensual from their sleep
> Of Death, and win the vacant and the vain
> To noble raptures; while my voice proclaims
> How exquisitely the individual mind
> (And the progressive powers perhaps no less
> Of the whole species) to the external World
> Is fitted:—and how exquisitely, too—
> Theme this but little heard of among men—
> The external World is fitted to the Mind;
> And the creation (by no lower name
> Can it be called) which they with blended might
> Accomplish:—this is our high argument.
>
> William Wordsworth, *The Recluse:*
> *Home at Grasmere*, 1800.

In the previous chapter we gave the main outline of the history of the "philosophical poem," and the place which *The Excursion* occupies in the general scheme. We shall now give a more particular account of this poem before going on to consider the problems which it discusses. We have already said that there is frequent mention of *The Excursion,* under the title of *The Pedlar,* in Dorothy Wordsworth's *Journals* from October 10, 1801, to July 8, 1802, the long series of entries winding up on the last mentioned date, July 8, 1802, with the surprising statement that Dorothy wrote it out and that it was only two hundred and eighty lines long.[1] But, before this date, in October, 1800, Coleridge speaks of *The Pedlar* as a long blank-verse poem which he and Wordsworth intended to publish with *Christabel*.[2] This design was dropped, and an-

---

[1] *Journals of Dorothy Wordsworth,* I, 136.
[2] *Letters of Samuel Taylor Coleridge,* Edited by E. H. Coleridge, 2 vols., 1895. I. 337; Arthur Turnbull, *Biographia Epistolaris,* 2 vols., 1911, I, 206.

other plan was formed to publish it with *The Yorkshire Wolds Poem*.[3] For some years we hear nothing of the publishing of *The Pedlar*, until, on April 24, 1814, we are told the surprising news that nine books are being printed, and this turns out to be *The Excursion* as we know it, not the comparatively short poem we have heard so much of under the title of *The Pedlar*.

In the long note on *The Excursion* Wordsworth gives us some additional details. The part of the poem which was first written are lines 871 to 916 of Book I, beginning with the line:

> Nine tedious years,

and ending with the line:

> Last human tenant of these ruined walls.

These were composed in 1795 at Racedown. The next in order was the rest of the story of Margaret, several passages of which are derived from Wordsworth's observation of actual people at Racedown and Alfoxden from the year 1795 to 1798. From the evidence which we derive from a letter of Coleridge's to Joseph Cottle, dated March 8, 1798, the story of Margaret was about twelve hundred lines long, and was in blank verse, "superior, I hesitate not to aver, to anything in our language which anyway resembles it."[4] This story of Margaret, as everyone knows, became an important part of Book I.

The next passage which Wordsworth designates as early is lines 1207 to 1274 of Book IV, which is an important statement of the relations between "sanity of reason" and "science," but marked as early by the much balder assertion of "necessity" than he would have made in the years when the main body of the poem was composed.

Wordsworth tells us that the rest of the poem was chiefly composed when they were living at Allan Bank, Grasmere, 1809 to 1811; but no doubt it was retouched and altered up to its publication in 1814.[5] This is the history of the writing of *The Excursion* as we know it, in its final form, enlarged by the accretions from the main philosophical poem around the

---

[3] See footnote 36 of Chapter XI, page 211.
[4] A. Turnbull, *Biographia Epistolaris*, I, 152.
[5] The Fenwick note on *The Excursion*, dictated about 1843.

character of the *Pedlar,* and so becoming a part of the very texture of the poem itself, instead of an embroidery or accompaniment, as *The Pedlar* was clearly intended to be. It is now in order to indicate the place which is occupied by the poem in the development of the main theme of man, and nature, and human life.

The main problem of the poem is the re-establishment of Hope by the overcoming or avoidance of Despondency, through the re-establishment of real, genuine knowledge. This is done by bringing each individual into contact with the living forms of the world of men and things, with the consequent dislodgment of false hopes and despondency through the real knowledge which comes through individual contact with experience and which, because it is real, leads to reality and hope. This process is displayed in the poem by two methods: by philosophical analysis and by concrete illustrations. The philosophic discussion treats of the mutual relations of despondency and hope and their origins in the mind of man. This discussion occupies the third and fourth books, and consists of a dialogue between the despairing Solitary[6] and the cheerful Wanderer—the Pedlar of the projected briefer poem—on Despondency and Hope. In the eighth and ninth books this dialogue is followed up and applied to the reconstruction of the social and political life of England, and so the philosophical discussion comes to a conclusion.

In the first and second books are found the stories of the Wanderer, or Pedlar, and of Margaret, who had attained to Hope and Wisdom;[7] and of the Solitary, or Recluse, who had not so attained;[8] and between the fourth and eighth books there are narrated seventeen stories; one about the living, and sixteen about the dead who lie in the churchyard among the

---

[6] It is to be noted that the Solitary is the pessimist. This shows that Wordsworth did not always think of solitude as the way to wisdom, contrary to popular opinion and certain critics. Solitude, for instance, is thought of as a painful thing, and is classified with fear, and pain, and grief in *Tintern Abbey,* l. 44. In this he is anti-Rousseauistic; for, according to the Rousseauists, the Solitary should have been wise. But, as Wordsworth indicates in the *Argument* of Book IV, his solitude was "morbid." and therefore "pitiable."

[7] The story of the Wanderer is in Book I, 108-433; the story of Margaret in Book I, 434-916.

[8] The story of The Solitary is in Book II, and is continued in the dialogue of Book III.

mountains, some of whom attained to the wisdom of life and some of whom did not. The poet thus discusses the whole subject from both sides, as laid down in the fifth book; first by "abstraction" and "dispute," or argument, and second, by "solid facts" and "plain pictures." By both methods he attempts to show how Reason may be reached, as far as man can ever attain to it; for

> Reason, best reason, is to imperfect man
> An effort only, and a noble aim;
> A crown, an attribute of sovereign power,
> Still to be courted—never to be won.

Nevertheless it is to be sought; for all the truth to which we can attain is won by our individual efforts, and by no mere acceptance of a "mechanic structure" prepared for us by others, and acquired by recipe:

> Moral truth
> Is no mechanic structure, built by rule;
> And which, once built, retains a steadfast shape
> And undisturbed proportions; but a thing
> Subject, you deem, to vital accidents;
> And, like the water-lily, lives and thrives,
> Whose root is fixed in stable earth, whose head
> Floats on the tossing waves.

Thus the attainment of Reason is no simple process, because of the elusive nature of Truth itself in this fluid world, where nothing is found in fixity; and it is made much more difficult by the multiplex nature of man:

> But how acquire
> The inward principle that gives effect
> To outward argument; the passive will
> Meek to admit; the active energy,
> Strong and unbounded to embrace, and firm
> To keep and cherish? How shall man unite
> With self-forgetful tenderness of heart
> An earth-despising dignity of soul?
> Wise is that union, and without it blind![9]

This is the problem of *The Excursion*. One year later, when he issued his poems in a collected edition, he expressed the problem in aesthetic terms, as he here expresses it in ethical

---

[9] These quotations are taken from *The Excursion*, V, 485-579.

and religious terms. He is discussing the relationship of knowledge and the individual, and objects to the term "taste" as expressive of a power which must be active in essence. "Therefore," he says, "to create taste is to call forth and bestow power, of which Knowledge is the effect, and *there* lies the true difficulty."[10]   So here, the difficulty is how to acquire the inner impulse, the "inner principle," which will give a motive to the activity of mind and heart which results in a new outlook and a substitution of high for low and true for false.[11] This aspect of Wordsworth's problem must be kept in mind when we deal with the stories in the poem, for Wordsworth does not tell them with the idea that the impulse derived from the hearing or reading of them can pass directly to the hearer or reader, and so influence his conduct. Far from it: they are rather told as instances of the many and devious ways in which victory is won or lost; they are not told because they have a certain pathos or human sorrow, or creed, or morality common to all of them and in virtue of which they can directly "convert" or correct the hearer or reader. Knowledge and reason are not so simply won as that, for these come by indirection; and emotion in turn, is derived from Knowledge. Wordsworth's doctrine is far removed from both the sentimentalism of Shaftesbury and the melancholy of the school of taste from which he revolted. There is no specific "moral sense," in Wordsworth's doctrine, nor is there the special efficacy in sorrow, suffering, or melancholy, such as is ascribed to them by both the school of taste and the school of Rousseau.[12] Wordsworth's psychology is much more complicated than that of either of these schools, as the statements which we have

---

[10] *Essay Supplementary to the Preface of Lyrical Ballads*, 1815.

[11] This "inner principle" is the active side of the mind—the "active powers" of Hartley. They are the "pleasures and pains," the moral energies or active phenomena, of human nature, as contrasted with the intellectual faculties of the human mind.

A clear statement of Hartley's philosophy is given in G. S. Bower, *David Hartley and James Mill*, 1881. Excellent, brief statements of the various English philosophers will be found in James Seth, *English Philosophers and Schools of Philosophy*, 1912. Professor Seth is one of the few historians of philosophy who give any adequate account of Hartley. A more detailed study of Hartley is to be found in Howard C. Warren, *A History of the Association Philosophy*, 1921, Ch. III and VI, but rather strictly from the standpoint of psychology.

[12] See the discussion of *Peter Bell* in Chapter X.

quoted from *The Excursion* and the *Essay Supplementary to the Preface* show.

It is no accident or oversight that the Solitary does not attain Hope within the limits of the poem. Wordsworth is not preaching a doctrine here so much as narrating the results of experience. The Solitary is on a false tack in cutting himself off from his kind and indulging in morbid solitude. He must be cured by a course of conduct which will correct the very currents of his being, or go through some experience which will induce "a healthful state of association"; and so the "restoration" cannot be represented within the frame of the present poem, but must be reserved for another, as the Fenwick note to *The Excursion* states. The method of restoration there outlined is once more the method of the three ages: The Wanderer was to be taken to his native hills and there see a religious ceremony which he had been familiar with in his early childhood, and so have his heart dissolved in tenderness, and so make a beginning on the recovery of faith, contentedness, and cheerfulness, which mark every mind which has had its normal development.

We shall now follow the "abstract" discussion of the problem of Hope as it is carried on in the fourth book. In the third book the Solitary is represented as having fallen into despair through the failure of the French Revolution, and through the discovery that his false learning had led him to believe impossible things both of civilized and savage man. He is disillusioned because the Utopia in which the false, revolutionary thought had led him to believe, does not exist, and the "noble savage" which had been held up to him as the apex of human development turns out, on actual knowledge, to be "a creature squalid, vengeful, and impure, remorseless, and submissive to no law but superstitious fear, and abject sloth."[13] The result is despondency, the loss of faith in man, and the only surviving impulse is the desire for extinction.

The fourth book contains the answer to the difficulties that have been raised by the story of the Solitary, and in general this answer is the vindication of Hope, or Optimism—"Despondency Corrected." It begins in the very same way as the

---

[13] *The Excursion*, III, 944-955.

Ode. Intimations of Immortality, in allowing many of the arguments of the Solitary, but argues in turn that these are inevitable; common to all men; are the experience of the optimists as well as the pessimists; and so are not germane to the question.   He, himself, the Wanderer answers, has gone through the experiences of the Solitary, but he knows that these are the result of the inevitable processes of life.   Infancy was followed by youth, youth by maturity, and in natural sequence the "cloud" of infancy was succeeded by the "visionary" powers of youth, which in turn faded with the coming of age.[14]   This is once again the three ages of man, and the argument proceeds as it did in previous examples of the use of this form of argument.   This fading of the "fervent raptures" of youth is perfectly natural, the Wanderer continues; but the result should be not despair, but rather hope.   What are things eternal, or permanent?   Surely they do not have their existence in any particular period of life, or state of mind.   Powers depart and possessions vanish; infancy, youth, opinions, and passions change.[15]   The permanent cannot exist in these. Duty, aspiration, hope exist outside all these changes and accidents, and are eternal.   Man is of dust, but his hopes are ethereal; and if he aspires in accordance with the highest that is within him he cannot end in despondency, hard though the way of the mature man is, deprived of the bright visions of his youth:

> Those fervent raptures are for ever flown;
> And, since their date, my soul hath undergone
> Change manifold, for better or for worse:
> Yet cease I not to struggle, and aspire
> Heavenward; and chide the part of me that flags,
> Through sinful choice; or dread necessity
> On human nature from above imposed.
> 'Tis, by comparison, an easy task
> Earth to despise; but, to converse with heaven—
> This is not easy:—to relinquish all
> We have, or hope, of happiness and joy,
> And stand in freedom loosened from this world,
> I deem not arduous; but must needs confess
> That 'tis a thing impossible to frame

---

[14] *Op. cit.,* IV, 66-139.
[15] *Op. cit.,* IV, 66-70.

> Conceptions equal to the soul's desire;
> And the most difficult tasks to *keep*
> Heights which the soul is competent to gain.[16]

Thus progress is no easy thing to attain and keep, but if hope seems hard, despondency is still less justifiable, for it negatives the very nature of man:

> Man is of dust: ethereal hopes are his,
> Which, when they should sustain themselves aloft,
> Want due consistence; like a pillar of smoke,
> That with majestic energy from earth
> Rises; but, having reached the thinner air,
> Melts, and dissolves, and is no longer seen.
> From this infirmity of mortal kind
> Sorrow proceeds, which else would not; at least,
> If grief be something hallowed and ordained,
> If, in proportion, it be just and meet,
> Yet, through this weakness of the general heart,
> Is it enabled to maintain its hold
> In that excess which conscience disapproves.
> For who could sink and settle to that point
> Of selfishness; so senseless who could be
> As long and perseveringly to mourn
> For any object of his love, removed
> From this unstable world, if he could fix
> A satisfying view upon that state
> Of pure, imperishable, blessedness,
> Which reason promises, and holy writ
> Ensures to all believers?—Yet mistrust
> Is of such incapacity, methinks,
> No natural branch; despondency far less;
> And, least of all, is absolute despair.
> —And, if there be whose tender frames have drooped
> Even to the dust; apparently, through weight
> Of anguish unrelieved, and lack of power
> An agonizing sorrow to transmute;
> Deem not that proof is here of hope withheld
> When wanted most; a confidence impaired
> So pitiably, that, having ceased to see
> With bodily eyes, they are borne down by love
> Of what is lost, and perish through regret.
> Oh! no, the innocent Sufferer often sees
> Too clearly; feels too vividly; and longs
> To realize the vision, with intense
> And over-constant yearning;—there—there lies

---

[16] *The Excursion*, IV, 123-139.

The excess, by which the balance is destroyed.
Too, too contracted are these walls of flesh,
This vital warmth too cold, these visual orbs,
Though inconceivably endowed, too dim
For any passion of the soul that leads
To ecstasy; and all the crooked paths
Of time and change disdaining, takes its course
Along the line of limitless desires.
I, speaking now from such disorder free,
Nor rapt, nor craving, but in settled peace,
I cannot doubt that they whom you deplore
Are glorified; or, if they sleep, shall wake
From sleep, and dwell with God in endless love.
Hope, below this, consists not with belief
In mercy, carried infinite degrees
Beyond the tenderness of human hearts:
Hope, below this, consists not with belief
In perfect wisdom, guiding mightiest power,
That finds no limits but her own pure will.[17]

The "venerable Sage" thus appeals to a higher court than the "domineering faculties of sense," and endeavors to arouse the Solitary from his despair and loss of faith in aspiration and self.

He now turns to another aspect of despondency—the loss of faith in "social man"; or, as we should say, the loss of faith in democracy. He calls the Solitary back to real knowledge concerning men, and appeals from the false "transports" of the age to solid truth:

　　　　　For that other loss,
The loss of confidence in social man,
By the unexpected transports of our age
Carried so high, that every thought, which looked
Beyond the temporal destiny of the Kind,
To many seemed superfluous—as, no cause
Could e'er for such exalted confidence
Exist: so, none is now for fixed despair:
The two extremes are equally disowned
By reason: if, with sharp recoil, from one
You have been driven far as its opposite,
Between them seek the point whereon to build
Sound expectations. So doth he advise
Who shared at first the illusion; but was soon
Cast from the pedestal of pride by shocks

---

[17] *Op. cit.*, IV, 140-196.

Which Nature gently gave, in woods and fields;
Nor unreproved by Providence, thus speaking
To the inattentive children of the world:
"Vain-glorious Generation! what new powers
On you have been conferred? what gifts, withheld
From your progenitors, have ye received,
Fit recompense of new desert? what claim
Are ye prepared to urge, that my decrees
For you should undergo a sudden change;
And the weak functions of one busy day,
Reclaiming and extirpating, perform
What all the slowly-moving years of time,
With their united force, have left undone?
By nature's gradual processes be taught;
By story be confounded! Ye aspire
Rashly, to fall once more; and that false fruit,
Which, to your over-weening spirits, yields
Hope of a flight celestial, will produce
Misery and shame. But Wisdom of her sons
Shall not the less, though late, be justified."[18]

The revolutionists are here asked very hard questions; they have forgotten that man's nature cannot be changed in a day. Their knowledge is not based on facts. Hence the world suffers its fate justly, for the bad have more unity among themselves and a greater faith in their unhallowed principles than the good; Wisdom is surely justified of her children! The Wanderer proceeds:

"Such timely warning," said the Wanderer, "gave
That visionary voice; and, at this day,
When a Tartarean darkness overspreads
The groaning nations; when the impious rule,
By will or by established ordinance,
Their own dire agents, and constrain the good
To acts which they abhor; though I bewail
This triumph, yet the pity of my heart
Prevents me not from owning, that the law,
By which mankind now suffers, is most just.
For by superior energies; more strict
Affiance in each other; faith more firm
In their unhallowed principles; the bad
Have fairly earned a victory o'er the weak,
The vacillating, inconsistent good.
Therefore, not unconsoled, I wait—in hope
To see the moment, when the righteous cause

[18] *The Excursion*, IV, 260-294.

Shall gain defenders zealous and devout
As they who have opposed her; in which Virtue
Will, to her efforts, tolerate no bounds
That are not lofty as her rights; aspiring
By impulse of her own ethereal zeal.
That spirit only can redeem mankind;
And when that sacred spirit shall appear,
Then shall *our* triumph be complete as theirs.
Yet, should this confidence prove vain, the wise
Have still the keeping of their proper peace;
Are guardians of their own tranquillity.
They act, or they recede, observe, and feel;
'Knowing the heart of man is set to be
The center of this world, about the which
Those revolutions of disturbances
Still roll; where all the aspécts of misery
Predominate; whose strong effects are such
As he must bear, being powerless to redress;
And that unless above himself he can
Erect himself, how poor a thing is Man'."[19]

This is the lesson men must learn: they must learn to know man, and each man must learn to know himself, if they are to find happiness and satisfaction both in their private lives and in social institutions. Hope and happiness cannot be founded on the "illusion" of false knowledge.

---

[19] *Op. cit.*, IV, 294-331. The quotation at the end is from Samuel Daniel. Wordsworth's own note is as follows:
"The passage quoted from Daniel is taken from a poem addressed to the Lady Margaret, Countess of Cumberland, and the two last lines, printed in Italics, are by him translated from Seneca. The whole poem is very beautiful. I will transcribe four stanzas from it, as they contain an admirable picture of the state of a wise Man's mind in a time of public commotion.

'Nor is he moved with all the thunder-cracks
Of tyrant's threats, or with the surly brow
Of Power, that proudly sits on others' crimes;
Charged with more crying sins than those he checks.
The storms of sad confusion that may grow
Up in the present for the coming times,
Appal not him; that hath no side at all,
But of himself, and knows the worst can fall.

Although his heart (so near allied to earth)
Cannot but pity the perplexed state
Of troublous and distressed mortality,
That thus make way unto the ugly birth
Of their own sorrows, and do still beget
Affliction upon Imbecility;
Yet seeing thus the course of things must run,
He looks thereon not strange, but as fore-done.

But the great weakness of despondency is apathy: and here begins a new step in the argument. As we have noted in previous chapters, an essential quality of the normal adult mind is *activity:* and here Wordsworth makes use of this principle. If man is to erect himself, he must do it by his own activity. But how? The answer is that he must begin at the level which he occupies. Let him identify himself with the "inferior kinds" of creation: bird, animal, things which "call forth and best sustain these pure sensations," such as may be found in rural life. As the prose argument puts it, apathy is weakness, and so any activity that is healthy is recommended, especially any activity that leads the mind along the ways of direct, real, natural knowledge, which is the way to "tranquillity."[20]

> "Happy is he who lives to understand,
> Not human nature only, but explores
> All natures,—to the end that he may find
> The law that governs each; and where begins
> The union, the partition where, that makes
> Kind and degree, among all visable Beings;
> The constitutions, powers, and faculties,
> Which they inherit,—cannot step beyond,—
> And cannot fall beneath; that do assign
> To every class its station and its office
> Through all the mighty commonwealth of things;
> Up from the creeping plant to sovereign Man.
> Such converse, if directed by a meek,
> Sincere, and humble spirit, teaches love:
> For knowledge is delight; and such delight

> And Whilst distraught ambition compasses,
> And is encompassed, while as craft deceives,
> And is deceived: whilst man doth ransack man,
> And builds on blood, and rises by distress;
> And th' Inheritance of desolution leaves
> To great-expecting hopes: He looks thereon,
> As from the shore of peace, with unwet eye,
> And bears no venture in Impiety.

> Thus, Lady, fares that man that hath prepared
> A rest for his desires; and sees all things
> Beneath him; and hath learned this book of man,
> Full of the notes of frailty; and compared
> The best of glory with her sufferings:
> By whom, I see, you labour all you can
> To plant your heart! and set your thoughts as near
> His glorious mansion as your powers can bear.' "

[20] *Argument* to Book IV.

Breeds love: yet, suited as it rather is
To thought and to the climbing intellect,
It teaches less to love, than to adore;
If that be not indeed the highest love!"
"Yet," said I, tempted here to interpose,
"The dignity of life is not impaired
By aught that innocently satisfies
The humbler cravings of the heart; and he
Is still a happier man, who, for those heights
Of speculation not unfit, descends;
And such benign affections cultivates
Among the inferior kinds; not merely those
That he may call his own, and which depend,
As individual objects of regard,
Upon his care, from whom he also looks
For signs and tokens of a mutual bond;
But others, far beyond this narrow sphere,
Whom, for the very sake of love, he loves.
Nor is it a mean praise of rural life
And solitude, that they do favour most,
Most frequently call forth, and best sustain,
These pure sensations; that can penetrate
The obstreperous city; on the barren seas
Are not unfelt; and much might recommend,
How much they might inspire and endear,
The loneliness of this sublime retreat!"21

Then follows a long speech by the Sage, urging the Solitary to live a normal country life where the human, animal and inanimate might wean him from false theories, judgments, and books, and so from his despair.22

Roused by the enthusiasm of the Sage, the Solitary exclaims that it would be joyous to have the vitality of vigorous health and to identify one's vigor with that of nature. But the speech is so important for the answer which it elicits that it must be given entire:

The Solitary lifted toward the hills
A kindling eye:—accordant feelings rushed

---

21 *The Excursion*, IV, 332-372.

22 *Op. cit.*, IV, 373-504. This marvelous speech must yield its quality to any reader who is sensative to poetic effects: to one who is even in a slight degree familiar with the face of the hills and valleys and tarns depicted, it must seem to be a sublimation of a hundred experiences in all seasons, in storm and shine, where lamb and rook and rainbow and cloud are a part of the experiences. It is the very experience itself, to a degree rarely realized in poetry.

16

Into my bosom, whence these words broke forth:
"Oh! what a joy it were, in vigorous health,
To have a body (this our vital frame
With shrinking sensibility endued,
And all the nice regards of flesh and blood)
And to the elements surrender it
As if it were a spirit!—How divine,
The liberty, for frail, for mortal, man
To roam at large among unpeopled glens
And mountainous retirements, only trod
By devious footsteps; regions consecrate
To oldest time! and, reckless of the storm
That keeps the raven quiet in her nest,
Be as a presence or a motion—one
Among the many there; and while the mists
Flying, and rainy vapours, call out shapes
And phantoms from the crags and solid earth
As fast as a musician scatters sounds
Out of an instrument; and while the streams
(As at a first creation and in haste
To exercise their untried faculties)
Descending from the region of the clouds,
And starting from the hollows of the earth
More multitudinous every moment, rend
Their way before them—what a joy to roam
An equal among mightiest energies;
And haply sometimes with articulate voice,
Amid the deafening tumult, scarcely heard
By him that utters it, exclaim aloud,
'Rage on, ye elements! let moon and stars
Their aspects lend, and mingle in their turn
With this commotion (ruinous though it be)
From day to night, from night to day, prolonged!' "[23]

"Yes," answered the Wanderer, "you are on the way to hope and tranquillity; for you are speaking of what you once experienced. In your youth you experienced just such transports and you indulged just the fancies which you now express. Go to Garry's hills, the scene of your youth, and indulge in Fancy." Here we are once again plainly in the general method of the three ages of man. If we but once have felt strongly or had a vivid sensation or experience we have exercised and cultivated power which we shall be able to exercise again. If but once we have been strong, power abides with us.[24]

[23] *The Excursion*, IV, 505-539.
[24] *The Prelude*, XII, 264-277. See Chapter VIII, *The Active Principle*.

"Yes," said the Wanderer, taking from my lips
The strain of transport, "whosoe'er in youth
Has, through ambition of his soul, given way
To such desires, and grasped at such delight,
Shall feel congenial stirrings late and long,
In spite of all the weakness that life brings,
Its cares and sorrows; he, though taught to own
The tranquillizing power of time, shall wake,
Wake sometimes to a noble restlessness—
Loving the sports which once he gloried in."[25]

This reply is a very clear enunciation of the principle by which the unity of the mind is maintained, and is a preparation for the next step. This is the statement of the principle that it is essential to keep the mind in activity; and since the Wanderer has been aroused by memories of his youth, he should begin at that point to renew and restore his mind. That is to say, he must exercise the faculty accorded to youth: that is, the Fancy. The Fancy is its own justification to Youth; and this doctrine we have seen fully developed in the reply to "Mathetes."[26] But the advice he now gives is advice with a difference. "Mathetes" was a youth; and Wordsworth advised him accordingly; but the Solitary is an adult. Yet the advice is given him that he must exercise the faculties of youth none the less. Now, if the Solitary were a man whose development had not been arrested, the natural faculty would have been the imagination. But he is not developed: he is not in possession of the higher faculty of imagination. He must therefore do the only thing he can: he must exercise the fancy, which will lead up to the higher faculty in time. Thus even the adult, if he but have the impulse to activity, may arrive, albeit somewhat belated, at the goal of reason, imagination, and hope. As the prose *Argument* states the problem: "If the elevated Imagination cannot be exerted, try the humbler fancy."[27]

The dialogue continues:

Compatriot, Friend, remote are Garry's hills,
The streams far distant of your native glen;
Yet is their form and image here expressed
With brotherly resemblance. Turn your steps

[25] *The Excursion*, IV, 540-549.
[26] Chapter V.
[27] In the edition of 1814.

Wherever fancy leads; by day, by night,
Are various engines working, not the same
As those with which your soul in youth was moved.
But by the great Artificer endowed
With no inferior power. You dwell alone;
You walk, you live, you speculate alone;
Yet doth remembrance, like a sovereign prince,
For you a stately gallery maintain
Of gay or tragic pictures. You have seen,
Have acted, suffered, traveled far, observed
With no incurious eye; and books are yours,
Within whose silent chambers treasure lies
Preserved from age to age; more precious far
Than that accumulated store of gold
And orient gems, which, for a day of need,
The Sultan hides deep in ancestral tombs.
These hoards of truth you can unlock at will:
And music waits upon your skilful touch,
Sounds from the wandering shepherd from these heights
Hears, and forgets his purpose;—furnished thus,
How can you droop, if willing to be upraised?[28]

I have said that the same advice is given to the Solitary as
was given to "Mathetes," but with a difference. The Wanderer is an adult, and any exercise of the youthful fancy would
seem false. Now it happens that exercise of the unreason
which we call fancy is well known in human history, and we
call it *superstition*. To superstition then, the dialogue turns,
and especially to its place and value in human development;
for, surprising as it may seem, Wordsworth claims for it a
peculiar value: it has the same value in the race as Fancy has
in the individual. The pathway to Truth is indirect and winding, and Truth does not exact the same service of all:

A piteous lot it were to flee from Man—
Yet not rejoice in Nature. He, whose hours
Are by domestic pleasure uncaressed
And unenlivened; who exists whole years
Apart from benefits received or done
Mid the transactions of the bustling crowd;
Who neither hears, nor feels a wish to hear,
Of the world's interests—such a one hath need
Of a quick fancy and an active heart,
That, for the day's consumption, books may yield
Food not unwholesome; earth and air correct

---

[28] *The Excursion*, IV, 550-574.

His morbid humour, with delight supplied
Or solace, varying as the seasons change.
—Truth has her pleasure-grounds, her haunts of ease
And easy contemplation; gay parterres,
And labyrinthine walks, her sunny glades
And shady groves in studied contrast—each,
For recreation, leading into each:
These may he range, if willing to partake
Their soft indulgences, and in due time
May issue thence, recruited for the tasks
And course of service Truth requires from those
Who tend her altars, wait upon her throne,
And guard her fortresses. Who thinks, and feels,
And recognizes ever and anon
The breeze of nature stirring in his soul,
Why need such man go desperately astray,
And nurse "the dreadful appetite of death?"
If tired with systems, each in its degree
Substantial, and all crumbling in their turn,
Let him build systems of his own, and smile
At the fond work, demolished with a touch;
If unreligious, let him be at once
Among ten thousand innocents, enrolled
A pupil in the many-chambered school,
Where *superstition* weaves her airy dreams.[29]

Then follows the surprising statement by the Wanderer:

Life's autumn past, I stand on winter's verge;
And daily lose what I desire to keep:
Yet rather would I instantly decline
To the traditionary sympathies
Of a most rustic ignorance, and take
A fearful apprehension from the owl
Or death-watch: and as readily rejoice,
If two auspicious magpies crossed my way;—
To this would rather bend than see and hear
The repetitions wearisome of sense,
Where soul is dead, and feeling hath no place;
Where knowledge, ill begun in cold remark
On outward things, with formal inference ends;
Or, if the mind turned inward, she recoils
At once—or, not recoiling, is perplexed—
Lost in a gloom of uninspired research;
Meanwhile, the heart within the heart, the seat
Where peace and happy consciousness should dwell,

---

[29] *Op. cit.*, IV, 575-610.

> On its own axis restlessly revolving,
> Seeks, yet can nowhere find, the light of truth.[30]

Wordsworth's comment on this is to be found in the *Argument* of the book: "Superstition better than apathy"; for superstition is at least based on first-hand knowledge. Then the Wanderer proceeds to show that the ages which produced what we call superstitions were not divided from actual facts; and so, though their findings were false, as those of fancy and youth are false, they point out the true way to reality. He then runs through ancient history and shows how the Jew, the Persian, the Babylonian, the Chaldean, and the Grecian developed a sort of truth of their own.[31]

To this the Sceptic, or Solitary, objects; for such a course of reasoning does not take cognizance of error. We live by Admiration, Hope, and Love, to be sure; but the Wanderer allows a value to these "favorite vassals" of Fancy which can be given only to Reason; and he asks the question,

> Love, Hope, and Admiration—are they not
> Mad Fancy's favourite vassals? Does not life
> Use them, full oft, as pioneers to ruin,
> Guides to destruction? Is it well to trust
> Imagination's light when reason's fails,
> The unguarded taper where the guarded faints?[32]

And then he demands that the Wanderer clear up the relationships of error, truth, and intellectual rank:

> Stoop from those heights, and soberly declare
> What error is; and, of our errors, which
> Doth most debase the mind; the genuine seats
> Of power, where are they? Who shall regulate,
> With truth, the scale of intellectual rank?[33]

The Sage in reply appeals to the experience of the Wanderer himself for the answer. The Wanderer, of all men, should know the answer; for he passed his early years among the hills, where men lived with the fewest wants, and where the imagination worked within the simplest and healthiest confines—the confines of actual experience. And if the working of

---

[30] *The Excursion*, IV, 611-630.
[31] *Op. cit.*, IV, 631-762.
[32] *Op. cit.*, IV, 768-773.
[33] *Op. cit.*, IV, 774-778.

the Imagination brings results that are not approved of by sophisticated men who have "unthinking minds," that is, men who take knowledge at second-hand and without self-activity, they are the person's own, and serve as guides of conscience, and populate the great spaces of the hills.[34]

Then follows the famous explanation of the origin of Greek myths, introduced to show that it is from such activity of mind that man has always nourished the highest emotions and ideas of the race by the means at hand and from first-hand knowledge and experience. The Greeks are taken as a famous case of this transmutation of first-hand experience into moral and ethical judgments; and by this use of the Greek mythology the Wanderer assures the Solitary that if he will throw aside his Voltaire and drink at the fountains of living experience and reality as the Greeks did, he too will arrive at a proper attitude towards life and its problems:

> Once more to distant ages of the world
> Let us revert, and place before our thoughts
> The face which rural solitude might wear
> To the unenlightened swains of pagan Greece.
> —In that fair clime, the lonely herdsman, stretched
> On the soft grass through half a summer's day,
> With music lulled his indolent repose:
> And, in some fit of weariness, if he,
> When his own breath was silent, chanced to hear
> A distant strain, far sweeter than the sounds
> Which his poor skill could make, his fancy fetched,
> Even from the blazing chariot of the sun,
> A beardless Youth, who touched a golden lute,
> And filled the illumined groves with ravishment.
> The nightly hunter, lifting a bright eye
> Up towards the crescent moon, with grateful heart
> Called on the lovely wanderer who bestowed
> That timely light, to share his joyous sport:
> And hence, a beaming Goddess with her Nymphs,
> Across the lawn and through the darksome grove,
> Not unaccompanied with tuneful notes
> By echo multiplied from rock to cave,
> Swept in the storm of chase; as moon and stars
> Glance rapidly along the clouded heaven,
> When winds are blowing strong. The traveller slaked
> His thirst from rill or gushing fount, and thanked

---

[34] *Op. cit.*, IV, 779-846.

The Naiad.   Sunbeams, upon distant hills
Gliding apace, with shadows in their train,
Might with small help from fancy, be transformed
Into fleet Oreads sporting visibly.
The Zephyrs fanning, as they passed, their wings,
Lacked not, for love, fair objects whom they wooed
With gentle whisper.   Withered boughs grotesque,
Stripped of their leaves and twigs by hoary age,
From depth of shaggy covert peeping forth
In the low vale, or on steep mountain-side;
And, sometimes, intermixed with stirring horns
Of the live deer, or goat's depending beard,—
These were the lurking Satyrs, a wild brood
Of gamesome Deities; or Pan himself,
The simple shepherd's awe-inspiring God!"[35]

To this the Solitary answers that it is well that the Wanderer is not in Scotland, or he would be prosecuted for heresy.   In reply, the Wanderer declares that his ancestors and the Greeks alike had found the essence and unity of life, even though they were "far misled."   In this they were much in advance of many people who were far advanced in the thinking of the day, who may know many facts at second-hand, but do not connect their knowledge and know the world as a living whole:

Enquire of ancient wisdom; go, demand
Of mighty Nature, if 't was ever meant
That we should pry far off yet be unraised;
That we should pore, and dwindle as we pore,
Viewing all objects unremittingly
In disconnection dead and spiritless;
And still dividing, and dividing still,

---

[35] *The Excursion*, IV, 847-887.   This passage was much admired by Keats, and not improbably had a profound influence on his interpretation of Greek myth in *Endymion*.   For an invaluable study of the relations between Wordsworth and Keats see Sir Sidney Colvin, *John Keats*, 2 vols. 1917. *passim*.   See also E. de Sélincourt, *The Poems of John Keats*, 1905.

Nearly everyone has heard the story of Keats reading to Wordsworth the *Hymn to Pan*, now found in the first book of *Endymion*, and Wordsworth's remark, "A pretty piece of Paganism."   If we keep in mind Wordsworth's own use of such "Paganism" we can see what he meant.   Such is the voice of fancy, or youth; and so, while it may be pretty, it cannot be ultimate.

Even late in life Wordsworth was interested in this phenomenon of mythologizing.   *Love Lies Bleeding* and *Companion to the Foregoing*, published in 1842 and probably composed then, deal with the problem of solving puzzles in natural objects by seeking a cause "not in Nature's laws, but in Man's fortunes."   This is exactly Fancy, and so could never be considered as ultimately true by Wordsworth.

Break down all grandeur, still unsatisfied
With the perverse attempt, while littleness
May yet become more little; waging thus
An impious warfare with the very life
Of our own souls!

       And if indeed there be
An all-pervading Spirit, upon whom
Our dark foundations rest, could he design
That this magnificent effect of power,
The earth we tread, the sky that we behold
By day, and all the pomp which night reveals;
That these—and that superior mystery
Our vital frame, so fearfully devised,
And the dread soul within it—should exist
Only to be examined, pondered, searched,
Probed, vexed, and criticised?—Accuse me not
Of arrogance, unknown Wanderer as I am,
If, having walked with Nature threescore years,
And offered, far as frailty would allow,
My heart a daily sacrifice to Truth,
I now affirm of Nature and of Truth,
Whom I have served, that their Divinity
Revolts, offended at the ways of men
Swayed by such motives, to such ends employed;
Philosophers, who, though the human soul
Be of a thousand faculties composed.
And twice ten thousand interests, do yet prize
This soul, and the transcendent universe.
No more than as a mirror that reflects
To proud Self-love her own intelligence;
That one, poor, finite object, in the abyss
Of infinite Being, twinkling restlessly![36]

The Wanderer continues, urging that the Solitary depend upon other guides, better than the scoffings of Voltaire, which he has learned in youth;[37] and promises a restoration of the soul's original activity, which leads to Hope and drives out despair, if the Solitary will but do what he should:

Within the soul a faculty abides,
That with interpositions, which would hide
And darken, so can deal that they become
Contingencies of pomp; and serve to exalt
Her native brightness. As the ample moon,
In the deep stillness of a summer even

---

[36] *The Excursion*, IV, 957-994.
[37] *Op. cit.*, IV, 995-1034.

Rising behind a thick and lofty grove,
Burns, like an unconsuming fire of light,
In the green trees; and, kindling on all sides
Their leafy umbrage, turns the dusky veil
Into a substance glorious as her own,
Yea, with her own incorporated, by power
Capacious and serene. Like power abides
In man's celestial spirit; virtue thus
Sets forth and magnifies herself; thus feeds
A calm, a beautiful, and silent fire,
From the encumbrances of mortal life,
From error, disappointment—nay, from guilt;
And sometimes, so relenting justice wills,
From palpable oppressions of despair.[38]

Touched by these eloquent words, the Solitary asks: "But how begin? Is not your advice like advising the creature without wings to fly?" The Wanderer answers that just as there are manifold ways of falling and manifold degrees of guilt and shame, there are manifold and various ways of restoration. But the universal way to peace and hope is by the human way to knowledge, which leads to imagination—imaginative will—the highest activity of the soul. The Solitary's weakness is that he depends on the false conclusions of the reasoning power,—conclusions which he himself has not tested, and which lead to false hopes, because they close the passages through which the ear converses to the heart. In other words, the Wanderer's advice is a sublimation of the advice which Wordsworth himself gave to "Mathetes"—to follow the natural way to knowledge and keep the senses open and the mind active in the assimilation of experience, not deaden the mind's activity by the acceptance of alien, untried knowledge. Thus by natural, human activity, by intercourse with men, and an interest in life as a whole, we build up our

---

[38] *The Excursion*, IV, 1058-1077. Many critics seem to misunderstand the introduction of Voltaire and his *Candide* into *The Excursion*. It seems to be commonly supposed that Wordsworth makes him the pattern of the mocker at things sacred; and this opinion has support in the hard things said of Voltaire in the poem. But Wordsworth and Voltaire agree in condemning *cheap optimism*. Wordsworth disapproves of Voltaire's method and spirit. He is as firmly convinced as Voltaire that this is not "the best of possible worlds"; but he is also convinced that this is the only possible world—"the world of all of us, where we find happiness, or not at all." He does not think that mockery can laugh away that fact, even though it be the mockery of the "laughing sage of France."

Being, and arrive at last at Reason, Hope, Imagination, and Power.[39] In the words of the prose *Argument,* the Wanderer claims that it is happy for us "that the imagination and affections in our own despite mitigate the evils of that state of intellectual slavery which the calculating understanding is so apt to produce,"[40] and to claim that the ideal state of man's mind is "a legitimate union of the imagination, affections, understanding, and reason."

In the year after the publication of *The Excursion,* he composed a sonnet which summarizes the teaching of the fourth book. It attaches the same value to the imagination and expresses the same conviction of the necessity of aspiration to the healthy, normal mind:

> "Weak is the will of Man, his judgment blind;
> Remembrance persecutes, and Hope betrays;
> Heavy is woe;—and joy, for human-kind,
> A mournful thing, so transient is the blaze!"
> Thus might *he* paint our lot of mortal days
> Who wants the glorious faculty assigned
> To elevate the more-than-reasoning Mind,
> And color life's dark cloud with orient rays.
> Imagination is that sacred power,
> Imagination lofty and refined:
> 'T is hers to pluck the amaranthine flower
> Of Faith, and round the sufferer's temples bind
> Wreaths that endure affliction's heaviest shower
> And do not shrink from sorrow's keenest wind.[41]

---

[39] *Op. cit.,* IV, 1106-1274. It is the modest hope of the writer that this exposition of *The Excursion* will do something to clear up Wordsworth's differentiation of reason and the "false, secondary power." The first is real, the second is sham. The first is the result of real experiences built up into the highest forms of "pure" thoughts by association; the second is the result of apathetic borrowing, without any real relationship to the person who holds such opinions. If we grasp this important and fundamental distinction, we shall be saved from such a judgment as that delivered by G. M. Harper, *William Wordsworth,* II, 226: "The real antithesis is not reason, but apathy, as he virtually admits in his Argument to the Fourth Book; yet it is reason, after all, which he attacks in the text." Both of these statements are wrong: Apathy is contrasted not with imagination, but with superstition, i. e., fancy; and reason, as I hope I have abundantly shown, is never attacked by Wordsworth.

[40] In the 1814 edition.

[41] *Miscellaneous Sonnets,* Part I, No. XXXV. On the interpretation of this part of *The Excursion,* the reader will do well to consult W. Hale White, *An Examination of the Charge of Apostasy against Wordsworth,* 1898.

The dialogue on the attainment of hope and happiness is resumed in the eighth book, after the stories of the Pastor have been told; and in this book the question of reconstruction is taken up in the general, rather than the personal, aspect. The evils of manufacturing are discussed, with its breaking up of the family life and the "long captivity" of the child in the mill, leading to the disintegration of English society through crime, ignorance, poverty, and beggary.[42]   Moreover, the country boy is also left in ignorance; and yet we dare to call our country one which assures *liberty,* when it does not assure *liberty of mind* through education.[43]   The ninth book begins with the familiar idea of activity, reminding us that "an active principle" is assigned to "all things," "all natures," and the conclusion is drawn that this principle is best seen in man, through childhood, youth and maturity.[44]   Therefore Man must never be regarded as a *passive* thing, nor forced to be such.   No man must be oppressed, but all must be free

> to obey the law
> Of life, and hope, and action.[45]

This principle of the human mind implies the cultivation of man's birthright, Reason; and the social programme which logically results from it means the putting down of ignorance through the education of every child in England. This is Wordsworth's ideal—education for all, as he expresses himself in this well-known passage, and it will be noted, education by the State:

> O for the coming of that glorious time
> When, prizing knowledge as her noblest wealth
> And best protection, this imperial Realm,
> While she exacts allegiance, shall admit
> An obligation, on her part, to *teach*
> Them who are born to serve her and obey;
> Binding herself by statute to secure
> For all the children whom her soil maintains
> The rudiments of letters, and inform
> The mind with moral and religious truth,
> Both understood and practised,—so that none

---

[42] *The Excursion,* VIII, 196-391.
[43] *Op. cit.,* VIII, 391.
[44] *Op. cit.,* IX, 1-44.
[45] *Op. cit.,* IX, 127-128.

However destitute, be left to droop
By timely culture unsustained; or run
Into a wild disorder; or be forced
To drudge through a weary life without the help
Of intellectual implements and tools;
A savage horde among the civilised,
A servile band among the lordly free!
This sacred right, the lisping babe proclaims
To be inherent in him, by Heaven's will,
For the protection of his innocence;
And the rude boy—who, having overpast
The sinless age, by conscience is enrolled,
Yet mutinously knits his angry brow,
And lifts his wilful hand on mischief bent,
Or turns the godlike faculty of speech
To impious use—by process indirect
Declares his due, while he makes known his need.
—This sacred right is fruitlessly announced,
This universal plea in vain addressed,
To eyes and ears of parents who themselves
Did, in the time of their necessity,
Urge it in vain; and, therefore, like a prayer
That from the humblest floor ascends to heaven,
It mounts to reach the State's parental ear;
Who, if indeed she own a mother's heart,
And be not most unfeelingly devoid
Of gratitude to Providence, will grant
The unquestionable good—which, England, safe
From interference of external force,
May grant at leisure; without risk incurred
That what in wisdom for herself she doth,
Others shall e'er be able to undo.[46]

Thus the way to both personal and social regeneration is pointed out: the soul's integrity and activity in the individual through strenuous individual effort, and the chance to be active and integral in soul to every child in England. This is the cure for false hopes which lead to despair in the individual and to the destruction of the nation. This is as far as the demonstration goes in *The Excursion,* but he tells us in a note that he intended to carry the case of the Solitary to the point where a cure for his despair was found. It is to be noted that of this unexecuted plan the three ages formed an essential part. The note reads as follows, referring to the lines

---

[46] *Op. cit.,* IX, 293-335.

> But turned not without welcome promise made,
> That he would share the pleasures and pursuits
> Of yet another summer's day, consumed
> In wandering with us:[47]

When I reported this promise of the Solitary, and long after, it was my wish, and I might say intention, that we should resume our wanderings, and pass the Borders into his native country, where, as I hoped, he might witness, in the society of the Wanderer, some religious ceremony—a sacrament, say, in the open fields, or a preaching among the mountains—which, by recalling to his mind the days of his early childhood, when he had been present on such occasions in company with his parents and nearest kindred, might have dissolved his heart into tenderness, and so to have done more toward restoring the Christian faith in which he had been educated, and, with that, contentedness and even cheerfulness of mind, than all that the Wanderer and the Pastor, by their several effusions and addresses, had been able to effect. But alas!

> 'mid the wreck of *IS* and *WAS*,
> Things incomplete and purposes betrayed
> Make sadder transits o'er thought's optic glass
> Than noblest objects utterly decayed.[48]

We shall now turn to the stories which are told in the poem by the Pastor and others.[49] These are placed in various parts of the poem: (1) The stories of the Wanderer, and Margaret in Book I; (2) The Story of the Old Man in Book II, 73-895,

---

[47] *The Excursion*, IX, 775-777.

[48] Fenwick note to *The Excursion*, 1843. The quotation at the end is from the sonnet *Malham Cove*, composed in 1818 and published in 1819, *Miscellaneous Sonnets*, Part II, No. XXXIV.

[49] I have not said much regarding the literary relationships of *The Excursion*. Two such relationships, however, should be briefly signalized.
(1) I have already spoken of the *English Eclogues*, 1799, of Robert Southey. Several of these are strikingly like some of the stories in *The Excursion*. *The Doctor*, 1834-1847, also contains a story much like Wordsworth's, entitled *The Two Orphans*. There must have been considerable give and take between Wordsworth, Southey, Coleridge, Lamb, Thelwall and others of that interesting group from 1793-1798.
(2) This list includes one name especially linked with *The Excursion*. John Thelwall published *The Peripatetic* in 1793, a prose and verse miscellany gathered around the general plan of a series of excursions about the neighborhood of London. There are a philosopher ("Ambulator"), a poet, and a cynic ("Arisor"). Stories of a sad nature are told, four of them being told in Fulham churchyard. Crabb Robinson, writing to John Thelwall in 1815 seems to imply that Wordsworth borrowed from Thelwall in composing *The Excursion*. At any rate, he says Wordsworth borrowed "without acknowledgment." *Diary* I, 248. See also Charles Cestre, *John Thelwall*, 1906.
The Excursion in its essential originality of argument and spirit is not involved in any relationship with the work of either of these authors.

and of the Solitary in Books II and III; (3) the story of the Quarryman and his Wife, told by the Pastor in Book V; followed by (4) the group of stories dealing with certain graves in the Grasmere Churchyard, told by the Pastor;—accounts of the Rejected Lover, the Miner, the Prodigal, the Jacobite and Hanoverian, the Unamiable Woman, the Amiable Woman (Ellen), Wilfred Armathwaite, the Widower who did not re-marry, the Widower who did re-marry,[50] in Book VI; and the stories of the Sporting Parson, the Virtuous Parson ("Wonderful" Walker), the Deaf Man, the Blind Man, and the vigorous Timberman (who is not dead, but passes with his team and timber wain), the Infant Girl, the Volunteer Oswald, and the Knight, in Book VII. Of the living and the dead, of the characters who actually appear in the poem and of those who do not appear save through their biographies, there are narrated twenty-two stories, four concerning the living and eighteen concerning the dead.

These stories are an integral part of the poem, giving rise to the philosophical discussion, or arising out of it, and illustrating it. In order, therefore, to judge the purpose of the stories, it is essential to keep clearly in mind the purpose of the whole poem, and thus to judge of the stories as a whole in their connection with the development of this purpose. We shall consider these stories in the order in which we have named them.

The story of the Wanderer[51] is told by the author, and is developed in accordance with the method of the three ages of man, as we have noted in Chapter V. It is the story of a man who has had a normal development, and so has arrived at true knowledge, and so to a proper ethical outlook on life, with the result that his is a philosophy of Hope. He is thus a fitting character to represent the central idea in this poem, which preaches the "sanity of Hope." As a contrast to this story, there follows the story of Margaret.[52] According to Words-worth's own testimony, a part of the story was composed at

<hr />

[50] The story of the Widower who married again and redeemed his fields was omitted in the edition of 1827, appearing only in the editions of 1814 and 1820.

[51] *The Excursion*, I, 108-433.

[52] *Op. cit.*, I, 1-37; 438-956.

Racedown in 1795,[53] and was completed by 1798. Thus the
story extends over the period of the drama, *The Borderers,*
1795-1796; *Poor Susan,* 1797; *Peter Bell,* 1798; and the poems
published in the first edition of the *Lyrical Ballads,* 1798, with
the exception of *The Female Vagrant,* 1791-1794, *The Convict,*
1793; and probably *Lines Left Upon a Seat in a Yew-Tree.* It
is also contemporaneous with Coleridge's *The Three Graves,*
Lewti, and *The Ancient Mariner,* as well as with Southey's
English Eclogues, and shares with them certain striking characteristics. We know the artistic motive which led to the composition of some of these poems: Wordsworth has made it
clear that he intended to show the workings of "the primary
laws of our nature" when the characters are displayed under excitement.[54] Thus we find several poems on the maternal passion
and the wifely passion. This connects closely with *Margaret,*
bringing this poem and *The Thorn, The Mad Mother, The
Idiot Boy,* and *The Complaint of a Forsaken Indian Woman*
into one group, which also includes nearly all of Southey's
English Eclogues, one of which is called *The Ruined Cottage,*
which is the other name of Wordsworth's *Margaret.* In the
same manner, the theme of a soul under a curse connects
Goody Blake and Harry Gill, The Ancient Mariner, and *The
Three Graves* into another group; and the "passion of property" and "the love of property" is the central idea of still another set of poems. It is clear that *Margaret* belongs to the
first group, and that it is the study of a wife and mother, who
had been widowed through her poverty, which was caused by
war and famine; whose husband, unmanned by poverty, had
abandoned her, enlisted in the army or navy, and gone to a
distant land. Beaten down by her misfortunes, she neglects
her house and garden and children, and for nine tedious years
thinks only of her husband, for whom she vainly waits in "tor-
turing hope." Whether Wordsworth had formulated his theory
of the primary human passions as early as 1795 we cannot say,
but it is a fact that the part of the story which most clearly

---

[53] *The Excursion,* I, 871-916.
[54] *Preface* of 1800. See Ch. IX.

shows the wifely passion was composed the first.[55]   As the
Wanderer says, in introducing the story,—

> 'Tis a common tale,
> An ordinary sorrow of man's life,
> A tale of silent suffering, hardly clothed
> In bodily form.[56]

As a tale of "silent suffering" it is closely connected with
certain of the poems already mentioned, which show the dumb
acceptance of sorrow and wrong; for instance with *The Mad
Mother,* who also looks for her husband and her child's father
to return—and in vain,—without resentment and in like "tor-
turing hope"; with *The Last of the Flock;* with *Simon Lee,*
who suffered neglect and poverty, not resentful at the spectacle of "man's inhumanity to man," which left the poet
mourning; with *The Complaint of a Forsaken Indian Woman;*
with *The Thorn;* with *The Old Man Travelling;* as well as
with Coleridge's *The Three Graves;* and Southey's *Hannah,
The Ruined Cottage, The Sailor's Mother,* and *The Old Mansion House.*   Truly, if we consider the number of poems
which this group of related men wrote on this theme, and add
to them the stories of Crabbe, Lamb, De Quincey, Fawcett, and
Thelwall, such a situation was a "common tale, an ordinary
sorrow," in literature as well as in life.

The relation which the story bears to the poem of which it
forms a part is indicated by the discussion between the Wanderer and the poet.   This tale ought not to be told, except for
the good results which it will bring.   It has the disadvantage
of turning the minds of the listeners from "natural comfort,"
and "natural wisdom" to a story which leads us, "with un-
toward mind," to feed on disquiet and thus to disturb the "calm
of nature with our restless thoughts";[57] and it also has the disadvantage of seeming to "hold vain dalliance with the misery"
of the dead, and to extract from it "a momentary pleasure."
But such is not our case; for in the "mournful thoughts"
which are evoked by such a story there may be "a power to
virtue friendly," which is marked by reason, and productive

---

[55] Lines 871-916.
[56] Lines 636-639.
[57] Lines 593-604.

17

of "future good."[58] It is to be noted that the Wanderer says that such power might always be found in such stories. On what does this power depend? Why do he and the poet not deserve the "severe reproof" demanded for those who, in their "wantonness," and for the sake of a mere "momentary pleasure," violate the sanctities of the dead? Because the "pleasure" which they derive from it is not a momentary one, but one which has "future good" and is approved by reason. That is to say, the "pleasures" which are derived from the painful thoughts, which, according to the law of association, are transformed to pleasure and are approved of reason, are the "pleasing thoughts that spring out of human suffering," of the *Ode*. At the end of the tale, this principle is expounded in the concluding discussion of the first book.

> The old Man ceased: he saw that I was moved;
> From that low bench, rising instinctively
> I turned aside in weakness, nor had power
> To thank him for the tale which he had told.
> I stood, and leaning o'er the garden wall
> Reviewed that Woman's sufferings; and it seemed
> To comfort me while with a brother's love
> I blessed her in the impotence of grief,
> Then towards the cottage I returned; and traced
> Fondly, though with an interest more mild,
> That secret spirit of humanity
> Which, 'mid the calm oblivious tendencies
> Of nature, 'mid her plants, and weeds, and flowers,
> And silent overgrowings, still survived.[59]

This was the first effect of the tale on the Poet: "the impotence of grief" at the spectacle of the survival of the "secret spirit of humanity" even in the ruins of what was once a human habitation.

But this is a mere luxuriating in passive emotion, and it must not be allowed to become a habit. Enough if the impression be made; for the mind must not be subdued into mere passivity, but must maintain its own healthful activity. The sorrows we feel for the sufferings of Herbert and his daughter Idonea, of Simon Lee, the old huntsman, of Ruth, of Martha Ray, of the forsaken Indian Woman, and of all virtuous per-

---

[58] Lines 625-636.
[59] Lines 917-930.

sons, are healthful only when we have the strength to rise above the "impotence of grief" and out of it create health of mind and happiness.

The Wanderer sums up this wisdom of life in his closing speech. The grief which the painful case of Margaret caused is far in the past, and for him has been transformed into the high pleasure of intellectual judgment; not the merely surface "natural wisdom," and "natural comfort" which do not arise out of deep experience and meditation, but derived merely through the illusory appearances of external nature which speaks to us only in analogies and not in facts. The Wanderer observes the emotion and "weakness" of the younger man; and continues his speech:—

> The old Man, noting this, resumed, and said,
> "My Friend! enough to sorrow you have given,
> The purposes of wisdom ask no more:
> Be wise and cheerful, and no longer read
> The forms of things with an unworthy eye:
> She sleeps in the calm earth, and peace is here."[60]

This is the conclusion of the Hartleian Wanderer; the impression is made, and the processes of life will transform the sadness into cheerfulness and wisdom. To show how this process is carried on he cites his own case. Oppressed by the uneasy thoughts which the case of Margaret had stirred within him, he once saw the very same ruins and weed-grown walls which the young man now sees in grief, and the peace of the scene entered into his heart. This peace, "factitious" at first, asserted its power, and, under the processes of life, in accordance with which the good grows greater and the evil less, became transformed into the higher powers of the mind, and resulted in sympathy, wisdom, enlightenment, and happiness:

> I well remember that those very plumes,
> Those weeds, and the high spear-grass on that wall,
> By mist and silent rain-drops silvered o'er,
> As once I passed, into my heart conveyed
> So still an image of tranquillity,
> So calm and still, and looked so beautiful
> Amid the uneasy thoughts which filled my mind,
> That what we feel of sorrow and despair

---

[60] Lines 931-936. This is the text of the Edition of 1814.

> From ruin and from change, and all the grief
> That passing shows of Being leave behind,
> Appeared an idle dream, that could not live
> Where meditation was. I turned
> And walked along my road in happiness.[61]

This is the justification of the presence of the story of Margaret's sufferings in this poem, the theme of which is Hope and Optimism, and it is at once cast in the terms of Hartleian associationism and of the discussion of Hope in the fourth book. I wish to note especially that it is cast in the terms of Hartley and associationism; for in a recent paper by Professor O. J. Campbell, already referred to in the tenth chapter, the most thorough discussion of this and related stories of Wordsworth, the story of Margaret is interpreted in a somewhat different manner.[62] Professor Campbell makes the tale teach a *sentimental* morality, and at the same time connects it with the philosophy of Hartley. Professor Campbell has defended his position by quotations from Hartley, chiefly from those sections of the *Observations on Man* which deal with sympathy; but he does not take account of Hartley's doctrine of association, in the light of which the doctrine of sympathy must be interpreted. I have stated the fundamental principles of this process in that part of Chapter III where I deal with the differences between Hartley and the other important and opposed system of Shaftesbury. I may be permitted to state them in summary fashion once more, on account of the important issues involved. According to Hartley, the results of hearing such a tale are not immediate, especially in the young or youthful, for before the moral judgment can come into being there must be a complex development in accordance with the law of association, before the experience can come to its full growth as sympathy, theopathy, or the moral sense. Only in the highly developed cases of moral judgment is there an immediate transference of such judgments.[63] The sentimentalists, on the contrary, as represented by Shaftesbury, Hutcheson, and Butler, held that there is a "moral sense" in man, to which appeal can be made inde-

---

[61] Lines 942-956. The version of the edition of 1814 is here given.
[62] O. J. Campbell, *Sentimental Morality in Wordsworth*, University of Wisconsin Studies in Language and Literature, No. 11, 1920.
[63] *Observations on Man*, I, 497.

pendently of reason and the experience of the individual. Moreover, they held that this moral sense is to be identified with public good. Hence sympathy is given a very important role; it is superior to reason, and by virtue of the identity of the moral sense and public weal it is the instrument by which man indulges in expansive identification with all outside himself, and places the standard of morality not within himself but without him. Adding to these characteristics of the moral sense school, their conception of virtue as absolutely disinterested and so independent of a God, we have the resulting trust in emotion and the expansive feeling, and the exaltation of these feelings into the place of the theistic conception of Hartley.

These are the characteristics of sentimental morality. But they are not those of the philosophy of Hartley, nor of Wordsworth, as I have attempted to show in my statement of what I conceive to be the purpose of this and related poems, as well as by my discussions of the fundamentals of Wordsworth's thought. Professor Campbell does well to lay stress on the words of the Wanderer:

> But we have known that there is often found
> In mournful thoughts, and always might be found,
> A power to virtue friendly;[64]

But it must be pointed out that in interpreting these lines we must interpret them in accordance with Wordsworth's whole doctrine; and this principle demands that we interpret them in accordance with Hartley's system and not in accordance with Shaftesbury's: that is with associationism, not with sentimentalism.[65]

In another aspect I find Professor Campbell's article insufficient for my purpose. In this chapter, I am studying *The Excursion* as a whole, and I must regard any theory of the stories as inadequate which does not include all the stories, but only a limited number. Now, all the stories are not such as give rise to

[64] Lines 632-634.
[65] A very useful differentiation between sentimentalism as opposed to intellectualism, and sentimentalism as opposed to associationism, will be found in the Introduction to L. A. Selby-Bigge: *British Moralists*, 2 vols., 1897. The distinction between the sentimental and associationistic interpretation of virtue is clearly expressed in James Seth, *English Philos-*

262   UNIVERSITY OF WISCONSIN STUDIES

"mournful thoughts," but to those of a quite different nature, and yet the stories must serve a common, general purpose in the plan of the poem. Hence, even though Professor Campbell did explain certain of the stories considered individually, his theory is defective as a method of explaining the stories as a whole. The next story, that of the old man who died as the result of exposure to a storm in the mountains, is the mournful tale of one who had reached "The still contentedness of seventy years," and who meekly and apathetically bore the severe labor which he was called upon to do and died without a murmur.[66] The story is told by the Solitary to illustrate the heartlessness that is not seldom found in this valley, which might seem to harbor none but those who might belong to the golden age. It illustrates "man's inhumanity to man," but it is lightened by the description of the sunshine in the storm—"heaven's pomp is shed on ground which British shepherds tread." It is followed by no comment, save that the Solitary characterizes it as "a dolorous tale."

Next comes the autobiography of the Solitary,[67] the story of one who has missed Hope by the perversion of his powers induced by the passive yielding to grief, which first divorced him from his kind, then led him to have false hopes in the French Revolution, and to fall into despair when the dawn of a new day which it promised, faded into primeval, hideous night. Thence followed loss of faith in God and man and the dominion of misanthropy and despair. At this point the story ceases, for it is the opening of the great debate on the sanity of Hope, which occupies the whole of the fourth book and about half of the fifth. The debate has reached the final point in the actual attainment of Hope, when the question is raised as to how the "active energy" of mind will lead to wisdom, even when necessity restricts the development of the in-

ophers and Schools of Philosophy, pp. 188-217. Many critics of Wordsworth would do well to acquaint themselves with the simple and fundamental distinction between these two systems of thought. It is difficult to conceive that anyone who realizes the distinct characteristics of each can identify Wordsworth with the sentimentalists.

[66] Lines 729-895.

[67] Lines 480-991. The original of this character, Joseph Fawcett, is interestingly discussed in the Fenwick note to The Excursion. I have gathered some information concerning him in my edition of his Art of War, University of Wisconsin Studies in Language and Literature, No. 2, 1918.

dividual; for if the "active principle" operates, the "necessity" will become "benign."[68] The Solitary utters some ironical words in praise of such necessity, and he demands that the Pastor give them "solid facts" in place of the "abstractions" in which they had been dealing.[69] The Pastor responds by telling of a Quarryman and his wife[70] who, under the stress of "necessity" rendered "benign" by their diligence, live a life of wholesome fact and cheerful acceptance of their fate. He does not get very far in his story, for he is interrupted by the Wanderer, who completes it. It is not tragic, but just such a tale as could have been told of many a toiler on the fells of the district.

But the cynicism of the Solitary is not quieted, and he declares that he knew but one such contented man,[71] for they are "thinly sown," most of them being marked rather by "selfishness, and cruelty, and vice." This is what the boasted solitude of the Lakes breeds, or at least what it has not the power to cure.[72]

Not answering or offering any opposition to this opinion, the Pastor proceeds to tell the stories of some of the graves in the churchyard, beginning with the Rejected Lover.[73] This is the story of a young man who was disappointed in love, but who possessed the requisite powers of mind to prevent the apathy of grief from mastering him. He resorted to books and natural science "searching for truth with keener appetite and closer industry"; and so, in spite of grief and disease, he conquered his restless thoughts and found harmony.

> The powers, that had been lost
> By slow degrees, were gradually regained;
> The fluttering nerves composed; the beating heart
> In rest established; and the jarring thoughts
> To harmony restored.[74]

Next follows the story of one who "achieved a humbler victory," the Miner,[75] who sought for years gold in the hills, and

[68] *The Excursion*, V, 562-601.
[69] Lines 601-656.
[70] Lines 670-837.
[71] Lines 862-877.
[72] Lines 838-890.
[73] *Op. cit.*, VI, 95-211.
[74] Lines 192-196.
[75] Lines 212-254.

was at last successful. But his good fortune was too much for him, and he fell into bad habits and disappeared. However, his great qualities of hope and perseverance remain in the path which is still to be seen between his cottage and the mine, for it is called "The Path of Perseverance."

Next follows the Prodigal, who thrice ventured forth into far countries and thrice returned; who repented and was buried in the quiet churchyard. Strange contrasts there are in human life!

"But," says the Solitary, "it is strange that this man should have made himself known; are there none here who would rather shun than seek the fellowship of kindred mould?" "Yes," answers the Pastor, and tells the story of the Jacobite and the Hanoverian,[76] who had come to spend their last days in the vale and finally became reconciled to each other, and were buried together by the monumental sundial which they had erected in common, away from other men.

The poet desires

> To have *one* Enclosure where the voice that speaks
> In envy or detraction is not heard;
> Which malice may not enter; where the traces
> Of evil inclinations are unknown;
> Where love and pity tenderly unite
> With resignation; and no jarring tone
> Intrudes, the peaceful concert to disturb
> Of amity and gratitude.[77]

To this the Pastor answers,

> "Thus sanctioned,"
> The Pastor said, "I willingly confine
> My narratives to subjects that excite
> Feelings with these accordant; love, esteem,
> And admiration; lifting up a veil,
> A sunbeam introducing among hearts
> Retired and covert; so that ye shall have
> Clear images before your gladdened eyes
> Of nature's unambitious underwood,
> And flowers that prosper in the shade. And when
> I speak of such among my flock as swerved
> Or fell, those only shall be singled out

---

[76] *The Excursion*, VI, 405-521.
[77] Lines 638-645.

Upon whose lapse, or error, something more
Than brotherly forgiveness may attend;
To such will we restrict our notice, else
Better my tongue were mute.
                    And yet there are,
I feel, good reasons why we should not leave
Wholly untraced a more forbidding way.
For, strength to persevere and to support,
And energy to conquer and repel—
These elements of virtue, that declare
The native grandeur of the human soul—
Are ofttimes not unprofitably shown
In the perverseness of a selfish course:
Truth every day exemplified, no less
In the grey cottage by the murmuring stream
Than in fantastic conqueror's roving camp,
Or 'mid the factious senate unappalled
Whoe'er may sink, or rise—to sink again,
As merciless proscription ebbs and flows."[78]

Thus he tells of those who attain and those who do not. The first case is that of the Unamiable Woman,[79] who was torn between "two passions" which had degenerated into vices, avaricious thrift and maternal love, but who was softened into meekness, and sank with resignation into the grave.

In contrast with this story is the story of Ellen, the Amiable Woman,[80] who was seduced by a villain and left with her infant in poverty. But her mother instinct survived disgrace and separation, and she died in peace and in resignation to her fate.

The story of Wilfred Armathwaite[81] is next in order, the tale of one who broke his marriage vow, and found no forgiveness in himself nor could endure the weight of his own shame.

Next in order is the story of the Widower who devoted himself to the care of his six daughters, repressing all other desires,[82] which is succeeded by the story of the Widower who married a second wife, and by her goodness and "prudential

[78] Lines 645-674.
[79] Lines 675-777.
[80] Lines 787-1052.
[81] Lines 1079-1113.
[82] Lines 1114-1191.

habits" redeemed his fields, which are still held by his eldest son.[83]

At this point the poet notes five graves close together and encroaching on the playgrounds of the village school. The Pastor now tells the story connected with them; the story of the Clergyman[84] who came from the great world, a dissipated and disappointed man; but who through frank acceptance of the facts of life, won a spiritual victory and peace.

Then the story of the Other Clergyman,[85] "Wonderful" Walker, is told—a veritable "good parson," the living exemplar to the world of temperance, industry, self-denial, forbearance, and charity in deed and thought.

People of bodily infirmity are buried in the churchyard, and the stories of two of these are told; the story of the Deaf Man,[86] and the Blind Man,[87] both of whom found true wisdom, hope and peace, in spite of bodily weaknesses.

Here the necrology is interrupted by the appearance of the hearty old Timber man,[88] a man "of cheerful yesterdays and confident tomorrows," whose joy consists in felling the great trees for ships and mines and factories, regardless of any associations they might have for those who loved them.

Next is the story of the influence of An Infant[89] in its life and death in humanizing parents, brothers, and grandsire.

The Volunteer's story is now begun,[90] a glowing account of patriotism; and the series is completed by the tale of a Knight, Sir Alfred Irthing,[91] who labored amid a time as full of strife and ferment as the present, to redress human wrongs and to enact the law of gentleness.

---

[83] *The Excursion*, VI, 1193-1267. Only in the editions of 1814 and 1820.

[84] *Op. cit.*, VII, 38-291.

[85] Lines 291-360. The story of the remarkable man who was the original of this character is told at some length in Sonnets XVII and XVIII of the sonnet series, *The River Duddon*, (1820) and in the long note appended.

[86] Lines 395-481.

[87] Lines 482-536.

[88] Lines 537-631.

[89] Lines 632-694.

[90] Lines 695-890.

[91] Lines 921-1057.

Thus the series teaches what it set out to teach—

> words of heartfelt truth,
> Tending to patience when affliction strikes;
> To hope and love; to confident repose
> In God; and reverence for the dust of Man.[92]

This is the way to Truth, and Hope, and Virtue; it is the way of experience; the way of life, by which way alone man acquires the final wisdom so hardly won and so precious in the having. This has been illustrated in argument and in story, and those spirits who are maimed by the false transports and their inevitable consequences, dejection and degradation, would do well to listen. For the only way of perfection is the culture of the individual: mere generous feeling and expansive emotion will not suffice. Self-discipline, self-knowledge, self-control—these mark the way to truth. For Wordsworth always keeps clearly in mind the principle that the moral state of the individual is made possible only by individual morality. To attain morality, growth of the individual is necessary, and hence Wordsworth's great programme of education for every child in England. Self-activity, he holds, is the only preservative of mental health; and every child whose development is checked by neglect on the part of the State so that he becomes merely a passive thing is a menace to the state itself. Education is the instrument of individual development and activity; thence education *for all* is the prime necessity. This is his scheme of reconstruction for his age. This was the high argument of his Great Philosophical Poem, as he himself expressed it in words which are at once the sublimation of philosophic thought, ethical fervor, and poetry:

> On Man, on Nature, and on Human Life,
> Musing in solitude, I oft perceive
> Fair trains of imagery before me rise,
> Accompanied by feelings of delight
> Pure, or with no unpleasing sadness mixed;
> And I am conscious of affecting thoughts
> And dear remembrances, whose presence soothes
> Or elevates the Mind, intent to weigh
> The good and evil of our mortal state.
> —To these emotions, whencesoe'er they come,

[92] *Op. cit.*, VII, 1054-1057.

Whether from breath of outward circumstance,
Or from the Soul—an impulse to herself—
I would give utterance in numerous verse.
Of Truth, of Grandeur, Beauty, Love, and Hope,
And melancholy Fear subdued by Faith;
Of blessed consolations in distress;
Of moral strength, and intellectual Power;
Of joy in widest commonalty spread;
Of the individual Mind that keeps her own
Inviolate retirement, subject there
To Conscience only, and the law supreme
Of that Intelligence which governs all—
I sing:—"fit audience let me find though few!"
So prayed, more gaining than he asked, the Bard—
In holiest mood. Urania, I shall need
Thy guidance, or a greater Muse, if such
Descend to earth or dwell in highest heaven!
For I must tread on shadowy ground, must sink
Deep—and, aloft ascending, breathe in worlds
To which the heaven of heavens is but a veil.
All strength—all terror, single or in bands,
That ever was put forth in personal form—
Jehovah—with his thunder, and the choir
Of shouting Angels, and the empyreal thrones—
I pass them unalarmed. Not Chaos, not
The darkest pit of lowest Erebus,
Nor aught of blinder vacancy, scooped out
By help of dreams—can breed such fear and awe
As fall upon us often when we look
Into our Minds, into the Mind of Man—
My haunt, and the main region of my song.
—Beauty—a living Presence of the earth,
Surpassing the most fair ideal Forms
Which craft of delicate Spirits hath composed
From earth's materials—waits upon my steps;
Pitches her tents before me as I move,
An hourly neighbour. Paradise, and groves
Elysian, Fortunate Fields—like those of old
Sought in the Atlantic Main—why should they be
A history only of departed things,
Or a mere fiction of what never was?
For the discerning intellect of Man,
When wedded to this goodly universe
In love and holy passion, shall find these
A simple produce of the common day.
—I, long before the blissful hour arrives,
Would chant, in lonely peace, the spousal verse
Of this great consummation:—and, by words

Which speak of nothing more than what we are,
Would I arouse the sensual from their sleep
Of Death, and win the vacant and the vain
To noble raptures; while my voice proclaims
How exquisitely the individual Mind
(And the progressive powers perhaps no less
Of the whole species) to the external World
Is fitted:—and how exquisitely, too—
Theme this but little heard of among men—
The external World is fitted to the Mind;
And the creation (by no lower name
Can it be called) which they with blended might
Accomplish:—this is our high argument.
—Such grateful haunts foregoing, if I oft
Must turn elsewhere—to travel near the tribes
And fellowships of men, and see ill sights
Of madding passions mutually inflamed;
Must hear Humanity in fields and groves
Pipe solitary anguish; or must hang
Brooding above the fierce confederate storm
Of sorrow, barricadoed evermore
Within the walls of cities—may these sounds
Have their authentic comment; that even these
Hearing, I be not downcast or forlorn!—
Descend, prophetic Spirit! that inspir'st
The human Soul of universal earth,
Dreaming on things to come; and dost possess
A metropolitan temple in the hearts
Of mighty Poets: upon me bestow
A gift of genuine insight; that my Song
With star-like virtue in its place may shine,
Shedding benignant influence, and secure,
Itself, from all malevolent effect
Of those mutations that extend their sway
Throughout the nether sphere!—And if with this
I mix more lowly matter; with the thing
Contemplated, describe the Mind and Man
Contemplating; and who, and what he was—
The transitory Being that beheld
This Vision; when and where, and how he lived;—
Be not this labour useless. If such theme
May sort with highest objects, then—dread Power!
Whose gracious favour is the primal source
Of all illumination,—may my Life
Express the image of a better time,
More wise desires, and simpler manners;—nurse
My Heart in genuine freedom:—all pure thoughts

> Be with me;—so shall thy unfailing love
> Guide, and support, and cheer me to the end!

This is the argument, not only of his philosophical poem, but of his whole work. In all his mature work he speaks of no world but "the world of all of us"; he knows of no knowledge but the knowledge of experience; he knows of no joy but the "joy in widest commonalty spread"; he knows of no virtue save that which is within the experience of all of us; he knows no ideal save the ideal which is "the simple produce of the common day." If he repudiates hopes, ideals, and promises, he repudiates them because they are not founded on fact and on reality. He repudiates the hopes of the French Revolution, not because he repudiates idealism and hope, but because he believes that the facts of human nature make such hope impossible and fantastic. He is the "lost leader" and the "apostate" only to those who have not advanced in the knowledge of life far enough to know that we cannot ignore the facts of human life and the world without incurring the certain fate of the despondency which follows upon the fading of fallacious hope. He deserts the cause of what he conceives to be surface idealism because he owes allegiance to truth; to the higher truth which is found in the heart of man. In thus turning from the "false, secondary" knowledge which was proclaimed by the youthful and by the surface thinkers of the day as the ultimate truth, and turning to the ultimate reality of experience, he builds hope on a sure foundation as deep as the foundations of life itself. The "great philosophic poem" in which these foundations are laid, is thus the culmination of his work; and at the same time most clearly points out the historical relationships which it holds in the realm of thought.[93] In the spirit of searching enquiry for a foundation of fact, as contrasted with a foundation of theory, it is in the great tradition of English philosophy, in which Bacon and Locke and Hume are conspicuous figures, a movement which resulted in Utilitarianism and all its beneficent endeavors on behalf of the common man. This endeavor was always Wordsworth's; and he found

---

[93] To avoid any possible misunderstanding, I wish to point out that I am speaking of the Wordsworth of *The Excursion*. His later Toryism is a separate question, which I do not discuss here.

in David Hartley this beneficent desire expressed congenially
to his own spirit and supported by a system of thought which
commended it to his reason. Furthermore, it commended itself
to his imagination as well, and as a result we have his poetry,
at once a product of the imagination and the reason; or, as
Wordsworth himself expresses it, "of Reason in her most exalted mood."

CHAPTER XIII

CONCLUSION

His *fame* belongs to another age, and can neither be accelerated nor retarded. How small the proportion of the defects are to the beauties, I have repeatedly declared; and that no one of them originates in deficiency of poetic genius. Had they been more and greater, I should still, as a friend to his literary character in the present age, consider an analytic display of them as *pure gain;* if only it removed, as surely to all reflecting minds even the foregoing analysis must have removed, the strange mistake, so slightly grounded, yet so widely and industriously propagated, of Mr. Wordsworth's turn for *simplicity!* I am not half so much irritated by hearing his enemies abuse him for vulgarity of style, subject, and conception; as I am disgusted with the gilded side of the same meaning, as displayed by some affected admirers, with whom he is, forsooth, a *sweet, simple poet!* and *so* natural, that little Master Charles and his youngest sister are *so* charmed with them, that they play at "Goody Blake," or at "Johnny and Betty Foy!"

Samuel Taylor Coleridge,
Biographia Literaria, 1817.

We place these words of Coleridge at the head of this chapter for the reason that they express very clearly and strikingly the general aim of the present study.

In the first place, we have made it as plain as it is possible for us to do so, that Wordsworth is a philosophical poet, and a philosophical poet not merely in the general sense of a contemplative or meditative poet, but a philosophical poet who expresses a distinctive philosophy. That is to say, we have tried to show that he is the poet of the English philosophy of Locke and his school in general, and of the English associationistic philosophy in particular.

In the second place, we have fully recognized that such a method of interpretation brings with it certain necessary consequences, one of which is the clear perception of the falsity of the idea which is fully as widely propagated today as in Coleridge's time, that Wordsworth is a simple writer. This point of view also puts into our possession an intelligent and consistent solution of these difficulties. Every careful reader of Wordsworth must recognize the profundity and difficulty of many parts of this poetry and prose; and when the critic attempts to solve these difficulties he will find that it does not help to declare that there is no system of philosophy, no philosophy at all. On the contrary, he speedily finds that he is without any key to the difficulties that the poet presents, as the example of some eminent critics has demonstrated. Arnold's attempt to establish the fame of the poet by ignoring his philosophy is a conspicuous example of this mode of procedure; and while in this particular case it has had a popular success, it achieves that success by ignoring most of the poet's verse and all his prose. That Arnold had to gain his success in this manner is a sure indication that the use of a system of philosophy in the interpretation of Wordsworth does not create difficulties which would never occur to anyone who has no philosophy. The simple fact is that the critic in the present volume does not put the philosophy into the poet, as it has been charged against others; he merely extracts the philosophy from the poet's own utterances in prose and verse, and uses it as a clue to follow the windings and intricacies of his thought. Hence there is no apology necessary for the attempt to read the poet's mind in the light of a method which he himself indicates; and Arnold's curse on all critics of Wordsworth who take any account of his philosophy, must be borne as cheerfully as may be. Indeed, the curse must inevitably be borne; for the philosophy is there: it furnishes the clue to many difficulties in Wordsworth, and we therefore, plead that the poet and not the critic must in this case be held responsible for any blame that may fall on the head of either the critic or the poet who speaks of philosophy in connection with poetry.

However, in spite of our claim that the associationistic philosophy is plainly stated as well as implied in Wordsworth, we are perfectly aware of the newness of our approach to his poetry: and in defence of it we may instance not only the rather obvious fact that the poet is avowedly a philosophic poet and must be studied as one having a philosophy, but also certain

18

definite advantages which it affords of judging him as a poet and prose writer. We shall consider four advantages: Wordsworth's alleged neglect of beauty both in theory and in practice; the roots of his autobiographical-psychological method marked by reminiscence; characteristics of his style which arise from sense-impressions and reality; the connections between his prose and his poetry.

The poet began his career by the striking statement that he wished his poetry to be judged by its naturalness and truth to fact.[1] For this he has been blamed over and over again as proclaiming his lack of allegiance to something which seems to many to be more closely connected with poetry, namely, beauty. But this first declaration was consistently maintained throughout his whole career as poet and critic. In all his works there are no claims on his part to "inspiration," "afflatus," "genius," or any such thing. In 1800 he has this to say of the nature of poetry:

> Poetry sheds no tears "such as Angels weep," but natural and human tears; she can boast of no celestial Ichor that distinguishes her vital juices from those of prose; the same human blood circulates through the veins of them both.[2]

This statement he supplements in 1802 in a definition of the poet,—a definition which has dissatisfied many:

> He is a man speaking to men: a man, it is true, endued with more lively sensibility, more enthusiasm and tenderness, who has a greater knowledge of human nature, and a more comprehensive soul, than are supposed to be common among mankind; a man pleased with his own passions and volitions, and who rejoices more than other men in the spirit of life that is in him; delighting to contemplate similar volitions and passions as manifested in the goings-on of the Universe, and habitually impelled to create them where he does not find them. To these qualities he has added a disposition to be affected more than other men by absent things as if they were present; an ability of conjuring up in himself passions, which are indeed far from being the same as those produced by real events, yet (especially in those parts of the general sympathy which are pleasing and delightful) do more nearly resemble the passions produced by real events, than anything which, from the notions of their own minds merely, other men are accustomed to

---

[1] *Advertisement* to *Lyrical Ballads*, 1798.
[2] *Preface* to the Second Edition of *Lyrical Ballads*.

feel in themselves; whence, and from practice, he has acquired a greater readiness and power in expressing what he thinks and feels, and especially those thoughts and feelings which, by his own choice, or from the structure of his own mind, arise in him without immediate external excitement.[3]

This seems to place the poet on a humble plane; and because it does so criticisms have been heaped upon it as well as on similar definitions of the poet and of poetry. However, if we have in mind the primary notion which Wordsworth holds of poetry,—that is, truth,—we shall be able to see the matter in a true perspective. The supreme test of poetry is truth; and in the highest moments of imagination the poet is but exercising "Reason in its most exalted mood."

In the second place, if we remember that Wordsworth's poetry is fundamentally influenced by Locke and associationism we can easily understand why he adopts the psychological, autobiographical method so generally used in his poetry. The idea of the development of the individual consciousness as expressed in what we have named the three ages indicates at once the interests of the poet in psychological manifestations as indications of the growth of the mind from stage to stage and his affiliation with associationism, the psychology which is most closely related to the method displayed in the poet's work. From his associationistic connections come his methods of conducting *The Prelude*. It is biographical in a sense, but not purely or mainly so: it is a psychological, or philosophical, poem, which gives a sketch of the chief factors in the development of a mind from childhood to maturity. Many events are but slightly touched on which would be marked for rather full treatment in a simple autobiography, such as the death of his mother, the death of his father, and his love affair in France. For his reticence in *The Prelude* with regard to the last event he has been severely blamed, as by Señor Madariaga, who condemns him for the suppression of facts. He demands:

Is it conceivable in the name of poetic truth, that an episode so essential in the formation of the poet's mind as his first conflict with sex should be omitted from such a poem? The point need hardly be developed. In so far as this all-important episode is ab-

---

[3] *Preface to the Third Edition of Lyrical Ballads.*

sent from the Prelude, the Prelude is poetically false, and its author, as a truth-seeker, stands condemned.[4]

Such a judgment assumes that the poem is an autobiography, which it is not; and further it assigns a value to an event which is not that of the author, with the charge of a departure from the truth of it if the author's evaluation does not correspond with that of the critic. But, as we have already pointed out, the poem is not an autobiography in the strict sense of the term; and it must be remembered that if this event does not play a part in his poem neither do many distressing events of his childhood such as his mother's death, his poverty, and his separation from his beloved sister. In his memory of the events which seemed to him in his maturity to be important factors in his development, those which seemed very trivial at the time seem very important and those which play a large part in the conventional autobiography shrink into insignificance. That a chance meeting with a sheep by a dry wall should be a more vivid experience than the death of a father may seem to some to be absurdly impossible. It was not so to Wordsworth; and if we but search our own experience it is possible that we ourselves may be able to parallel such inversions. If we remember that the poet is giving us psychological truth and the poetry that is based on it, we shall be able to appreciate his presentation of the events of his life more truly.

Moreover, it is only by regarding Wordsworth as a philosophical poet who directs his reasonings along the route marked out by associationism that we can appreciate the "way of the soul" as it is expounded in the fourth book of *The Excursion;* that book which is devoted to the problem of placing the soul of the Solitary in the way of health and sanity. This we have shown at length in the twelfth chapter, and we do nothing more at this place than refer to the full treatment of this very difficult and highly Wordsworthean problem.

In the third place, the realization that Wordsworth places a value on simple sensations and experiences, which is exactly that which is given it by associationism will go a considerable

---

[4] *Shelley and Calderon and Other Essays*, 1921, p. 156. For a judicious treatment of this episode, consult G. M. Harper, *Wordsworth's French Daughter*, 1921.

way to explain that characteristic of his style which is felt by all discriminating critics. This quality is clearly set forth by Pater:

To read one of his longer pastoral poems for the first time, is like a day spent in a new country: the memory is crowded for a while with its precise and vivid incidents:—

> The plaint harebell swinging in the breeze
> On some grey rock;—
>
> The single sheep and the one blasted tree
> And the bleak music from that old stone wall;
>
> And in the meadows and the lower grounds
> Was all the sweetness of a common dawn;—
>
> And that green corn all day is rustling in their ears.

Clear and delicate at once, as he is in the outlining of visible imagery, he is more clear and delicate still, and finely scrupulous, in the noting of sounds; so that he conceives of noble sound as even moulding the human countenance to nobler types, and as something actually "profaned" by colour, by visible form, or image. He has a power likewise of realizing, and conveying to the consciousness of the reader, abstract and elementary impressions—silence, darkness, absolute motionlessness: or, again, the whole complex sentiment of a particular place, the abstract expression of desolation in the long white road, of peacefulness in a particular folding of the hills.[5]

The same aspect of Wordsworth is dealt with by Arnold, when he analyzes his unique quality:

The right sort of verse to choose from Wordsworth, if we are to seize his true and most characteristic form of expression, is a line like this from *Michael:*—

> And never lifted up a single stone.

There is nothing subtle in it, no heightening, no study of poetic style, strictly so called, at all; yet it is expression of the highest and most truly expressive kind. . . . Nature herself seems, I say, to take the pen out of his hand, and to write for him with her own bare, sheer, penetrating power. This arises from two causes: from the profound sincereness with which Wordsworth feels his subject, and also from the profoundly sincere and natural character of his

---

[5] *Appreciations, Wordsworth,* 1889. The essay was first published in *The Fortnightly Review,* April, 1874.

subject itself. He can and will treat such a subject with nothing but the most plain, first-hand, almost austere naturalness.[6]

The same aspect of Wordsworth's style has never been more subtly explained than by Coleridge; and, even though his words are well known, they must be quoted here. He classifies Wordsworth's excellences, of which the fourth is:

The perfect truth of nature in his images and descriptions, as taken immediately from nature, and proving a long and genial intimacy with the very spirit which gives the physiognomic expression to all the works of nature. Like a green field reflected in a calm and perfectly transparent lake, the image is distinguished from reality only by its greater softness and lustre.[7]

There is no doubt that this wonderful use of plain sensations is a part of Wordsworth's peculiar organization; but, on the other hand, we must keep in mind that he was a conscious artist, who quite deliberately chose how he might write. As an associationist he valued sensations as the real materials out of which experience is built, and as such should be treasured accordingly. He is a thorough sensationalist when he speaks of impressions of sense as "half-creating" experience,[8] and when he dwells on

> Those hallowed and pure motions of the sense
> Which seem, in their simplicity, to own
> An intellectual charm.[9]

When we realize that Wordsworth holds such opinions regarding the value of semi-impressions, we can easily understand why he should cultivate his sensitiveness to them and his power of expressing their strange quality to such a height that over and over again he gives us, not a description of a scene or object, but the very experience itself and the object in its reality.

Finally, if we accept Wordsworth as the poet of associationism, we have the point of view from which we can see the author as a whole; that is, we can see the connection between the poetry and his prose, his practice and his theory, the one supporting and explaining the other. In the course of our enquiry

---

[6] *Essay on Wordsworth*, 1879.
[7] *Biographia Literaria*, Ch. XXII.
[8] *Tintern Abbey*, 142.
[9] *The Prelude*, I, 551-553.

we have pointed out the high quality and importance of much of Wordsworth's prose, and its importance not only in itself but as an explanation of the method and content of his poetry. Before the real quality of Wordsworth can be perceived, the prose must be studied in connection with the poetry. If this is done, and if the results thereby gained are viewed in those relations which are very clearly indicated by the poet himself, we shall have a new Wordsworth, restored to the integrity of a philosophic poet, a title to which he always laid claim, and firmly established as the noblest exponent and poet of man and nature and human life, mainly as interpreted in their origins, development, and mutual relations by the English philosophy of associationism.

INDEX

active principle, the, 141-142.
Akenside, Mark, 43, 52.
Alison, Archibald, 33, 34(note), 35, 40, 43, 146.
Anti-Jacobin, The, 56(note).
Arnold, Matthew, 11-12, 183, 273, 277-278.
Association of ideas, 43-46, 100-115.

Babbitt, Irving, 15, 107(note), 121 (note), 120-124.
Bacon, Francis, 95.
Bartram, George, 136.
Beaupuy, Michel, 21.
Beattie, James, 52(note).
Berkeley, George, Bishop, 59, 95, 115-116, 137, 141, 143.
Bible, The, 165.
Blair, Alexander, 82.
Blair, Sir Hugh, 33, 34(note), 34-35.
Bower, G. S., 233(note).
Bowles, W. L., 92, 95.
Bradley, A. C., 14-15, 186-188.
Bridges, Robert, 67(note).
Bruce, Michael, 196.
Butler, Samuel, 260.

Caleb Williams, 25.
Campbell, O. J., 194(note), 260-262.
Candide, 250(note).
Carlyon, Clement, 93.
Carver, Jonathan, 135.
Cestre, Charles, 254(note).
Chateaubriand, François René, 125, 136.
Chaucer, Geoffrey, 39, 56, 57.
Coleridge, Samuel Taylor, 42 (note), 47, 50, 59, 69, 92-94, 95, 112(note), 148, 151, 167-168, 169 (note), 198-199, 201, 202, 229, 256, 257, 272, 278.
Collins, William, 56.
Colvin, Sir Sidney, 248(note).
Condillac, Étienne Bonnot de, 162.
Cooper, Lane, 136(note).

Cottle, Joseph, 92.
Cowper, William, 56(note).
Crabbe, George, 257.

Daniel, Samuel, 50-56, 239-240 (note).
Darwin, Erasmus, 33-34, 34 (note), 35, 41, 52, 53-56, 56 (note), 95.
De Quincey, Thomas, 94, 257.
de Selincourt, E., 248(note).
d'Holbach, 23, 122.
Dicey, A. V., 13, 81(note), 195 (note).
diction, poetic, 49-61.
Dowden, Edward, 22(note), 67-68(note).
Dryden, John, 51.

Edwards, Bryan, 135.
Elton, Oliver, 67(note).
emotion, derived from intellect, 104-107, 184.
emotion, extrinsic, 72, 147, 149.

Fawcett, Joseph, 21, 29(note), 257, 262(note).
fancy and imagination, 153-169.
   fancy, 124-136, 153-157, not creative, 165-166.
   imagination, 157-159.
   theory of Coleridge *vs.* Wordsworth, 167-169.
feeling, See emotion.

Gibson, James, 114(note).
Godwin, William, 17, 20-31, 32, 89, 90, 91, 96.
Goethe, Johann Wolfgang, 11.
Goldsmith, Oliver, 39, 51.
Gray, Thomas, 51.
Grey, Viscount, of Falloden, 195 (note).
Grosart, Alexander B., 12, 13 (note).

Harper, G. M., 21(note), 89 (note), 251(note), 276(note).
Harris, J., 58, 168(note).

UNIVERSITY OF WISCONSIN STUDIES
IN LANGUAGE AND LITERATURE
NUMBER 17

WILLIAM WORDSWORTH

HIS DOCTRINE AND ART IN THEIR HISTORICAL
RELATIONS

BY

ARTHUR BEATTY

ASSISTANT PROFESSOR OF ENGLISH

MADISON
1922

UNIVERSITY OF WISCONSIN STUDIES

NUMBER 28   LANGUAGE AND LITERATURE NO. 17

DECEMBER, 1922   PRICE, $2.00

Published bi-monthly by the University of Wisconsin at Madison, Wisconsin. Entered as second class matter August 31, 1919, at the postoffice at Madison, Wisconsin, under the Act of August 24, 1912. Accepted for mailing at special rate of postage provided for in Section 1103, Act of October 3, 1917. Authorized September 17, 1918.

The Studies may be obtained from the Secretary of the Regents, University of Wisconsin, to whom checks and money orders should be made payable.